Financial Management and Control in Higher Education

There is no doubt that financial issues within higher education (HE) are of critical importance, and with the ongoing expansion of the HE sector, this emphasis on finance will continue to increase. However, successful financial management is not easy to achieve.

This book explains the key issues in HE finance and financial management and provides practical guidance. It is a professional handbook, authoritative and comprehensive enough for finance professionals, yet written in an engaging and accessible style that will be understood by those who do not have a background in finance.

Full of tried-and-tested case material, examples and useful illustrations, this book considers the latest developments and covers all aspects of financial management – from the macro-allocation of funding down to the management of individual budgets.

Financial Management and Control in Higher Education is an invaluable guide for anyone in higher education with a level of financial responsibility, and will be a source of advice that is referred to again and again.

Malcolm Prowle has worked in universities and has many years' experience as a senior management consultant working in the HE sector. He specialises in financial management and financial strategy and is the author of numerous books on finance and management.

Eric Morgan is former Director of Finance and Governor of Nottingham Trent University and is currently a consultant to a number of HE institutions.

Financial Management and Control in Higher Education

Malcolm Prowle and Eric Morgan

RoutledgeFalmer
Taylor & Francis Group

NEW YORK AND LONDON

First published 2005
by RoutledgeFalmer
2 Park Square, Milton Park, Abingdon, Oxon OX14 4RN

Simultaneously published in the USA and Canada
by RoutledgeFalmer
270 Madison Ave, New York, NY 10016

RoutledgeFalmer is an imprint of the Taylor & Francis Group

© 2005 Malcolm Prowle and Eric Morgan

Typeset in New Baskerville by
Newgen Imaging Systems (P) Ltd, Chennai, India
Printed and bound in Great Britain by
The Cromwell Press, Trowbridge, Wiltshire

British Library Cataloguing in Publication Data
A catalogue record for this book is available from the British Library

Library of Congress Cataloging in Publication Data
A catalog record for this book is available from the Library of Congress

ISBN 0–415–33538–8 (hbk)
ISBN 0–415–33539–6 (pbk)

Contents

List of figures

List of tables

List of case studies

Foreword

Not so long ago, universities and colleges of higher education (collectively 'Higher Education Institutions' or 'HEIs') were perceived to be important to the country in terms of their education and research roles, but a niche interest due to the small numbers of institutions and students, and also their relatively low profile among the general public. A description of financial and management control in higher education could have been a fairly slim volume.

The last two decades have brought many changes which have left HEIs not an important but small sector, but important and big. They remain centres for teaching and research but are now recognized as being central to the economy as well. This recognition is reflected in increased public awareness and scrutiny of their finances. Student numbers have also increased significantly, with nearly half the young people in the UK going on to study in higher education.

Along with these changes has come a considerable change in Government policy, including quality inspections, the introduction of undergraduate fees in the mid 1990s following the Dearing enquiry, and the prospect of the introduction of variable fees. Also, there is a new drive for sustainability and full economic costing which will change the landscape of the funding of research.

The growth of the sector has been accompanied by a much greater diversity of activity. There has been a significant growth in its international business, through recruitment of students from overseas and the launching of new ventures based overseas. There has been the growth of technology transfer or 'third leg' activities, of which there may be more to come. There has also been growth in the number of self-financing teaching and research activities funded by sponsors other than the Government.

What this means is that the financing of higher education matters to more people now than it has ever done before, and is also more complex, with more stakeholders involved. HEIs are not businesses, but they certainly need to be more businesslike in the way they conduct their financial affairs.

This volume sets the scene for those with an interest in the finance of HEIs. It covers the ground in a comprehensive fashion and many readers will find material to their benefit in it. Among other examples, the emerging areas of costing and pricing, and of variable fees are described with great clarity. For financial professionals in the sector, there is material on the higher education finance function, and the role of the Finance Director.

As the authors say, matters are not going to stand still from here on. The sector can expect much further change, but this compendium will bring people up to date and be a base for the future. Elements of the material relate specifically to the system in England but readers throughout the UK and beyond will find valuable material on effective practice for managing the finance of HEIs.

The authors and the other contributors are to be congratulated for their clarity and their thoroughness.

H. James Hunt
Finance Director of the University of Warwick
Deputy Chairman, British Universities Finance Directors Group

Preface

Higher education (HE) in the UK has gone through a period of great change and will undoubtedly face yet more change in years to come. Just a few of the issues facing HE managers and academic staff over the next few years include:

- the expansion of the HE sector in terms of student numbers;
- the implementation of student top-up fees;
- the need for Higher Education Institutions (HEIs) to develop links with business and diversify their income streams;
- the need for HEIs to improve management practices;
- changes to HE resource allocation methods particularly in relation to teaching and research.

All of these (and other) changes will have significant financial implications. As a consequence of this, there is an increasing emphasis on high-quality financial management and control in HEIs. Not surprisingly, therefore, many staff in HEIs feel the need for a book which outlines the complexities of finance and its management in the HE sector.

The book is aimed at four classes of reader. Firstly, HE managers and academics in HEIs who have a limited financial background but require a working knowledge of HEI finance and financial systems. Secondly, the HE finance professional who needs a reference book about various aspects of HE financial management. Thirdly, Governors of HEIs most of whom will not be finance professionals. Fourthly, students who may be pursuing MBAs, undergraduate degrees or diploma courses in public sector management or professional courses, and who need a primer in various aspects of HE finance.

In addition to providing comprehensive coverage of all aspects of HE financial management and control the book also incorporates a series of case studies within many of the areas covered.

Our thanks are due to James Lacey, Head of Finance at Nottingham Trent University, Terry Heffer, formerly Director of Finance at De Montfort University, and Paul Large, Director of Finance and Legal Services at Oxford Brookes University, who have read drafts of the various chapters. However, the views expressed in the book are those of the authors and not their employing organisations. Also, any errors remain the responsibility of the authors.

Eric Morgan
Malcolm Prowle

Abbreviations

ABC	Activity Based Costing
AHRB	Arts and Humanities Research Board
AME	annually managed expenditure
AOC	Association of Colleges
ASC	Accounting Standards Committee
ASC	academic subject category
BUFDG	British Universities Finance Directors' Group
BBSRC	Biotechnology and Biological Sciences Research Council
CASE	Co-operative Awards in Science and Engineering
CCLRC	Council for the Central Laboratory of the Research Councils
CPD	Continuous professional development
CSR	Comprehensive Spending Review
DCF	discounted cash flow
DEL	Departmental Expenditure Limit
DEL	Department of Education and Learning (Northern Ireland)
DfES	Department for Education and Skills
DOF	Director of Finance
DOH	Department of Health
DTI	Department of Trade and Industry
EPSRC	Engineering and Physical Sciences Research Council
ERDF	European Regional Development Fund
ESF	European Social Fund
ESRC	Economic and Social Research Council
EU	European Union
FD	foundation degree
FE	further education
FEC	further education college
fEC	Full Economic Cost
FM	Financial memorandum
FRC	Financial Reporting Council
FRS	Financial Reporting Standard
FTE	full time equivalent
GDP	gross domestic product
GO	Government office
HE	higher education
HEFCE	Higher Education Funding Council for England
HEFCW	Higher Education Funding Council for Wales

HEI	Higher education institution
HEIF	Higher Education Innovation Fund
HESA	Higher Education Statistics Agency
HNC/D	Higher National Certificate/Diploma
HR	human resources
IP	intellectual property
JANET	Joint Academic Network
LSC	Learning and Skills Council
MRC	Medical Research Council
NAW	National Assembly for Wales
NERC	Natural Environmental Research Council
NPV	net present value
ODPM	Office of the Deputy Prime Minister
OECD	Organisation for Economic Co-operation and Development
OJEU	Official Journal of the European Union
OST	Office of Science and Technology
OU	Open University
PFI	private finance initiative
PG	post-graduate
PGR	post-graduate research
PGT	post-graduate taught
PPARC	Particle Physics and Astronomy Research Council
PPP	public private partnerships
PVC	Pro Vice-Chancellor
QAA	Quality Assurance Agency for HE
QR	quality research
RAE	research assessment exercise
RAM	resource allocation model
RDA	Regional Development Agency
SCOP	Standing Conference of Principals
SHEFC	Scottish Higher Education Funding Council
SLA	service-level agreement
SRIF	Science Research Investment Fund
SSAP	Statement of Standard Accounting Practice
SWOT	Strengths, Weaknesses, Opportunities, Threats
TCS	teaching company scheme
TMR	Total Managed Expenditure
TTA	Teacher Training Agency
UCAS	Universities Central Admissions Service
UG	undergraduate
UUK	Universities UK
VC	Vice-Chancellor
WP	widening participation

Chapter 1

Introduction

Overview

This book aims to provide a comprehensive overview of financial management and control in the UK higher education (HE) sector for both the specialist finance professional and the non-financial academic or manager. Financial issues cannot be considered in isolation from the organisational context in which they are applied and although much of the practice of financial management and control is generic to all organisations the detailed aspects of practice will vary substantially according to the type of organisation involved. Every type of organisation has its own specific approach to managing its financial affairs and the particular style, techniques and systems used depend largely on four main factors:

- the organisational structure and the financial information required within the organisation;
- the management arrangements and processes in place;
- the organisational culture;
- the external environment within which the organisation must operate and the policies and trends effecting that environment.

Consequently, the approach to financial management and control in the HE sector cannot be discussed in isolation from the factors listed above and we have therefore placed financial management and control within the context of the much broader aspects of HE organisation, culture, policy and management. Therefore, this book starts by considering a number of contextual issues in which financial management and control is set.

Organisation of the HE sector

The organisation of what might be called the HE sector in England is complex and involves many different organisations. In Figure 1.1, we present a picture of the links between HEIs and other organisations which illustrates the central and pivotal role the HE sector plays in the economic and

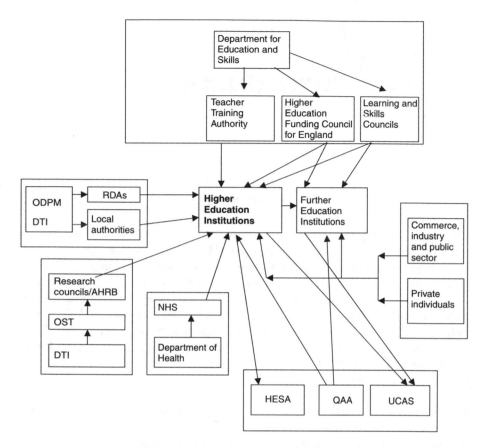

Figure 1.1   *Organisation of the HE sector*

public life in this country. The various organisations and linkages are then discussed below in a series of groupings.

Education policy group

Department for Education and Skills (DfES)

This is the Government department with overall responsibility for HE in England, headed by the Secretary of State for Education and Skills. Outside England the various Parliaments and Assemblies in Scotland, Wales and Northern Ireland have responsibility for education matters.

Higher Education Funding Council for England (HEFCE)

HEFCE is a non-departmental public body accountable to the Secretary of State for Education and Skills and responsible for implementing Government policy in the HE sector and for providing public funds for teaching and research to HEIs. HEFCE also funds the delivery of HE provision in a number of FE institutions.

Teacher Training Agency (TTA)

TTA is a non-departmental public body accountable to the Secretary of State for Education, which is responsible for implementing Government policy with regard to teacher training and for providing public funds for the delivery of teacher training in HEIs.

Learning and Skills Council (LSC)

The LSC is the successor to the Further Education Funding Council (FEFC) and the Training and Enterprise Councils (TEC) and is the main funder of FE provision in England. However, since some of the new universities are providers of some FE programmes they are in receipt of LSC funding.

HE provider group

In this grouping we include those organisations that actually provide HE services to individuals and organisations.

Higher Education Institutions

In total there are around 130 HEIs in England (and approximately a further 40 in the other parts of the UK) but this number is constantly changing due to various mergers taking place. HEIs various enormously in terms of age, location, size and so on, and there are numerous different ways of classifying them. For the purposes of this introductory chapter we have applied the following classification:

- **'Old' universities** – used to describe those universities in existence prior to 1992 when former polytechnics obtained university status. They include ancient universities (e.g. Oxford and Cambridge), the big civic universities (founded in the nineteenth century), the newly built 'Robbins' universities (built in the 1960s) and the former Colleges of Advanced Technology which obtained university status in the 1970s. Within this group are the 'Russell Group' which comprises seventeen self-appointed elite institutions.
- **'New' universities** – in April 1989, polytechnics became independent of local authority control. In 1992 polytechnics obtained university status and are now referred to as the 'new' universities. Since 1992 a number of former colleges of higher education also obtained the title university or university college. Although from different backgrounds, with the passage of time the distinction between old and new universities has tended to fade.

- **Federal universities** – in England there is the federal University of London and in Wales the federal University of Wales. These are the formal degree-awarding bodies but tuition is undertaken in a number of separate and largely independent HEIs, which are, in effect, separate organisations.
- **Open University** – this is one of the largest providers of distance learning HE in the world.
- **Colleges of higher education** – these are designated HEIs which do not have a university charter nor, with some exceptions, degree awarding powers, but which do deliver a wide range of HE programmes and also undertake a certain amount of research.

Further Education Institutions

HE provision (at degree and sub-degree levels) is also delivered by a large number of further education colleges (FECs). An FEC might have set up a separate HE department or HE provision might be delivered from its existing departments. Such HE provision in FE is funded in two main ways:

- some FECs are directly funded by HEFCE to deliver HE provision;
- some HEIs sub-contract the delivery of some aspects of their HE provision to FECs. This is usually termed franchising.

Regional/local government group

Department of Trade and Industry (DTI)

Along with the Office of the Deputy Prime Minister (ODPM), the DTI has responsibilities for economic development activity in the regions of England.

Office of the Deputy Prime Minister (ODPM)

The Government department with responsibility for regional and local government in England. It funds the various activities of local authorities.

Regional Development Agencies (RDA)

RDAs were formed with responsibilities relating to economic sustainability and regeneration in their particular region. Not surprisingly, RDAs see HEIs as significant players in relation to the local economies and have tried to establish strong links with the HEIs in their region. This has often manifested itself in RDA funding being received by HEIs.

Local authorities

The main involvement of local authorities in the HE sector concerns the payment of student fees to HEIs and FECs. However local authorities may also purchase HEI training and consultancy services and be partners in matters of economic regeneration.

Research group

Department of Trade and Industry

The DTI is also the Government department with overall responsibility for scientific and technological research in the UK.

Office of Science and Technology

The OST is headed by the Government's chief scientific advisor who has responsibility for promoting scientific and technological research and to whom the Director-Generals of the science research councils report.

Science research councils

The science research councils, listed in Chapter 2, come under the auspices of the OST. They have substantial funds available for scientific research most of which is allocated, in different ways, to a limited number of universities.

Arts and Humanities Research Board

The AHRB was formed following the recommendations of the Dearing Committee on higher education. It funds research into arts and humanities subjects in HEIs in an analogous way to the science research councils. In due course the Board is to be designated a research council.

Health group

Department of Health

As the Government department responsible for health services in England the DOH has responsibilities for the training of medical, nursing and other NHS staff. Since the bulk of this training is undertaken by HEIs then the DOH has a major involvement with the HE sector. However, whereas the training of doctors and degree-level nurses is financed by HEFCE through the normal funding mechanisms the training of non-degree nurses and other staff is dealt with through NHS organisations contracting with HEIs.

NHS organisations

The various organisations comprising the NHS enter into contractual arrangements with HEIs to train agreed numbers of different types of health service professionals such as nurses, health visitors and radiographers. At the time of writing these were termed Workforce Development Confederations (WDC) but the organisational arrangements of the NHS are in a constant state of flux and the WDCs are being absorbed into Strategic Health Authorities.

Agency group

Universities Central Admissions Service (UCAS)

UCAS is, effectively, a private sector organisation owned by HEIs which provides a centralised admissions service for full-time students (domestic and overseas) wishing to enter HE in the UK. Thus all HEIs and a significant number of FECs are stakeholders of UCAS. UCAS recovers its costs through application fees charged to potential students and capitation fees charged to institutions. As well as conventional HE applications, the umbrella body of UCAS is also responsible for admissions into teacher training, nursing and midwifery and social work training.

Higher Education Statistics Agency (HESA)

Again HESA is, effectively, a private sector body owned by HEIs. Its primary role is to collect raw data and produce statistical information about the HE sector on:

- student numbers;
- staffing;
- resources and costs.

The running costs of HESA are financed by subscriptions paid by HEIs.

Quality Assurance Agency for HE (QAA)

The QAA is the body responsible for monitoring quality standards of HE teaching in both HEIs and FECs. Following teaching quality assessments (TQA), HEIs are able to publish the scores they obtain as an incentive to potential students to enrol in the institution. The levying of charges on the institutions themselves funds the activities of the QAA.

Private group

Commerce, industry and public sector

These organisations will interface with HEIs in a number of ways:

- an HEI may undertake research or consultancy for the organisation in return for payment;
- the HEI may deliver some form of educational provision for the employees of the organisations. Some of these activities may be part-financed by HEFCE and part financed by the client organisation itself or totally financed by the client organisation.

Private individuals

The most obvious interface between private individuals and HEIs will be as students, potential students or past students via the institution's alumni association.

Other structures

For completeness there are three other structural issues which should be described but which are not shown in Figure 1.1.

- **HE companies** – HEIs are empowered to create or purchase wholly or partly owned companies with ownership of the company resting wholly or partly with the HEI. Such companies may be used by the HEI for a variety of purposes such as:
  - The protection, promotion and realisation of intellectual property developed by the HEI.
  - To act as an HEI's trading arm for training and consultancy purposes, and so on.
  - Tax avoidance purposes.
- **HE consortia** – some HEIs have formed formal consortia with one or more FECs in their area to deliver local HE provision. Although such consortia may have no separate legal existence they involve the creation of managerial and supervisory arrangements and are likely to become of increasing importance as contributors to the widening participation policy discussed later.
- **HE representative organisations** – there are two national organisations, which represent HEIs and can be regarded as 'pressure groups' for HE providers. These are:
  - Universities UK (UUK) – comprising the vice-chancellors of universities, representing universities;
  - Standing Conference of Principals (SCOP) – representing Colleges of HE.

Management arrangements in HEIs

Management arrangements in each HEI are likely to be different, the range of the differences depending on factors such as:

- age of the institution;
- mission of the institution;
- geographical location.

Thus it is only possible to describe here some of the models of management arrangements which exist in the HE sector. Initially we make some generic points, which will be applicable to all or most HEIs.

Chief executive role

Every HEI will have a 'chief executive' whose usual title will be Vice-Chancellor (VC) (English and Welsh universities) or Principal (Colleges of Higher Education). Usually the VC/Principal will have a substantial academic background in HEIs although there are examples of VCs from outside the HE sector.

Academic unit structure

The academic units of an HEI can be organised in a number of different ways. However, two distinct models can be identified:

- **Faculty based structure** – Some HEIs have a faculty structure (e.g., science faculty, humanities faculty) with each headed by a Dean and within which there are a number of discrete departments each with a head of department (HOD). The relative balance of power between a Dean and HODs will vary between HEIs. The faculty tier may have relatively little power and little resources at its disposal or the reverse may be true. Differences exist in the ways in which Deans and HODs obtain their posts. In the older and more traditional universities, post holders are often elected by their academic colleagues to hold the posts for a finite period of years. In other HEIs the post holders will have been appointed for an indefinite period. The increasing resource pressures in HEIs have led to a more robust management style which has led to an increased prevalence of appointed Deans and HODs.
- **School based structure** – Many HEIs have no faculty structure but instead have a simplified structure consisting of a number of Schools each with its Head. In recent years the School structure model has become more common since it reduces the numbers of tiers in the organisation and therefore saves costs.

Senior management arrangements

There will be numerous variations of organisational structure below the VC/Principal level and it is not possible to classify all of the variations which might exist. However, the following models frequently occur and are illustrative of the diversity within the sector:

- *Model 1* Under the VC the senior management team may comprise a number of Pro Vice Chancellors (PVC) with academic responsibilities in relation to research, teaching, and so on. The PVCs will generally have an academic rather than a managerial background and there may also be a powerful post of Registrar who has responsibility for all of the non-academic activities of the HEI. The responsibilities of the Registrar, probably with a managerial background, may encompass finance, accommodation, student services, catering, computing, and so on.

- *Model 2* Under the VC there might be two PVCs. The PVC (Academic) will be responsible for all academic matters and will have managerial responsibility for heads of schools. The PVC (Resources) will have responsibility for a variety of non-academic activities including finance, accommodation, student services, catering and computing.
- *Model 3* This is a managerial model where the senior management team may comprise a number of directors such as, for example,
  - Director of Academic Affairs;
  - Director of Finance;
  - Director of Estates and Facilities;
  - Director of Human Resources;
  - Director of IT.

Where there is a faculty structure, the Deans of Faculties might also be members of the senior management team.

The organisational culture of HEIs

The organisational culture of an HEI is substantially different from that in most commercial organisations. It also differs substantially from that in most public sector organisations although there are some broad similarities with the NHS. The following aspects of HEI organisational culture should be noted.

Academic freedom

Academic staff in UK HEIs have traditionally enjoyed what is termed 'academic freedom' and this freedom is jealously guarded. Basically this means that individual members of academic staff have freedom to decide what areas of scholarship they should pursue and what research activities they should undertake without any form of national or institutional direction. In some more traditional universities this academic freedom might also extend to deciding what courses they should teach. The outcome of this academic freedom is that, to a large extent, individual members of academic staff can decide what hours they should work, on what, and where. Furthermore, there is often only limited information about exactly what hours academic staff work and what they do with their time since no data on this is collected (with the exception of the transparency exercise discussed in a later chapter).

Academic freedom creates a different organisational culture to that in most other organisations (public or private) although there are some similarities to the concept of 'clinical freedom' to be found in the NHS. In most organisations, individual employees only have limited freedoms and there is some degree of managerial direction and control about what hours staff work and

what they do with their time. In consequence there is often difficulty in getting individual academic staff to pursue activities such as course development
or income generation since this would conflict with academic freedom.
Similarly it is often difficult to get individual academics to accept managerial
(and financial) responsibility for certain activities.

Significant variations exist between HEIs in the degree of academic freedom,
academic staff at new universities having less academic freedoms than
those in more traditional universities although generally academic freedom is
probably more limited than it was ten years ago.

Consensual decision-making

In most organisations, decisions about such matters as recruitment, staff
deployment and expenditure commitments would be delegated to individual
managers, who would naturally consult as appropriate, but with more strategic decisions being taken at higher levels of management. Although good
management practice would suggest that managers would always be wise to
consult their peers and subordinates about these decisions, the final responsibility for the decision rests with the individual manager. In many (and particularly the more traditional) HEIs decision-making is often less focused on
the individual and is more consensual in nature with individual decisions
being made by committees or groups of academics. As noted above, in many
HEIs even the posts of HODs are elected by academic staff of the department
rather than being appointed by senior management of the institution.

Managerial implications

In terms of management practice (including financial management), HEIs
are, therefore, very different to most other types of organisation. Although
individual HEIs can develop strategic plans, the freedoms enjoyed by academic staff can make implementation difficult. Furthermore, the practice of
consensual decision-making can often result in slower (and maybe poorer)
decision-making than in other types of organisation. However, although these
features clearly exist, they should not be over-emphasised and there are
substantial variations within the HE sector regarding their effect.

Policies and trends in the HE sector

The HE environment has changed dramatically over the last ten years or so
and it is beyond the scope of this book to provide a comprehensive recent
history of the HE sector. However, some of the changes to be highlighted
include the:

- growth in the numbers of HEIs having university status;
- growth in the number of HEIs undertaking research activities;

- substantial growth in overall student numbers;
- development of part-time HE student provision;
- huge extension in the range of course and subject offerings;
- development of modularisation of course offerings;
- development of the research assessment exercise and the link to research funding;
- implementation of teaching quality assessments;
- reduction of over 50 per cent in the unit of funding for home under-graduate students;
- increasing emphasise on the role of HEIs in economic development both regionally and nationally;
- effective loss of tenured posts for most academic staff.

Looking ahead, a number of possible trends can be discerned some of which will be as a direct result of Government policies and others which will be driven by other social, economic or technological factors. The most obvious are:

- expansion in domestic student numbers;
- increased numbers of overseas students;
- increased financial contributions from students through the use of top-up fees;
- changes to student finance support arrangements;
- changes in research configuration and research funding;
- changes in teaching and learning methods;
- some reconfiguration of the numbers and types of HEIs;
- enhanced partnership arrangements between HEIs and other organisations;
- changes in institutional resourcing patterns;
- ongoing pressure for efficiency improvements in the HE sector;
- improved management practices in HEIs.

All of these trends will have implications for finance and financial management and control and are discussed, in more detail, in Chapter 12.

Structure of this book

This book is structured as follows:

- Chapter 2 discusses the overall financing of the HE sector, undertakes some international comparisons and considers alternative financing arrangements.
- Chapter 3 discusses the various methods by which public resources available for HE are distributed among the various HEIs and FECs in the sector.
- Chapter 4 discusses the vital task of strategic planning in HEIs and considers the financial role in and contribution to strategic planning.

- Chapter 5 discusses the application of budgets and budgetary control systems in HEIs.
- Chapter 6 is concerned with costing and costing systems in HEIs.
- Chapter 7 discusses approaches to pricing in HEIs including the linkage to costing.
- Chapter 8 is concerned with financial control and audit arrangements in HEIs including the topical issues of corporate governance and risk management.
- Chapter 9 deals with statutory financial accounting and accountability in HEIs.
- Chapter 10 outlines the organisation and role of the finance function in an HEI covering both the central finance department and decentralised finance staff.
- Chapter 11 looks at the different ways in which the finance function in a HEI might contribute towards improved organisational performance.
- Chapter 12 looks ahead at likely future changes in the HE sector and their implications for financial management and control.

At the time of the writing of this book, the HE Bill, consequent on the HE White paper, is proceeding through Parliament. The final content of the proposed HE Act will have significant implications for the HE sector but the outcome of its passage through Parliament is unclear. Hence, an Appendix describes the latest situation regarding the Bill.

Finally we must emphasise that this book is based on financial management and control practices in the HE sector in England since the English HE sector dominates the overall HE sector in the UK. However, it must be noted that the HE systems in Scotland, Wales and Northern Ireland operate under different political systems and are the responsibility of the various Parliaments and Assemblies set up in those devolved parts of the UK. In addition, in each country there is an HE funding council responsible to the Parliament/Assembly with the exception of Northern Ireland where HEFCE fulfils the role of an HE funding council on an agency basis. Although there will, clearly be variations between the different parts of the UK regarding the organisation, funding, resource allocation and monitoring aspects of HE, in broad terms the approaches are similar to those in England. For those readers interested in the variations in practice in Scotland, Wales and Northern Ireland, reference should be made to the relevant web-site addresses shown at the end of the book.

Chapter 2

Financing the Higher Education sector

Introduction

Chapter 1 set out the organisation of the HE sector and the inter-relationships between HE providers and Government, business, other educational providers, the community and others. The financing structures reflect these complex inter-relationships and is outlined in this chapter under the following headings:

- The distinction between capital and revenue funding in HE.
- Sources of finance for HE.
- Public expenditure planning and control.
- Public/Governmental funds for HE.
- Non-Public/Non-Governmental Funds for HE.
- Capital funding.
- Private Finance Initiative (PFI) and Public Private Partnership (PPP) in HE.
- Institutional variations in HE funding.
- International funding comparisons.
- Alternative approaches to funding HE.

The distinction between capital and revenue funding in HE

In HE, as in most sectors, a distinction must be drawn between funds for capital expenditure and funds for revenue expenditure. Capital expenditure is defined by HEFCE in its Financial Memorandum (FM) as 'expenditure used to create or purchase a new fixed asset, replace an existing fixed asset, or refurbish or remodel an existing fixed asset'. A fixed asset could be a building, a piece of equipment, a vehicle and so on. Capital expenditure can, therefore, be clearly distinguished from revenue expenditure, such as costs of staff, costs of heating and maintaining buildings and so on, which is incurred in operating an institution on a day-to-day basis.

This distinction is an absolutely vital concept to grasp and confusion can arise through using other wording to describe these types of expenditures. For example, revenue expenditure is often referred to as recurrent expenditure and capital expenditure as non-recurrent expenditure even though some forms of non-recurrent expenditure (e.g., project management costs) are not capital in nature. Furthermore, individual HEIs determine the level at which to capitalise expenditure, and therefore capitalisation thresholds can range from £1,000 to over £30,000 in HEIs (unlike for example an NHS Trusts where the level of capitalisation is pre-defined and standardised). The median figure for capitalisation purposes in HEIs is now about £10,000.

Sources of finance for HE (public and private)

The total funding available for HE in the UK in 2001/02, from all sources, was approximately £14.49 billion, as shown in Table 2.1.

The English component supports

- 77 universities;
- 17 directly funded schools and institutions of the University of London;
- 37 HE Colleges;
- HE provision in 164 FE colleges in England.

This funding in 2001/02 was from many different sources as shown in Table 2.2, which relates only to England.

Since 1998/99 the student tuition fee element has required a contribution from the student. This was initially set at £1,000 per full-time undergraduate student with financial assistance being provided where parental income has been below prescribed levels. This topic is covered in greater detail in Chapter 3.

The above funding provided tuition in December 2002 for 962,350 full-time equivalent (FTE) home and EU students in England in the categories shown in Table 2.3.

Table 2.1 Total HE funding in the UK

	£ billion
England	11.84
Scotland	1.66
Wales	0.70
Northern Ireland	0.29
Total UK	14.49

Source: HESA Financial Statistics Return 2001/02

Table 2.2 Sources of finance for English Universities and Colleges, 2001/02

	£ million	%
Student Loans Company and LEA fees	403	3
HEFCE, TTA and LSC Grants	4,551	39
OST/Research Council grants + postgraduate fees	923	8
Other government grant – research	448	4
Other government grant – non-research	810	7
Other research income	367	3
UK Charities	504	4
Overseas student fees	763	6
Residences and catering	811	7
Other income	2,254	19
Total	11,834	100

Source: HESA Finance Statistics Return 2001/02

Table 2.3 Composition of students at HEIs, 2002

	Fulltime (%)	Part time (%)	Total (%)
Undergraduate	74	15	89
Postgraduate	5	6	11
Total	79	21	100

Source: HEFCE 'Realising a vision for higher education', Annual review 2002 03 (September 2003)

Public expenditure planning and control

In total, therefore, about 60 per cent of all funding into HE is provided ultimately by Government, the precise mechanism depending on the purpose for which the funding is to be used. The decision to allocate funds received from taxation to HE is formalised in the Government's budgeting processes which incorporate firm spending plans and detailed annual allocations. At the highest level the Government divides the 'cake' according to needs and political priorities using the mechanism of the Comprehensive Spending Review (CSR). This was introduced by the present Labour Government in July 1998 and set out the spending plans for the three years 1999/00 to 2001/02. It replaced the system of annual Public Expenditure Surveys which had operated previously.

The various spending departments in Government are provided with Departmental Expenditure Limits (DELs) within which to formulate strategies, a clear distinction being made between current and capital expenditure. Spending which does not fit easily into firm multi-year limits is included in Annually Managed Expenditure (AME) which, together with DEL, makes up

Table 2.4   Total managed expenditure, 2003–04

	£ billion
Current expenditure	420
Net investment	20
Depreciations	15
Total	455

Source: Public Expenditure Statistical Analyses 2002–03, Cm 5401, May 2002

Table 2.5   Departmental expenditure limits, 2003–04

	£ billion
Education and Skills	26
Health	62
Transport and the regions	16
Local government	41
Home Office	11
Lord Chancellor/Attorney General	3
Defence	25
Foreign and Commonwealth Office and International development	5
Trade and Industry	4
Environment, Food and Rural Affairs	2
Culture, Media and Sport	1
Work and pensions	8
Scotland	19
Wales	10
Northern Ireland Executive	6
Northern Ireland Office	1
Lord Chancellor's Office	2
Cabinet Office	2
Capital modernisation fund	1
Reserve	2
Budget 2002 addition	2
Total	249

Source: Public Expenditure Statistical Analyses 2002–03, Cm 5401, May 2002

Total Managed Expenditure (TME). For 2003/04 Government plans in May 2002 were for TME of £455 billion, as shown in Table 2.4.

DEL's within this figure totalled £249 billion and covered the areas shown in Table 2.5.

There are a number of roundings and so on in the above figures but they give an indication of the size of DELs given to departments, the planned level for DfES (Department of Education and Skills) being nearly £26 billion in 2003/04, at 2003/04 price levels (approximately £24 billion at 2000/01 price levels).

The difference of £206 billion between the TME of £455 billion and the DEL expenditure of £249 billion in the 2003/04 plans is accounted for by Annually Managed Expenditure (AME). This included £114 billion for social security benefits; £23 billion for Central Government gross debt interest; locally financed expenditure of £22 billion; depreciation and capital charges of £26 billion with the balance for planned expenditure on items such as public service pensions, housing revenue account subsidies and net payments to EU institutions.

The Government monitors actual out-turn for total planned expenditure in detail and issues the Public Expenditure Statistical Analysis (PESA) which reports on actual out-turn against plans and sets out future spending plans. The report for 2002/03 was published in May 2002 (Cm 5401).

Spending on HE comes primarily through the DfES department spending limit but elements, such as funding of DTI (Department of Trade and Industry) initiatives concerned with links with business and industry, can be funded from that source.

Resource accounting

The Government now accounts for its expenditure when it is committed on the same basis as commerce and industry and most parts of the public sector. It has moved away from a system of cash accounting to a system of accounting for resources when they are committed. Up until 2000/01 expenditure was controlled and accounted for on a cash basis but the new approach is now referred to as resource accounting.

Public/governmental funds for HE

These are provided through:

- HE and FE funding bodies;
- European funding;
- research council funding;
- other public funding.

HE and FE funding bodies

Earlier in this chapter the total funding available to HE in the UK in 2001/02 was shown. This totalled £14.49 billion of which funding council grants accounted for £5.69 billion, as shown in Table 2.6.

The main funding bodies are HEFCE, in England; SHEFC (The Scottish Higher Education Funding Council) in Scotland; HEFCW (The Higher

Table 2.6 HE funding from HE and FE funding bodies, 2001–02

	£ billion	%
England	4.55	80
Scotland	0.69	12
Wales	0.30	5
Northern Ireland	0.15	3
Total UK	5.69	100

Source: HESA Financial Statistics Return 2001/02

Education Funding Council for Wales) and DEL (The Department for Education and Learning) in Northern Ireland, although the Department has a service agreement with HEFCE under which the funding models and regulations of the latter are used. However, the HE funding council allocations will not precisely match figures in Table 2.6 for each country, as other funding bodies also provide funding. The two main ones are the TTA (The Teacher Training Authority) and the LSC (The Learning and Skills Council).

Funding from the HEFCE

This is the main source of governmental finance for most English HEIs. In 2003/04 the HEFCE distributed £5.07 billion in revenue funding and £0.41 billion of earmarked capital funding as shown in Table 2.7.

This total HEFCE funding of £5.48 billion was an increase in cash terms of 7.6 per cent over 2002/03 HEFCE funding and before allowing for price inflation included an increase of 3.8 per cent in funding for teaching. After adjusting for price inflation, the increase in funding for teaching was quoted by HEFCE at 1.6 per cent, but this increase in teaching funding included funding for an additional 19,700 FTE student places. Before adjusting for inflation, research funding was quoted by HEFCE as increasing by 10.9 per cent between 2002/03 and 2003/04.

This increase in overall funding for HE appears consistent with the Government's policy of viewing education, including HE, as a priority area for additional funding. However, the earmarking of many of the funds resulted in a real decline in funding available for core teaching activities and resulted in strong criticism of the Government from UUK (Universities UK) the body representing Vice-Chancellors.

Funding from the TTA

The TTA is the Government agency concerned with funding teacher training in English HEIs. In the year 2002/03 (in the case of the TTA to 31 March not 31 July as for HEFCE) the total expenditure was approximately £444 million,

Table 2.7 HEFCE funding, 2003/04

Purpose	£ billion	%
Funding for teaching	3.40	62
Funding for research	1.04	19
Special funding	0.45	8
Rewarding and developing staff	0.18	3
Total revenue funding	**5.07**	**92**
Earmarked capital funding	**0.41**	**8**
Total funding	**5.48**	**100**

Source: HEFCE Recurrent grants for 2003–04 (March 2003/10)

Table 2.8 TTA funding, 2002/03

	£ million	%
Initial teacher training		
Mainstream funding	187	42
Training bursaries	128	28
Other	7	2
Total ITT	*322*	*72*
Other		
In-service training	14	3
Employment based routes	52	12
Miscellaneous	17	4
Total other	*83*	*19*
Recruitment publicity and administration	*39*	*9*
Total TTA expenditure	*444*	*100*

Source: Financial Statements of the Teacher Training Agency, 2002–2003

with programme expenditure representing nearly £405m of this total. The ITT (initial teacher training) programme accounted for £322m of this of which £128m was spent on training bursaries. These bursaries included a £6,000 training bursary for all graduates entering full-time teacher training after September 2000 accompanied by the payment of no tuition fees. Also, all post-graduate trainees studying to teach secondary subjects in 'shortage' areas are entitled to 'golden hellos' of £4,000 in maintained schools or non-maintained special schools. These schemes have been extended to 2004/05.

Expenditure for the year to 31 March 2003 is shown in Table 2.8.

Funding for further education

The LSC is concerned primarily with funding post-16 education and training in FE colleges and other providers. The latter include many HEIs, particularly the newer universities and the Colleges of Higher Education undertake a significant amount of FE provision. Consequently they receive funding from the LSC. Of the £4.55 billion of grants received from funding councils by HEIs in England in 2001/02, £71 million (0.6 per cent of total funding) related to the provision of further education (FE) in HEIs.

European funding

European Union (EU) support is a form of public funding which HE receives in a number of different ways. In 2001/02 English HEIs received over £201 million (1.7 per cent of total funding) from the EU excluding any EU contribution to student fees. Support from the EU can be in the form of:

- **ERDF Grant (European Regional Development Fund)** – provides capital and revenue grants designed to stimulate economic development in the regions of the EU where income is below the EU mean. Support includes infrastructure investment, help for SMEs (small and medium enterprises), regional development initiatives, and initiatives linked to regional developments in areas such as environmental protection, tourism and cultural activities.
- **ESF Grant (European Social Fund)** – provides revenue grants to help develop the labour market, encourage entrepreneurship, encourage employment and develop the skills of individuals in the workforce.

Both of these funds are aimed at supporting specific EU policy objectives and up until 2000 there were five such objectives, namely:

- Objective 1 – to promote the development and structural adjustment of regions seriously lagging behind the EU average;
- Objective 2 – to convert regions or areas seriously affected by industrial decline;
- Objective 3 – to assist the long-term unemployed, the young and those considered 'excluded', for example, promoting equal opportunities between men and women;
- Objective 4 – to help employees adjust to changes in industry and production systems;
- Objective 5a – to help the agricultural and fisheries sectors to modernize;
- Objective 5b – to help to redevelop rural areas.

Funding under Objectives, 1, 2 and 5b was only available to certain areas of the UK and regional GOs (Government Offices) advised on which areas could qualify for such grants. However, following a review in 1997 the Objectives were reduced to three in number, as follows:

- Objective 1 – similar to previous Objective 1, to help develop regions with GDP at less than 75 per cent of the EU average.
- Objective 2 – to regenerate areas with structural difficulties such as those with a decline in their industry – fisheries, rural activities, and so on.
- Objective 3 – similar to the previous Objective 4, to help individuals re-skill, develop, and so on.

The administration of such grants is highly complex and GOs have key roles on advising if grants are applicable and how to obtain them. Detailed guidance is provided on expenditure covered and detailed monitoring of the actual expenditure takes place.

Expenditure on successful projects is not funded solely from EU sources, as a fundamental principal is that funding must also be obtained or provided directly by the HEI to secure the grant. This principle of 'matched funding' varies in its application, but generally, for an ERDF grant the EU will provide a maximum of 50 per cent of costs, although this can increase up to 75 per cent in Objective 1 regions. For ESF projects, the normal EU contribution is 45 per cent, although this can increase in Objective 1 regions and in exceptional cases can reach 100 per cent.

HEIs may also make use of a number of highly targeted EU funds. These include:

- Tempus – trans-European cooperation scheme for HE. This forms part of the overall programme for the EU for the economic and social restructuring of the countries of Central and Eastern Europe (the Phare Programme) and for economic reform and recovery in the New Independent States and Mongolia (the Tacis Programme);
- Socrates – designed to promote exchange of curriculum and authorial activities;
- Leonardo – which supports vocational programmes;
- Framework 5 – a programme for research and technological development for the period 1999–2002.

The complexity of bidding for and administering such grants is accompanied by significant dangers if procedures are not carried out correctly. The EU has the right to audit such schemes and numerous examples exist of HEIs having to repay grants where they have failed to comply with the attached conditions.

Funding from Research Councils

In 2001/02 the OST (Office of Science and Technology) and the Research Councils, together with the related post-graduate fees, contributed £923 million

(8 per cent) to the funding of HE in England. The seven Research Councils are:

- BBSRC – Biotechnology & Biological Sciences Research Council;
- CCLRC – Council for the Central Laboratory of the Research Councils;
- EPSRC – Engineering & Physical Sciences Research Council;
- ESRC – Economic & Social Research Council;
- MRC – Medical Research Council;
- NERC – Natural Environmental Research Council;
- PPARC – Particle Physics & Astronomy Research Council.

The Councils formulate policy objectives and provide funding, in a number of ways, to HEIs which are undertaking work in accordance with the priorities of the Councils. Funding will usually require the submission of project proposals to the Councils, often in the form of competitive bids between HEIs. The support from the Councils can be by way of recurrent funding of on-going research projects through grants and contracts and also through very significant capital funding for plant and equipment. The recurrent funding for research projects will usually meet all eligible direct costs as well as providing a contribution to indirect costs (overheads) of 46 per cent of the eligible direct costs of the staff employed on the project.

There is also the Arts and Humanities Research Board (AHRB) which finances research in the arts and humanities. Following proposals in the HE White paper this is to become a full Research Council.

It is sometimes suggested that the research element of HEFCE funds should be transferred from HEFCE to the Research Councils and the AHRB for them to distribute. This might have a number of implications including:

- Funds might be allocated to HEIs according to the financial needs of future research activity rather than on the basis of past research activity, as is the case with the RAE.
- Funding allocations might be more closely focused on achieving the research priorities of the Government by allocating funds to specific projects, subject areas, and HEIs. Under the RAE arrangements, funds are allocated to HEIs and the use of those funds within the HEI is a matter for its own discretion.

Other public funding

Other public funding comes from a number of diverse sources which include:

- income from the health authorities in respect of the funding of posts in HEIs and from contracts to provide training for nurses and teaching contracts relating to professions supplementary to medicine, such as physiotherapy and radiography.

- CASE (Co-operative Awards in Science and Engineering) – a scheme by which research councils and an external partner, usually a firm, share the cost of providing post-graduate studentships.
- TCS (formerly Teaching Company Schemes) – which are similar to CASE with an emphasis on research and technology transfer. It is used particularly in post-1992 HEIs.
- the public contribution, in respect of students whose families qualify financially for assistance with tuition fees.

Non-public/non-governmental funds

In the HE sector as a whole these are significant although definitions can vary and this can influence the quoted figures. The OECD figure for the UK was a 32 per cent contribution to HE from private sources in 2000. As not all under-graduates were then paying a tuition fee the current figure is undoubtedly higher and for 2001/02 shows a non-publicly-funded element approaching 40 per cent for English HEIs.

Sources of such income include:

- student fees;
- research income;
- income from Other Services;
- income from the use of facilities;
- investment interest earned.

Student fees

UK and EU tuition fees

This income totalled £1.84 billion (15.6 per cent) of total funding for English HEIs in 2001/02 and included both student and public contributions to undergraduate fees and post-graduate fees.

Overseas tuition fees

Another major source of income comes from overseas students. This totalled £763 million in 2001/02, over 6 per cent of the income of English HEIs. According to a survey undertaken by UK of over 100 HEIs, the median over-seas tuition fee, in 2002/03, for classroom-based courses was £7,170 for under-graduate courses, £7,350 for taught post-graduate courses and £7,325 for post-graduate research courses. For laboratory-based courses fees were £8,500, £8975 and £9,293 respectively, and for clinical courses £18,250, £18,100 and £18,125 respectively. However, there was significant variation around this median depending on the precise course and the market strength

Table 2.9   Overseas student fees compared to HEFCE price bands

Price band	Type of course	HEFCE Standard Resource (2001–02)	UG Overseas student fees (2001–02)
A	Clinical stages medicine/ dentistry and veterinary science	£12,623	£18,250
B	Laboratory subjects including pre-clinical medical/dental	£5,610	£8,500
D	All other subjects particularly classroom based subjects	£2,805	£7,170

Source: How the HEFCE allocates its funds, Guide 01/14 March 2001

of the HEI. For example, classroom-based fees ranged from about £5,000 to £10,000. The fee is often incorporated in an overall package which includes accommodation and sometimes even flights.

It is interesting to compare the above UG tuition fee levels with the 'standard resource' used by HEFCE for its various price bands. This is illustrated in Table 2.9.

The potential funding contribution from overseas students compared to domestic students is evident even allowing for the difference in years and the fact that domestic UG students pay a flat rate of just over £1,000 in fees. However, there are significant additional overheads and tuition costs associated with recruiting overseas students, which can considerably reduce the net contribution to the HEI.

The main countries sending students to the UK are those of South and East Asia, with China becoming increasingly more important. Although overseas fees are a significant source of income, the market is extremely competitive, with countries such as the USA and Australia being large recruiters. Markets can also be extremely volatile. A significant reduction in students from Asia followed financial difficulties there in the late 1990s and a number of countries are now providing more higher education places themselves or undertaking tuition locally using courses validated by overseas universities. The pattern of overseas recruitment is constantly changing but it is anticipated that the total recruitment of overseas students into the UK will continue to increase.

Other fee income

At £219 million in 2001/02 this represented nearly 2 per cent of total funding of English HEIs. It covers fees from courses not funded by one of the funding councils and ranges from fees for short courses to fees for certain post-graduate studies including MBAs.

Research income

UK industry, commerce and public sector organisations provided £209 million of funding for research grants and contracts in 2001/02 to English HEIs, just under 2 per cent of total income. UK based charities provided a further £504 million, over 4 per cent of total income, to English HEIs in 2001/02.

Income from other services

This includes both income from selling expertise in academic areas and non-academic related income, and totalled over £530 million in English HEIs in 2001/02. It included:

- fees from validation services, usually on a per capita basis where a UK HE provider agrees that another provider can offer the UK provider's qualification. The fee includes work undertaken to validate the quality of the provision;
- staff undertaking external consultancy work through the HEI, the latter retaining an agreed element of the surplus;
- the hiring/secondment of staff to external bodies;
- the receipt of licence and/or royalty payments related to intellectual property rights belonging to the University;
- the profits from spin-off companies, joint-venture arrangements established to capitalise on the value of the institutions intellectual property. Income from intellectual property rights was only £8 million in English HEIs in 2001/02.

Income from the use of facilities

Income can be earned by HEIs from the use of their physical facilities. Some examples include:

- many HEIs receive income from hiring out facilities for both academic (e.g. summer schools) and non-academic purposes such as for meetings of local societies, wedding receptions, and so on;
- the direct sale of items may take place.

This can range from renting accommodation to sales of farm produce in some institutions. A recent development has been the outsourcing of management of property, particularly of student accommodation. The types of schemes vary from provision of new student residences to the outsourcing of all an HEI's student residences. The impact on a HEI's finances will depend on the detailed scheme negotiated, but there are examples of cash-backed gains in excess of £20 million being recorded in the sector. Such funding gains can transform the financial position of the HEI concerned. It is also common for students to pay for certain items for example, photocopying, printing of theses, materials on certain courses such as art materials, costs associated with courses such as field trips. All these are classified as 'other income'.

Investment interest earned

Most HEIs have positive cash balances which can be invested to earn interest, and maximisation of the interest earned, within the rules laid down by the governing body, is an important function of the Director of Finance. Such earnings vary with prevailing interest rates, but in 2001/02 investment income totalled over £96 million in English HEIs, approaching 1 per cent of total income, and endowment income totalled £124 million, over 1 per cent of total income. However, endowment income is not spread evenly across English HEIs as the older established HEIs have had longer to establish such funds.

Capital funding for HEIs

In an earlier section we emphasised the distinction between capital and revenue expenditure. Clearly there must also be sources of capital funding for HEIs in the same way as there are sources for revenue funding. The main sources of capital funding are as follows.

Grants

HEIs may receive grants from a number of organisations to finance capital expenditure and part of the HEFCE funding is for capital purposes. However, other organisations, such as RDAs, may also make grants to HEIs for specific capital purposes. However, it should be noted that there is no interest charge associated with grants and HEIs do not, in normal circumstances, have to make any repayments.

Loans

Like other organisations, HEIs may take out loans to finance capital expenditure. Such loans may be of two types:

- **Commercial Loan** – the HEI may borrow money from a commercial organisation such as a bank. The loan will need to be repaid over an agreed period of time (e.g., 25 years) and interest will be paid, each year, on the outstanding balance of the loan. The rate of interest will be negotiable and will depend on a number of factors such as the size of the loan, the financial position of the HEI, and so on.
- **Interest-free loans** – in some cases the HEI may be able to obtain an interest-free loan from HEFCE. As it name suggests, there is no interest to be paid on this loan but the loan must be repaid over a period of years.

HEIs are not free to borrow unlimited amounts. Firstly borrowers will place limits on what they are prepared to lend, and secondly HEFCE places constraints on the level of longer-term borrowing of HEIs in that the annual servicing costs (interest and repayments) of long-term debt should not exceed 4 per cent of total institutional income without specific HEFCE consent being obtained.

Internal finance

In the course of undertaking its operational activities, an HEI will generally accumulate cash balances. These balances may be large or small dependent on the size of the HEI and its level of financial performance. Such cash balances may be used, in part, to finance capital expenditure and are often referred to as internal finance.

Leases

Leasing is not a way of purchasing a fixed asset but of obtaining the use of that asset in return for payment. It is, therefore, an alternative to purchasing an asset outright, as an HEI could arrange to lease a building, some equipment or a vehicle in return for an annual payment. Thus leases are effectively revenue expenditure rather than capital expenditure. However, a distinction must be drawn between two main types of lease:

- **operating leases** – leases that do **not** transfer, substantially, all the risks and rewards of ownership to the lessee are deemed to be operating leases. Under an operating lease the whole of the leased asset is treated as an asset of the lessor and the lessee (HEI) simply recognises the rental payments as an expense.
- **finance leases** – leases that **do** transfer, substantially, all the risks and rewards of ownership to the lessee are deemed to be finance leases. Accordingly, an asset is shown on the lessee's (HEI) balance sheet at the present value of the minimum lease payments (as defined) and a corresponding liability is recognised, similar to that of debt.

As a result of the different treatments, how leases are classified has important implications – for example, for reported levels of indebtedness, gearing ratios, return on assets employed and interest cover.

Private finance

The private finance initiative (PFI) has been a prominent means of financing public sector capital expenditure for over ten years. Basically it involves the private sector funding the creation of a fixed asset (e.g., a building) and leasing that asset back to the public sector organisation, or vice versa. 'Public private partnerships' is an umbrella term to describe other forms of partnership.

Constitutionally, since HEIs are private sector organisations and not public sector organisations it may seem a misnomer to refer to PFI and PPP in relation to HEIs. Nevertheless these are the terms used and the topic is discussed in more detail below.

Private finance initiative (PFI) and public private partnerships (PPP) in HE

Background

The preceding part of this chapter has set out sources of funds available to HE for undertaking core activities – teaching and research. However, there are many related activities, such as catering and student residential services, which although a fundamental part of HE life, cannot be classed as core activities.

Because of constraints on public finance, the Government introduced the PFI in 1992 as a means of introducing both private capital and management into capital projects in the public sector. Initially the PFI started in the NHS, which was not able to raise sufficient capital of its own, and in 1995 the HEFCE introduced the PFI concept into HE by making an evaluation of the PFI option part of its capital project appraisal system. The HEFCE has continued to back the PFI/PPP initiative and the consolidation of HEFCE funding into a single grant for both capital and revenue purposes in 1998/99 increased the scope for institutions to use this route.

Although many HEIs had successfully borrowed from banks and other commercial sources for a number of years, PFI was intended to bring the private sector in as a partner in projects, rather than an arm's length lender. The benefits of this approach were said to be:

- more effective management of services using private sector expertise;
- enabling HEIs to concentrate management efforts on core activities, i.e. keep their eye on the ball;
- to share risks between parties.

Both PFI and PPP, which cover areas such as procurement methods and contracting out of services, have been politically directed initiatives with significant Government input. The incoming 1997 Labour Government reviewed existing arrangements in June 1997 as initial PFI projects had suffered from both an insufficient clarity concerning the division of responsibilities between parties and the patchy presence of appropriate skill levels in the public sector. The review covered four sectors – institutional structure, improving the process, learning lessons and bid costs. These outcomes resulted in a Treasury Taskforce, appointed on 1 July 1997 to provide advice on best practice from practical PFI projects and HEFCE guidance on PFI incorporates this advice into a key document entitled 'Practical guide to PFI for Higher Education Institutions' (November 98/69 updated February 2004). However, an HEI must undertake a comprehensive evaluation of all the options before undertaking a proposed scheme, including seeking advice on all aspects of a possible PFI scheme.

HEFCE's support to PFI/PPP

HEFCE has made significant efforts to encourage PFI/PPP in the HE sector, both through providing expertise and providing financial incentives, albeit on a limited scale. HEFCE has established a specific Private Finance Unit which supports the HEFCE policy of encouraging PFI/PPP in the HE sector, both as a procurement method, a potential means of delivering better value for money and a means of spreading risk. Support methods can be summarised as follows.

Pathfinder projects

The HEFCE provides a maximum of 50 per cent of the professional fees on such projects up to the point of signing the contract. To be selected as a 'Pathfinder', projects must bring innovative features to the sector or must have features which can be replicated in other institutions.

Guidance/advice

Various guidance/advice is provided by HEFCE which includes the following:

- Guidance on Good Practice – publications, some of which are regularly updated, include:
  - Circular letter of March 2003 setting out HEFCE approach;
  - Practical Guide to PFI for HEIs (HEFCE 98/69);
  - PFI Case Studies (HEFCE 98/71);
  - Student accommodation projects (HEFCE 00/47);
  - Practical Guide (HEFCE 2004/11);
- A 'signing-off' procedure – in early schemes, private sector partners were sometimes deterred by only partly developed schemes. This process is aimed to provide reassurance.
- Advice – provided to both the private sector and to HEIs.

Before considering some of the advice/guidance in more detail, a brief review of what has been achieved provides an indication of the level of success of these initiatives.

PFI case studies

The examples set out below are quoted by the HEFCE in their published case studies included in HEFCE 98/71 and that on PPI/PPF Guidance issued in the spring of 2003. The first and last had 'pathfinder project' status. Not all were successfully completed but lessons were learned even from unsuccessful projects. The range of schemes is great and includes academically related projects.

- Falmouth College of Arts – successful completion of 156 unit student residential accommodation;
- University of Portsmouth Relocation of Business School – not successfully completed as bids did not represent better value for money than other options;
- Bournemouth University – Attempt to develop an arts media centre associated with lottery funding in a concert hall owned by the local authority. When the Arts Council Lottery Board did award funding the process was brought to a conclusion;
- Anonymous HEI – soft market testing used to assess the viability or otherwise of using a PFI approach;
- Oxford Brookes University – project to fund, design, construct and facilities manage a new 750 en-suite student residential unit which was to replace a 400-bed unit at the end of its useful life;
- The Nottingham Trent University – the construction of a 158-bed hotel and fitness gym on land owned by the University. The project provides the University with the ability to book early stage hotel accommodation for students on some high-profile courses such as those associated with its post-graduate law school. It has also provided a gym facility for students and staff.

HEFCE has also published details of three 'technical' PFI case studies as follows:

- School of Oriental and African Studies and University College London – the successful negotiation of a combined heat and power unit;
- Imperial College – the procurement of telecommunications services;
- University of Durham – outsourcing of management information systems.

Lessons learned from various case studies

PFI/PPP can involve very complex operational and legal agreements and it is important to identify lessons learned in order to assist others. From numerous case studies examined in HE the following lessons have been distilled:

- agree a realistic timescale with flexibility for revision;
- the importance of potential income streams to a private sector partner;
- ensure that top quality, experienced, responsive and proactive advisors and consultants are available;
- do not underestimate the different cultural viewpoints/backgrounds/ objectives of HE and private partners;
- senior managers will need to support the project;
- properly resource the project team;
- ensure that accurate cost models are produced and updated;
- use benchmarking against other services where possible;

- ensure suitable arrangements are in place for keeping control of contract developments during negotiations and over sub-contractors;
- once a scheme has been implemented continue to monitor and review, using external inputs, if necessary.

HEFCE practical PFI guidance

To conclude this section, it is helpful to briefly outline the steps set out by the HEFCE. These are the framework against which PFI activity should take place in order to minimise project difficulties.

- establishing the business need;
- appraising the options – choosing a procurement route;
- the business case and the reference project – assessing value for money;
- creating the project team – selecting advisers;
- deciding tactics;
- the OJEU notice – inviting expressions of interest;
- pre-qualification;
- short-listing;
- refining the original appraisal;
- the invitation to negotiate;
- evaluation of bids;
- selection of a preferred bidder – negotiation to financial close;
- contract award;
- contract management.

Institutional variations in HE funding

Given the widely different backgrounds of HEIs it is natural that the sources of funding vary widely. The 'pre-1992 universities' were historically funded to undertake a substantial amount of research work whereas the 'post-1992 universities' were historically not funded to undertake pure research, their research income coming from any applied research which they undertook. To some extent this distinction is breaking down with a number of new universities successfully competing for research funds in the Research Assessment Exercise (RAE). In 2000/01 the average funding for universities was as shown in Table 2.10.

However within these averages are significant variations. For example in relations to overseas tuition fees the funding variations shown in Table 2.11.

Again in respect of research grants and contracts institutional funding varies as shown in Table 2.12.

Although the funding streams through the funding councils are relatively stable, they are also inflexible, in that it is difficult to generate rapid increases in funding. This inflexibility coupled with a decline in the unit of resource per

Table 2.10   Average sources of funding for universities, 2000–01

	Pre-1992 universities (%)	Post-1992 universities (%)
Funding council grants	36	50
Undergraduate tuition fees	36	21
Post-graduate tuition fees, overseas student fees, investment income	23	11
Research grants and contracts	16	3
Residences and catering	9	6
Other	13	9
Total	100	100

Source: Calculation undertaken by Authors

Table 2.11   University variations in funding – overseas tuition fees, 2000–01

	%
Highest % of total funding	29
A 'pre-1992 university' next highest %	26
Highest 'post-1992 university'	12
Average – all universities	6
Lowest university ('post-1992 university')	1

Source: Calculation undertaken by Authors

Table 2.12   University variations in funding – research, 2000–01

	%
Highest % of total funding	38
Average – all universities	7
Highest 'post-1992 university'	17
Lowest 'post–92 universities'	0
Lowest university ('post-1992 university')	1

Source: Calculation undertaken by Authors

student, has encouraged universities to consider other sources of private funding to supplement the public sources.

International funding comparisons

In this section we undertake some comparisons between the HE sector in the UK and that in other countries.

International profile of HE

HE is found in all developed countries and the international market-place is becoming more and more competitive. The Organisation for Economic Co-operation and Development (OECD), which consists of 30 members with well-developed economies, has undertaken comparative studies on various aspects of HE. These include comparative studies on funding and also on participation and completion rates. The latter are interesting as they affect the efficiency of HE in member countries.

A critical issue is the 'entry rate' of the population into HE. This is the percentage of the population who are new entrants to tertiary (higher) education. The OECD calculation is based on data by single year of age for ages from 15 to 29 and on estimated data for 5-year age bands for older students. International comparisons are shown in Table 2.13.

The trend is for increasing participation in all countries and the UK Government's policy of increasing the percentage of the population having participated in HE is consistent with this trend.

In terms of completion rates, the percentage of those completing their studies divided by the number who commenced them, the UK compares very well. HE in the UK operates a tightly controlled entry system, unlike a number of OECD countries such as France which have very open entry systems. Some international comparisons are given in Table 2.14.

International funding comparisons

These can be undertaken at a number of different levels, from percentages of Gross Domestic Product (GDP) to costs of producing a graduate. These are illustrated in Figures 2.1 and 2.2.

These data indicate something of a funding gap between the UK and some of its major competitors, particularly the USA. Also, between 1995 and 2000

Table 2.13 International comparisons of entry rates into HE, 2001

	%
Australia	65
UK	45
USA	42
France	37
Turkey	20
OECD mean	47

Source: OECD Education at a Glance 2003

Table 2.14 International comparisons of completion rates in HE, 2000

	%
Japan	94
Turkey	88 (of a very low intake)
Ireland	85
UK	83
France	70
Italy	42
OECD mean	70

Source: OECD – Education at a Glance 2003

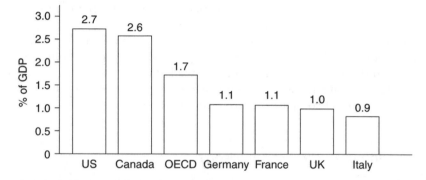

Figure 2.1 *Percentage of GDP spent on tertiary (higher) education (2000)*
Source: OECD Education at a Glance 2003

the UK's relative position had worsened as Table 2.15 showing the relative change between these years demonstrates.

Given the continuing debate on funding of HE in the UK and the Government emphasis on links with business and the community, the relative proportions of public and private funding in different countries is illuminating. In overall terms the graph in Figure 2.3 shows that the UK's private sector funding into HE was broadly in line with that of many OECD countries but it is well short of that in many of its competitors. In the USA, Japan, Australia and Canada in 2000 the private sector provided a much higher proportion of funding to HE than in the UK although the latter's proportion of 32 per cent private funding was above the OECD mean.

In terms of the cumulative expenditure per student over the average duration of tertiary (HE) studies, the UK is a cost effective performer. This is shown in Table 2.16 which shows the cumulative costs per student (year 2000) expressed in US dollars for all tertiary education in selected countries.

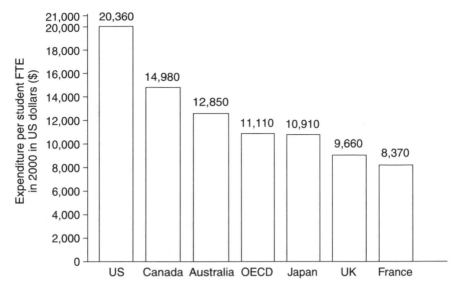

Figure 2.2   *HE expenditure per FTE student (2000) from public and private sources*
Source: OECD – Education at a Glance 2003

Table 2.15   Total tertiary education expenditure in 2000 taking 1995 expenditure as 100

Ireland	180
Canada	121
Australia	112
Japan	111
France	111
Germany	104
UK	101
Czech Republic	100
USA	n/a – figures between the years not comparable

Source: OECD – Education at a Glance 2003

The international HE market

The international nature of HE is well illustrated by the size of the student flows between countries and the associated funding flows. In addition to direct costs charged by HEIs, overseas students bring other economic benefits into countries.

So how large is the market? In the UK in 2000/01 there were over 126,000 full and part-time international students in UK HEIs, from over one hundred other countries. These figures represented approximately 7 per cent of the

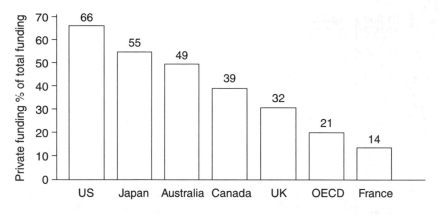

Figure 2.3   *Private HE expenditure as a percentage of total HE expenditure*
(2000)
Source: OECD – Education at a Glance 2003

Table 2.16   Cumulative costs per student
(year 2000) for all tertiary education

	Year 2000 $000
Sweden	69.6
Germany	53.0
UK	34.2
Australia	32.5
Spain	30.3
OECD mean (excluding USA and Canada)	40.4

Source: OECD – Education at a Glance 2003

total student population and there was an additional intake of over 100,000 EU students, representing a further 5 per cent of the total student population.

Greenaway and Hayes ('Funding Universities to meet National and International Challenges') suggest that in 1998/99 such students contributed £2 billion to British exports each year and boosted GDP by 0.26 per cent. Hence the drive to increase numbers both as a means of increasing funding and also of adding to the social environment dimension of HE in the UK. The main providers of non-EU overseas students in 2000/01 were as shown in Table 2.17.

This market is therefore very important and very competitive. The USA are the main providers but the UK is the second largest of the four main English-speaking competitors. In 1998/99 the total students from overseas to the USA, UK, Australia and Canada was over 804,000, as set out in Figure 2.4. The origin

Table 2.17 Sources of overseas students (non-EU) in the UK HE sector

Country of origin	% of total UK overseas students (non-EU)
USA	9.1
Africa (South of Sahara)	9.0
China	8.2
Malaysia	7.3
North Africa and Middle East	6.6
Hong Kong	6.5
India, Pakistan, Sri Lanka and Bangladesh	6.5
Japan	4.9
Singapore	3.7
Taiwan	3.2
Thailand	2.1
Other	32.9
Total	100.0

Source: HESA Student Data Return – December 2000

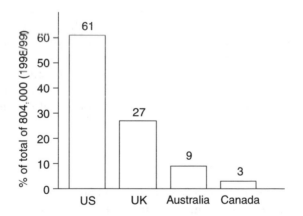

Figure 2.4 *Percentage of overseas students (1998/99) in main English-speaking countries*
Source: Authors from Confidential Survey

of these students was as shown in Figure 2.5. Although significant financial benefits can arise from overseas recruitment, there is greater volatility in this income stream. This was clearly demonstrated in the UK by the financial crisis in South-East Asia in the late 1990s which highlighted that a number of HEIs

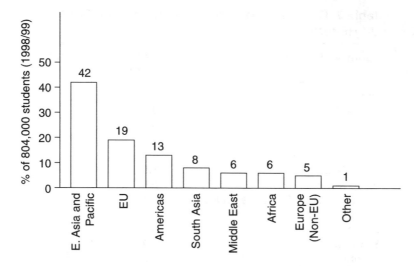

Figure 2.5   *Origin of overseas students studying in USA, UK, Australia and Canada*

Source: Authors from Confidential Survey

were over-dependent on this source of funding. Australia is particularly exposed in this respect, with over 80 per cent of its overseas students from East Asia and the Pacific, whereas the UK received 21 per cent from this region according to 1988/99 figures. Studies have been undertaken which have forecast an increase in the global market from about 2 million in 2000 to about 7 million in 2025 with UK HEIs well positioned to benefit significantly. Anthony Bohm, of IDP Education Australia, has estimated that the share of Asian students will increase from 43 per cent in 2000 to 70 per cent in 2025, the increase primarily being from China and India but with Turkey, Iran and Morocco also seeing significant growth in their students being taught overseas.

International staffing comparisons

OECD has carried out comparisons of the percentage of education expenditure on academic staff remuneration. The 2000 data showed that at 33 per cent of total HE expenditure, the UK had one of the lowest percentage expenditures on academic staff. The OECD average was 44 per cent. The total staff remuneration was also low at 58 per cent of HE expenditure against an OECD average of 69 per cent. These figures are reflected in the expenditure on core educational services per student in 2000 in OECD countries set out in Table 2.18. The staffing comparisons incorporate differences both in academic numbers and salaries and Greenaway and Hayes quote research which shows that in 1997/98 the UK lecturer earned, in real purchasing power terms, only 53 per cent of the US counterpart, the assistant professor.

Table 2.18 Core educational services per student, 2000

Country	Expenditure on core educational services per student (US$) – year 2000
USA	16,982
Australia	8,835
UK	5,950
OECD mean	6,701

Source: OECD – Education at a Glance 2003

Alternative approaches to funding HE

Previous sections of this chapter have highlighted the extent to which existing HEIs are funded from public and private sources. Two main drivers lie behind the desire of most HEIs to increase the proportion of non-state funding, namely:

- a wish to increase total funding available;
- a wish to be less dependent on state control.

The wish to increase available funding, both for teaching and research, has built up significantly since the early 1990s. The growth in student num bers accompanied by a decline in the average unit of resource per under graduate student has made it difficult for institutions to maintain their quality, which in turn has made the international standing of all UK HE and specifically of internationally benchmarked institutions difficult to sustain. The increase in public funding of HE, actual and planned, has been very real, increasing, at 2001/02 prices, from **£4.5 billion** in 1989/90 to approximately **£6.2 billion** by 2003/04, a real increase of about **40 per cent**. However, because of the rapid increase in student numbers in the 1990's the per capita support had fallen, at 2001/02 prices, from about **£8,000** per student in 1989/90 to **£5,000** per student in 2001/02, a fall of about **38 per cent** in unit funding.

In these circumstances, it is interesting and important to consider and evaluate alternative approaches to funding the HE sector. The following options are discussed below:

- increased public funding;
- increased income from users of HE;
- institutional endowment;
- other funding sources;
- alumni sources.

Increased public funding

The simplest way to increase HE funding would be for the Government to divert existing revenue from other services to HE or to increase its total revenue and direct some of this increase to HE. However, in the introduction to this section the 3 per cent reduction in funding per student in the period 1989/90 to 2001/02 was highlighted and it is unlikely that any Government will have the political will to more than marginally reduce this trend. This major political pressure to control public spending needs to be coupled to the Government's policy objective of an increase in participation in HE of 18 to 30 year olds of 50 per cent by 2009. The precise definition of 'participation' is unclear but the figure necessary to provide this increase, using the current participation profile is £1.9 billion per annum, according to Greenaway and Hayes. They calculate that this growth, together with a return to 1990/91 funding levels per student, would add an extra 3p in the pound on income tax. This option would be unlikely to receive the support of taxpayers, who felt they were not receiving direct benefit from such extra taxes and would probably, therefore, be politically unacceptable.

However the Liberal Democrat policy is to properly fund HE and also to promote access which, therefore matches this approach.

Strengths

- The existing system is well established and variations round the edges could provide additional funding benefits for example, a higher maximum, means-tested contribution. The implications of extra funding could, therefore, be easily modelled.
- It is administratively straightforward.

Weaknesses

- The political problems associated with higher public funding and taxation.
- The system does not encourage customers to press for improvements in the quality of provision which might be the case if the users were contributing a significant fee themselves.
- It may not increase total funding to the sector. In his paper 'Financing higher education: Comparing the options' of June 2003, Nicholas Barr of the LSE (London School of Economics and Political Science) argues that funding HE through taxation will always lead to a shortage of resources as HE will inevitably have a less powerful political case for extra resources than, say, the NHS.
- It may not assist widening access unless strong measures are also put in place to positively encourage wider access as the better-educated sections of the community will tend to obtain a disproportionate share of the resources available.

Increased income from users of HE

A direct alternative to increased public funding would be increased funding from the users of higher education, namely students, their parents or their employers. There are a number of ways in which this could be achieved:

- private universities;
- student fees;
- income-contingent graduate contributions.

Private universities

Apart from private US-linked HEIs the only entirely private HEI in the UK is the University of Buckingham, which was opened in 1976. This university offers a 2-year degree with students studying for 40 weeks each year. A very high staff: student ratio of 1 : 10 is provided, very much in the Oxbridge teaching style with face-to-face tuition in small groups. Tuition fees total £23,160 (at 2004 levels) for two years but they are offset by savings in student maintenance costs in view of the two-, as opposed to three-year study period to obtain an undergraduate degree. These savings, together with scholarships which are offered, can make the total cost for a student more competitive than might at first appear and the graduate is potentially earning a year earlier. The University of Buckingham calculates that the average cost to a student, assuming average graduate earnings while traditional students are in their third year, are about the same as for students following the three-year degree route.

However, the total provision at the University of Buckingham, of just over 700 students in 2002/03, represented only 0.1 per cent of the undergraduate population of UK universities and the university is international in flavour with under a quarter of the students being British.

So, although an interesting model, the concept seems likely to remain of limited applicability. However, given the finite nature of public funding, there has been some debate among a number of the Russell Group Universities about whether they might, probably as a last resort, become private universities independent of state funding.

Strength

- Makes the HEI truly independent of government funding and therefore able to determine its own HE policy.

Weakness

- Unlikely ever to provide sufficient funding for HE unless there are major political and cultural changes in the long term.

Student fees

This involves payments by students (or their parents or employers) for educational provision. Currently, HEIs already have discretion over the level of fees they will charge to post-graduate students and overseas students. Hence the debate about student fees concerns domestic UG students (including those from EU countries). Three different models can be envisaged:

- fixed UG student top-up fees;
- variable but controlled UG student top-up fees;
- de-regulated UG student fees.

Fixed UG student top-up fees

During the 1990s, as the unit of resource per student declined the concept of undergraduate top-up fees developed. The concept is a simple one – to charge an additional fee on a course and to use this 'top-up' to bridge the perceived shortfall in funding in the HEI. The possibility of unilateral action on top-up fees by some HEIs and the possible political fallout from such action led the previous Conservative administration, with support from the opposition, to set up a National Committee of Inquiry into Higher Education in May 1997. The Committee, chaired by Lord Dearing, reported its findings in July 1977 under the title *Higher Education in the Learning Society*. The terms of reference were extremely wide:

> to make recommendations on how the purposes, shape, structure, size and funding of higher education, including support for students, should develop to meet the needs of the United Kingdom over the next 20 years, recognising that higher education embraces teaching, learning, scholarship and research.

The recommendations were wide-ranging and recommendation 79 moved in the general direction of undergraduate students making a contribution to their tuition. It included the statement:

> On a balance of considerations we recommend to the Government that it introduces arrangements for graduates in work to make a flat rate contribution of around 25% of the average cost of higher education tuition, through an income contingent mechanism ...

Although many recommendations of the Dearing Report were not implemented, the door was beginning to creak open and the principle of students paying for a proportion of their tuition on a means-tested basis was introduced in 1998/1999. This involved undergraduate students paying a fee of £1,000 per annum which is updated for inflation each year. These fees have had to be paid at the commencement of a course but there are means by which such fees can be remitted for poorer students.

This approach to UG student top-up fees has two main aspects:

- the fee is fixed and is the same for all institutions and subjects. Thus individual HEIs have no discretion over the fee which is levied;
- the fee meets only a part of the cost of delivering HE provision – on average it represents approximately 25 per cent of the cost of one year's tuition.

Variable but controlled top-up fees

Many of the most prestigious universities met in the mid 1990s to consider their interests and the shortfall in funding. This became known as the Russell Group, after the London Hotel in which they met. They have been the most vociferous proponents of variable top-up fees and commissioned a report, commonly termed the Greenaway Report, which explored the inter-related issues of funding of universities and access to them. A number of options were examined, the favoured being for variable top-up fees. This was accepted by the Russell Group and its recommendation to Government was the need for high levels of top-up fees, where appropriate. In the run-up to the publication of the Government's White Paper in January 2003 entitled *The Future of Higher Education*, the Rector of Imperial College, Sir Richard Sykes, proposed top-up fees of £20,000 for certain subjects.

Chapter 12 explains that current Government policy (subject to Parliamentary approval) is to introduce variable top-up fees with effect from 2006/07. These specific proposals have the following key features:

- the maximum level of top-up fee to be levied on an undergraduate student is £3,000 per annum;
- within this constraint of £3,000, institutions have discretion as to the level of fees they set for different subjects, different modes and attendance methods;
- again, a fee of £3,000 meets only a part of the cost of delivering HE provision;
- though HEIs will charge these fees as and when students attend the institution, individual students will not start paying the fees until after they graduate (see next section on income contingent graduate contributions);
- fees can be remitted for poorer students;
- these arrangements only apply to domestic undergraduate courses. For post-graduate courses and overseas students, HEIs retain discretion to set their own fee levels.

What would this mean financially if an institution were allowed to retain the excess fee over the fixed fee of £1,100 (2002/03)? This would depend on the extent to which additional services were provided to 'justify' such additional fees and the level of student bursaries needed to assist less well off students to meet the increased tuition fee levels.

For example, consider HEI 'A' which had 15,000 full-time students and retained £1,900 per student in extra fee income but applied 60 per cent of the additional income to bursaries, improving facilities, and so on. It would receive a gross additional income of £28.5 million and a net additional income of £11.4 million. HEI 'B' with 5,000 full-time students, on the other hand only applies 40 per cent of additional income on bursaries, improving facilities, and so on, and would therefore receive additional gross income of £9.5 million and additional net income of £5.7 million. These simple examples demonstrate that a relatively small top-up fee could have a significant financial benefit for an institution, depending on the level of additional resources required in terms of bursaries and infrastructure provided.

Unregulated fees

Basically this would involve HEI setting undergraduate fees at whatever level they wished in the same way as for post-graduate students or overseas students. In setting fees, HEIs would need to take account of:

- the costs of HE provision;
- the level of student demand at different fees levels which in turn would influence income streams.

This approach would have the following aspects:

- there would be no maximum level of top-up fees to be levied on an undergraduate student per annum;
- institutions have complete discretion as to the level of fees they set for different subjects, modes and attendance methods;
- the pattern of HE provision would be driven by market forces;
- these fees could be charged up-front as and when students attend the institution or after they graduate;
- fees could be remitted for poorer students by some form of state subsidy or HEI bursaries.

So, what are potential strengths and weaknesses of charging unregulated student fees. Clearly these will vary according to the type of approach involved but the following points are pertinent.

Strengths

- large amounts of funding for HEIs could be raised by any of these methods;
- the precise yield would depend on the complex inter-relationship between private and government funding, means testing, fee models and scholarship arrangements;

- most such schemes are administratively complex to operate. However, the existence of student fee schemes in HEIs (fixed fee) means that any future development (e.g., variable top-up fees) should be *relatively* simple to administer since it would be a graft on to existing student fee arrangements;
- such an approach, particularly where HEIs charge different levels of fee, could provide greater diversity between institutions and greater choice to students;
- charging fees could generate increased pressure from the consumers – students and families – on the quality of estate, resources and tuition, which could increase the quality and efficiency of institutions. This is already the case in a number of post-graduate courses, where students pay significant amounts for tuition, for example, MBAs and LPCs (Legal Practice Courses).

Weaknesses

- such fees could act as a possible deterrent to potential students particularly those from disadvantaged backgrounds; clearly, the higher the fee, the greater the potential deterrent;
- the level of fee may affect students in their choice of subject. For example, the costs of a chemistry course will be much higher than a history course. If fees are set to reflect costs then the fees for chemistry will be much higher than for history. Arguably this may deter potential chemistry students and work against national workforce requirements;
- the levying of fees may affect graduate choices of employment. Evidence from the USA indicates reluctance among the better-calibre graduates to enter public service employment because of lower salaries;
- if the cap on such fees is set well below the costs of delivering different types of HE provision, then many or all HEIs could set their fees at the level of the cap. Thus there will be no price competition between HEIs;
- Given the Government's aim to increase participation of the low classified social groups, the disincentive effect of debt is of major concern. Would such fees be consistent with Government policy?
- Would the political effects on middle-income families be acceptable?
- Is the Government prepared for different tiers of HEI's which could result? Popular, highly graded HEI's might charge higher fees and be considerably better funded than those HEI's which are less favourably viewed in the market.

Income-contingent graduate contributions

Whatever undergraduate fee model is adopted, there are basically two ways in which students could pay their fees:

- up-front fees – the current approach based on a fixed fee;
- payment upon graduation – the approach proposed by the Government in relation to variable top-up fees.

There are two main variations of this graduate contribution model.

- Option 1 – requiring repayment of the accumulated fee debt from graduates through payroll deductions once their earnings exceed a specified threshold. This is basically the approach being proposed by the Government in relation to variable top-up fees.
- Option 2 – a flat-rate percentage levy on graduate income. Thus the more a graduate earned the more they would pay but the total amount of payments they make would have no relationship to the levels of fees they incurred. This is basically a graduate tax.

Strengths

- Administrative arrangements could be simplified if existing maintenance loans could be combined with the graduate contribution.
- The disincentive of up-front fees is removed, assisting social inclusion (although the spectre of a large debt remains).

Weaknesses

- Public funds required to replace current private contribution to fees. Therefore is there any guarantee of additional funding for the HE sector?
- Potential debt burdens still remain.
- Due to the accounting treatment of loans from public funds, only the subsidy element counts as public expenditure. For income contingent loans the relevant elements would be loans which were never repaid and any interest-rate subsidy. However, the loss of cash to the Government would have to be made good somewhere in its overall budget. Under the current arrangements, existing maintenance loans contain a 40 per cent to 50 per cent subsidy. An interest rate of 6 per cent on a loan would reduce this figure to below 20 per cent.
- If income contingent loans were made available to home students, such loans would also have to be offered to EU students, giving rise to administrative complexities in terms of repayment systems and, particularly, for high bad debt levels than for UK students.

Institutional endowment

This was an idea being investigated at one stage by the Conservative Party which is explained succinctly as follows in a UUK report:

> The Conservative proposals would raise interest rates on student loans to a market level, assumed to be 4.5 per cent real and 7 per cent nominal, and through securitisation accelerate Exchequer receipts. These receipts would permit sale of securities representing the loans at £1.6bn, which would be used to offer

universities endowments ('perpetual loans'). By investing these endowments in broad, pension-fund type portfolios, universities would obtain about 4.5 per cent real returns, which would replace their current income from funding council teaching grants.

This was the most fundamental of all options suggested to date and the income threshold for graduates to start repaying their loans was to be £20,000, although a new tax allowance of £3,500, worth £700 pa, was also to be introduced.

However the Conservative policy was revised in the spring of 2003 to one of abolishing all tuition fees. This is to be funded by retaining the HE system approximately at its current size with participation remaining at the current 43 per cent rather than increasing to the 50 per cent envisaged by the Government. Given the growth in the 17–20 year old population Nicholas Barr has calculated that in 2010/11 the participation rate would drop to between 36 per cent and 38 per cent if costs remain unchanged.

Strengths

- Some HEIs would become deregulated;
- It would assist market leaders to compete internationally with world-class HEIs and encourage leading UK HEIs to maintain/improve their international standing.

Weaknesses

- The assumptions on the return on investment are critical. The fall in world stock markets in recent years highlights how inaccurate such assumptions may be. Therefore, is it feasible?
- Major disruption caused to the existing system.
- A possible negative effect on less-well-off students as income dependent on fluctuating stock markets.

Other funding sources

- Increased research income – Throughout this book the Government's objective of encouraging international standards of research and of concentrating research funding on high-quality research in order to assist this objective is a constant theme. Most HEIs are striving to increase research funding whether it be from research councils, public bodies or from commerce and industry. The need to develop research is a major theme of the Lambert Review which is covered in outline in the following section and in detail in Chapter 12.
- Increased third stream income – All HEIs are attempting to increase this source of funding, generally by providing their external clients with tailored

products developed from their core educational activities. This can be in the form of courses, or from consultancy work, spin-off companies, and so on, as outlined earlier in this chapter. The Government is providing support and encouragement to HE to improve links between business and HE and this is another important component of its HE policy. So important, in fact, that the Chancellor of the Exchequer commissioned a review in November 2002, undertaken by Richard Lambert, a former editor of the *Financial Times*, into HEI/business links. Prior to publication of the review (Lambert Review of Business-University Collaboration) in early December 2003, the Prime Minister said 'One of the most important things happening in the British economy is an increasing link between universities and business. The university sector is no longer simply a focus of educational opportunity, it is also a very important part of the future of the British economy.'

Alumni sources

All of the above options can be assisted by 'alumni' providing funds to their university. In the USA it is an accepted part of an HEI's activities to run a very professional and well-staffed development office to oversee fund-raising, including fund-raising from alumni. A number of the top 'ivy league' universities generate hundreds of millions of dollars each year in this manner and an important part of the role of the president/principal/chief executive in such institutions is to be an integral part of this process with regular alumni functions and dinners. However, the culture for alumni donations is less well developed and organised in the UK and although this component of total funding is likely to increase in importance it is unlikely that it will ever match the importance of alumni funding to HEIs in the USA.

Chapter 3

Allocating resources in the HE sector

What is resource allocation about?

The process of resource allocation, at whatever level, can be a very contentious issue in many sectors and HE is no exception. The dictionary definition of to 'allocate' is to 'apportion' or 'share' and the allocation process, therefore, entails dividing the overall resource available between different entities, in this case HEIs. The allocation principle is not in itself contentious but resources are always limited and demand for resources will always exceed their supply. Therefore, whatever methodology is devised for allocating resources, there will inevitably be perceived 'winners' and 'losers'. In this last respect, the methodology for allocating research funding in the sector has been the subject of a particularly vigorous debate, as will be considered later.

Resources are allocated to deliver objectives and will usually only be retained if those objectives/conditions are met. The types of objectives can vary greatly, for example, from achieving recruitment targets to allocating Access Funds provided to assist students who face financial difficulties.

This element of setting objectives will in itself generate debate, as HEIs will differ in the priority given to various objectives and those objectives can be influenced by political considerations which may not necessarily be supported equally across all HEIs. The general aims and approaches underlying resource allocation are considered more fully below.

Resource allocation – general aims and principles

Taking into account the various pressures which are always present, a definition of a perfect resource allocation system might be:

> a methodology which provides the greatest overall satisfaction in meeting objectives while simultaneously constraining the use of resources exactly to those which are available.

This perfect world scenario can never be attained because of competing objectives, pressures and interests which exist in and surround HE and which compromise the perfect solution. The key player is ultimately the Government, which through its major financial input, is in overall control of HE policy. Its policies will often have been set out as manifesto promises prior to a general election and, therefore, the allocation of resources provided by Government is likely to be directed in ways which it feels will meet these promises, or those subsequently agreed as policy. A clear example of this has been the present Government's policy of increasing participation of 18–30 year-olds in HE to 50 per cent by the end of the decade which is having a major impact on resources allocation methodology in the HE sector. There exist, therefore, a cascade of policy objectives at different levels which influence the methodologies used. These include the following:

- **Government** will set overall policy objectives for HE per the White Paper of January 2003 as follows:
  - expansion of HE into less advantaged families;
  - better progress in harnessing knowledge to wealth creation, with the sub-text of backing world-class research;
  - providing a fair student support system, students not being deterred from entering HE through cost considerations.
- **Funding Councils** to deliver the above will:
  - attempt to devise methodologies which will deliver government objectives;
  - within different streams of funding, will produce resource allocation methodologies which are equitable between HEIs. Different methodologies will be devised for allocating teaching, research and other funds as appropriate;
- **HEIs** will devise internal methodologies which best assist delivery of their strategic objectives/missions.

Therefore, strategic objectives at different levels help drive allocation methodology, but what factors are taken into account in devising allocation formulae?

The two extremes in resource allocation methodology are inputs and outputs. The former will, for example, produce at one extreme a methodology for employing a certain number of staff, irrespective of what they achieve, whereas the 'output-driven' methodology will provide resources for the delivery of specific and quantifiable policy objectives. In practice, elements of both approaches are usually present. An input-based system may well be accompanied by a quality assessment mechanism which monitors that a threshold level of 'quality' is being provided. However, in other sectors, such as FE (further education) resource allocation systems have been very 'output/delivery driven'. Such 'aggressive' systems can have destabilising side effects in sectors with high fixed staffing costs, as expenditure adjustments cannot be made speedily to match any funding reductions. An additional element in such systems and any system in which there is likely to be a time-lag in adjusting expenditure to resources available, is that of 'moderation'. This is a mechanism for phasing in changes in resource allocation, which may have been caused by a reduction in student recruitment. Such phasing has the advantage of reducing the risk of an institution being placed in financial difficulty. The corollary is that other institutions are, in practice, subsidising the institution receiving the moderation funding and are, therefore, not receiving their full resource allocation while moderation is provided.

HE resource allocation in practice

In this section, consideration is given to how resources provided to the funding councils for HE purposes are allocated to the individual HEIs and FECs.

The main allocations are received through the HEFCE, with much smaller allocations from the TTA and from the LSC. The TTA funding covers primarily initial teacher training (ITT) which leads to a professional teaching qualification, and in-service training (INSET) for teachers who are already qualified. LSC funding is for FE level students who receive tuition in HEIs. In addition to funding for HEIs, £135 million is being provided in 2003/04 by HEFCE to FECs which were undertaking some HE level tuition. This includes teaching of foundation degrees, Post-graduate Certificate in Education (PGCE), CertEd (Certificate in Education), Higher National Diploma and Certificate (HND and HNC).

Finally, mention should be made of franchised HE provision whereby funds initially allocated to HEIs are passed by those HEIs to FECs who then deliver locally based HE provision.

HEFCE resource allocation

The HEFCE is the predominant allocator of funds to HEIs which are sub-divided into the objectives shown in the 2003/04 funding allocations as set out in Table 3.1.

Funds for 'rewarding and developing staff in HE' reflect a specific Government objective of increasing staff efficiency in HE and is covered further in a later section. Although HEFCE states that most of the funding is allocated between HEIs on a formula basis the main allocation between teaching (T) and research (R) funding, is very much historically based. Changes have been made at the margins but given the large infrastructures in existence to support such activities, a true zero-based approach in which no allocation would be made without full justification would be impractical.

The special initiatives element of 16 per cent of total funding is generally considered undesirable by HEIs who would prefer that this should be included in the T funding, and be allocated by using the agreed and

Table 3.1   HEFCE allocations, 2003/04

	£ billion	%
Teaching	3.40[a]	62
Research	1.04	19
Special funding	0.86	16
Rewarding and developing staff	0.18	3
Total	5.48	100

Note:
a The figure of £3.4 billion comprises core teaching of £3,064
  million, widening participation/access/retention of £265
  million and additional funded places of £71 million.

Source: Funding Higher Education in England; How HEFCE
  allocates its funds, HEFCE June 2003/29 guide

April–November	HEFCE discusses HE objectives and trends considered with DfES.
November (routine year)	Secretary of State announces HE funding.
December	HEIs and FECs provide student number data and data on research activity. These enable T & R grants to be calculated.
January	HEFCE agrees division between T, R and other funding.
February	Grant distribution agreed to individual universities and colleges for year from 1 August.
March (usually the first week)	Grant distribution announced to universities and colleges.

Figure 3.1   *HEFCE resource allocation timetable*
Source: HEFCE June 2003/29 guide

transparent T funding methodology. Particularly unpopular with many HEIs
are the bidding mechanisms associated with many of the special initiatives
which are covered in a later section on the weaknesses of the current system.

The timetable used by the HEFCE is subject to any changes in the Government's timetable and enables HEIs to co-ordinate planning and budget
processes with grant notification. The process shown in Figure 3.1 clearly indicates the inter-relationships with government.

The inter-relationships between HEIs, HEFCE and Government are a feature
of the English HE system and each year guidance is given to HEFCE, by the
Secretary for Education and Skills, of both the likely funding for the next
three years and of the policies which the Government wishes to pursue. Such
guidance from Government assists in setting priorities for future planning
purposes, and feedback from HEIs provided to HEFCE in December each
year provides the key information on student numbers which enables grant

allocations to be calculated. The letter covering 2003/04 and the period to 2005/06, entitled 'Higher Education Funding and Delivery to 2005/06' which was sent to the Chairman of HEFCE by the Secretary of State for Education and Skills is considered in a later section of this chapter.

The main elements of the funding allocations, namely teaching, research, special and others, including rewarding and developing staff, are supported by different principles which are examined separately in the following sections.

HEFCE teaching allocations

The funding allocation methodology used from 1998/99, which remained basically unchanged until 2004/05, was set out in HEFCE circular 21/96 of November 1996 entitled 'Funding Method for Teaching from 1998/99'. HEFCE has subsequently revised for 2004/05 aspects of the methodology which relate primarily to the weightings used but not to the basic principles. These are set out later in this chapter.

The general principles which underlie the allocation of T funds are:

- fairness – equal funding for equal activity level;
- transparency – HEIs can check the detailed calculations.

This is linked to an overall control on public funding through the bidding system for additional student numbers. This last point is relevant as teaching resources are derived from two sources:

- the HEFCE teaching (T) allocation;
- tuition fees.

The former is fixed (subject to the HEFCE tolerance band), whereas the latter, being a per capita element, which represents approximately 20 per cent teaching costs, varies with student numbers.

The outline calculation of the HEFCE T allocation is as shown in Figure 3.2. It is basically a very simple system, but as usual the 'devil lies in the detail'. Taking the elements in turn in more detail we have:

Step 1: calculate standard resource for a HEI

- **Student number calculation** – included in the calculation are:
  - home and EU students on undergraduate courses not funded from other public sources;
  - full-time PG taught students in year 1;
  - part-time PG students years 1 and 2.

Student numbers are converted to full-time equivalent units (FTE) the conversion based on the learning activity compared with a full-time student's. For example an undergraduate student on an industrial placement year will count as a 0.5 student FTE.

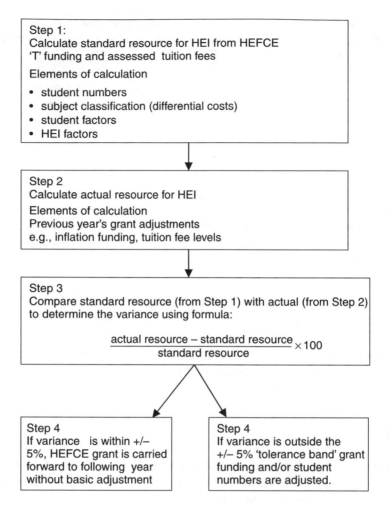

Step 1:
Calculate standard resource for HEI from HEFCE
'T' funding and assessed tuition fees

Elements of calculation

• student numbers
• subject classification (differential costs)
• student factors
• HEI factors

Step 2
Calculate actual resource for HEI

Elements of calculation
Previous year's grant adjustments
e.g., inflation funding, tuition fee levels

Step 3
Compare standard resource (from Step 1) with actual (from Step 2)
to determine the variance using formula:

$$\frac{\text{actual resource} - \text{standard resource}}{\text{standard resource}} \times 100$$

Step 4
If variance is within +/–
5%, HEFCE grant is carried
forward to following year
without basic adjustment

Step 4
If variance is outside the
+/– 5% 'tolerance band' grant
funding and/or student
numbers are adjusted.

Figure 3.2   *Outline of HEFCE teaching resource allocation methodology*
Source: Devised from HEFCE 2003/29 guide

• **Subject classifications** – resource inputs to different courses vary greatly
with laboratory-based subjects, which require significant infrastructure,
costing significantly more per student FTE than classroom-based subjects
such as English. HEFCE have determined four price bands which cover all
subjects and have allocated different relative cost weights to each price
band taking the lowest cost weight as 1.0. The price groups (bands) used
in the T funding model are as shown in Table 3.2.

These price groups do not precisely match individual subjects costs in each
band, the HEFCE view being that individual HEIs need not use these weightings
in internal resource allocation methodology. It can be argued that this very
broad categorisation of resource requirements and the questionable HESA

Table 3.2 HEFCE price bands for teaching allocations

Price band	Type of course	Relative cost weight	Price = Grant fee (2003–04)
A	Clinical stages medicine/dentistry and veterinary science	4.5	£12,636
B	Laboratory subjects including pre-clinical medical/dental	2.5 (HE) 2.0 (FE)	£5,616 £2,808
C	Subjects with part laboratory	1.5	£4,212
D	All other subjects particularly classroom based subjects	1.0	£2,808

Source: Funding higher education in England, How HEFCE allocates its funds, June 2003/29 guide

Table 3.3 HEFCE student factors for teaching allocations

Category	Premium (of weighted FTE) costs
Part-time students	+5% to cover additional costs
Mature undergraduates (over 25 at time of enrolment)	+5% to cover additional costs
Long courses – over 45 weeks per academic year (Excluding group A where already included)	+25% to cover additional costs

Source: Funding higher education in England, How HEFCE allocates its funds, June 2003/29 guide

data on which it was based are major weaknesses in this methodology which are considered further in a later section.

It is also interesting to note that the base unit of resource (grant + tuition fee) was £2,808 in 2003/04 against a figure of £2,870 in 2002/03, a reduction of over 2 per cent before inflation is taken into account. This is in spite of an overall increase in funding to the HE sector in 2003/04.

● **Student factors** – Minor variations in cost are covered by allocating additional premiums to cover the needs of different types of student. The main elements in 2002/03 were as shown in Table 3.3.

However, in **2003/04**, the only student premium which applied was the **'long course' premium**. Both HEIs and FECs qualify for appropriate premiums.

Table 3.4   HEI factors for HEFCE teaching allocations

Category	Premium (of weighted FTE) costs
London weighting – to cover greater costs in inner and outer London	+5% outer London
	+8% inner London,
Pensions – to reflect different academic staff pension schemes in the HE sector	+1.5%
Specialist institutions	Usually +10%, to reflect higher costs
Small institutions	Variable +%, to reflect proportionally higher infrastructure costs
Old and historic buildings	Variable +% to reflect proportionally high maintenance costs of less appropriate buildings for teaching purposes

Source: Funding higher education in England, How HEFCE allocates its funds, June 2003/29 guide

- **HEI Factors**: Once again, these are intended to produce, as far as possible, the 'level playing field' between institutions. For 2002/03 and 2003/04 these factors were as shown in Table 3.4.

From the above it will be seen that what started out as a very broad-brush resource allocation model based on only four cost groups/bands is tweaked very considerably at the margins, and the basis for some of the premiums is open to legitimate argument. This is considered in a later section.

So where have we got to? We have reached the fundamental stage of calculating the standard resource. This is the total grant plus tuition fees, which an institution should receive to be at 0 per cent in the +/−5 per cent funding tolerance band. The next stage is the calculation of the actual resource of the HEI.

Step 2: calculate actual resource for a HEI

A much simpler calculation than for the standard resource comprising:

- **Grant-related factors**
  - previous year's grant allocation;
  - adjustments to the previous year's allocation to reflect, for example, a failure to recruit to the agreed student contract numbers provided to HEFCE by government, less any efficiency gain required;
  - funding for additional student numbers (ASNs) following successful bids. Such numbers are received following a competitive bidding

process in which a good track record in attracting students in specified areas is essential. Any such funding is received at HEFCE's average unit of funding which can be very beneficial if the HEI only needs to incur marginal expenditure to teach such the additional students.

- **Plus: Fee-related factors**: calculation of estimated tuition fees paid to institutions from individual students, LEAs, Research Councils, commerce, and so on. The fee calculation does not include fees paid on courses which are 'not publicly funded'. Therefore, broadly speaking, fees from commercial courses are ignored. These fees represent, in overall terms, approximately 20 per cent of all resources paid to the HE sector but can vary from 100 per cent of the resources received for a course to approximately 38 per cent of the standard resource for a group D course to 9 per cent of a price group A course.

Step 3: the actual resource is now compared to the standard resource, and the per cent variance calculated

Let us say, the standard resource is £70 million, but for institutions A,B,C and D the actual resources are £68 m, £70 million, £72 million and £74 million. The calculations will result in the funding positions shown in Table 3.5.

Therefore, only institution D needs to receive extra student numbers and/or a reduction in grant to bring it back within the tolerance band. However, this example demonstrates that there is an 8.6 per cent difference of funding between A and C which could continue indefinitely. Is this an equitable situation as A is in effect cross-subscribing C and D?

HEFCE incorporates the outcome of the T grant calculations in Part 2 of the Financial Memorandum. This is the 'control element' by which an HEI contracts with HEFCE for the delivery of an agreed amount of teaching activity, and it is in this document that changes to the previous year's contract for institution D would be reflected.

Widening access/improving retention

The £265 million set aside for these purposes in 2003/04 represents nearly 8 per cent of HEFCE's teaching funding and is allocated outside the main

Table 3.5 Comparison of actual and standard in HEFCE teaching resource allocation method

	HEI A	HEI B	HEI C	HEI D
Actual minus standard resource (£70 m)	−£3 m	–	+£3 m	+£4 m
Variance as % of standard resource	−4.3%	–	+4.3%	+5.7%
% outside tolerance band	–	–	–	0.7%

Source: Authors' analysis

teaching funding methodology. It is allocated on a number of different bases which include:

- pre-entry qualifications and age to help prevent student drop-out;
- post code data to help meet the additional costs of attracting students from disadvantaged backgrounds.

Additional funded places

The £71 million set aside for this purpose in 2003/04 was also subject to an allocation methodology outside the allocation of the core teaching grant.

HEFCE research allocations

Following the Government's White Paper of January 2003, the research allocation methodology, which has been in place, albeit with modifications, since 1992, has been under fundamental review. To fully understand this debate it is necessary to outline the methodology which has been in place as this has had a major influence on the strategic direction and management behaviour of HEIs for this period. Given that teaching and research are seen by many as the two fundamental elements which determine university status, possible limitations on research activity can be interpreted as a threat to that status.

The HEFCE research allocation methodology is underpinned by a system of peer assessment of HEI research quality undertaken by assessment panels. This was established for the first Research Assessment Exercise (RAE) in 1992, which was followed by similar RAEs in 1996 and 2001. Although similar in principle, significant changes were made to the RAEs in funding weights applied to the different assessed quality ratings.

At £1,042 million in 2002/03, research funding represented 19 per cent of all HEFCE allocated funds. This is in addition to funds allocated by Research Councils for research through grants and contracts which totalled approximately £610 million in 1999/2000.

Because of this 'joint funding' of research from public sources, the system is known as the 'dual support system' in which HEFCE provides infrastructural support in terms of salaries, estate, equipment, IT, and so on. with Research Councils funding the direct costs of projects, and an element of the indirect costs (overheads). The percentage of indirect costs which is provided by Research Councils has long been a source of much debate. Currently indirect costs are, in principle, supported at 46 per cent of the direct staff costs.

To these needs be added privately funded research activity to fully appreciate the overall importance of research funding to HEIs.

HEFCE research allocation methodology

The £1,042 million research funding in 2003/04 is divided the amounts shown in Table 3.6.

Table 3.6 HEFCE research allocations, 2003/04

	£ million
QR – quality research of which	**1,020**
Mainstream QR	898
Research student supervision	71
London weighting	31
Quality supplement	20
Capability research	**20**
Veterinary research (with DEFRA)	**2**
Total	**1,042**

Source: Funding higher education in England, How HEFCE allocates its funds, June 2003/29 guide

Quality research (QR)

Mainstream QR

The fundamental elements in mainstream QR are quality and volume and Figure 3.3 shows the overall approach for allocating this quality-related funding.

The algorithm in Figure 3.3 shows, clearly, the importance of both the numbers of research-active staff and the RAE quality of the research undertaken. Managerially this has necessitated HEIs deciding on whether to try to obtain greater funding by submitting more staff at the possible expense of their RAE ratings, or whether to try to obtain the highest possible RAE rating with the submission of the minimum number of staff. Such decisions needed to be taken without any certainty of how the rest of the sector was performing in terms of research quality, or without knowing how the finite amount of research funding would be allocated across the RAE ratings. In the event, the 2001 RAE witnessed a significant upward movement in ratings, which resulted in an improvement of one grade in a rating assessment approximately equating to a stand still funding position. The quality funding weights used in the 1996 and 2001 RAEs demonstrate that research which would have been funded prior to the outcome of the RAE, at rating 3b, is not funded in 2003/04. In consequence a number of HEIs anticipating increased funding on the basis of improved RAE ratings were very disappointed by the outcome of the 2001 with many having reduced research funding. In financial management terms this resulted in a number of HEIs having commitments to employing research staff for which there was reduced, or no funding available. A number of options are available in such circumstances and include eliminating research activity in those UOAs, or finding alternative sources of funding in order to continue with that research.

London weighting

The £31 million London weighting funding (12 per cent inner and 8 per cent outer) is self-explanatory and is intended for London-based HEIs to reflect higher costs in the capital.

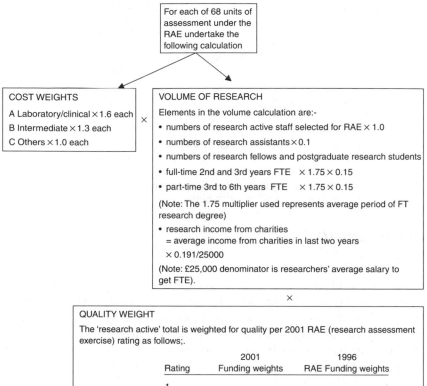

Figure 3.3   *Algorithm for calculating QR funding*

Source: Derived from information in Funding higher education in England, How HEFCE
allocates its funds, June 2003/29 guide

Supervision of post-graduate research students

The £71 million for the supervision of post-graduate research students (years
2–3 FT; Years 3–6 PT) is allocated in proportion to the weighted FTEs in
UOAs rated 3a and above. Again, the removal of funding from ratings of 3b
and below has necessitated decisions in many HEIs in relation to the continued
employment of post-graduate research students in such UOA.

Quality supplement

In line with the Government's wish to support the very best research, HEFCE has
set aside, for the first time in 2003/04, £320 million to be allocated to departments which achieved 5* ratings in both the 1996 and 2001 RAEs. This is being
allocated pro-rata to London-weighted QR funding for 2003/04 only, with con-
sultations likely during 2003/04 about the methodology to be used for 2004/05.

Capability research

In view of the financially damaging effects of the 2001 RAE outcome on many HEIs which had been encouraged to undertake research, a fund of £18 million has been established in 2003/04 to support research in seven units of assessment which are as not as well-established as more traditional research areas with a further £2 million being allocated later in the year. The units are:

- nursing;
- other studies and professions allied to medicine;
- social work;
- art and design;
- communication, cultural and media studies;
- dance, drama and performing arts;
- sports-related studies.

Special allocations

Approximately 17 per cent of HEFCE funding was earmarked for special and capital funding in 2002/03 and 16 per cent in 2003/04. However, including funding for 'rewarding and developing staff in HE', these figures arc 19 per cent for both 2002/03 and 19 per cent 2003/04. Thus, nearly a fifth of available funds is earmarked for initiatives which are not necessarily recognised as high priorities by all HEIs while the basic unit of teaching resource per student FTE is falling.

As government priorities influence such special initiatives many of these allocations change in nature over time. In 2003/04 the special funding comprised the elements shown in Table 3.7.

The 'strategic initiatives' include developing teaching and learning strategies and best practice in teaching (£65 million), widening participation in HE through projects (£31 million), projects with business and the community (£58 million), and setting aside funds to assist with collaboration and restructuring in the sector.

National facilities include support for the AHRB (£66 million), IT related infrastructure support, for example the Joint Academic Network (JANET – £15 million), and the Science Research Investment Fund (SRIF – £145 million).

The inherited activities category basically covers expenditure, usually related to HEI estates where previous changes in organisational structures have resulted in a commitment on HEFCE.

Capital funding in 2003/04 was primarily aimed at areas suffering from previous under-investment and inherited problems and included the SRIF, and funds for learning and teaching and IT. All HEIs in receipt of HEFCE grant receive part of this funding but through a more complex process than the basic teaching allocation.

The TPS compensation is to offset most of an increase in the employers' pension contribution for those HEIs which have non-academic staff in this 'unfunded' scheme.

Given the many different drivers behind the special funding, it is not surprising that different allocation methods apply to different initiatives. For

Table 3.7   Special allocations, 2003/04

Element	£ million
Strategic initiatives	217
National facilities	97
Inherited activities	95
Capital	401
Teachers' pension scheme (TPS) compensation	47
Sundry	5
Total	862

Source: Funding for higher education, How HEFCE allocates its funds, June 2003/29 guide

example, some inherited activities, are simply allocations to individual HEIs while many initiatives require detailed and time-consuming bids.

Rewarding and developing staff in HE

Government is keen to recruit and retain quality academic staff and wishes to ensure that HEIs are well managed and that management processes and training are consistent with best modern practices. Following the CSR of 2000, the Government set aside £330 million for the three years 2001/02 to 2003/04 for this purpose and this was augmented by another £167 million following the 2002 Government spending review. It was not made clear initially whether or not this money would become part of the recurrent funding in HEIs, and at £120 million in 2002/03 this represented 2 per cent of total HEFCE funding. In 2003/04 the amount increased to £178 million (£8 million of which is for TTA- funded staff) and HEFCE is to consolidate this amount into the teaching allocation from 2004/05. Although allocated to HEIs in 2003/04 in proportion to their total assumed resources for 2002/03, HEIs have to submit acceptable HR strategies before the funding is released.

Student support funding

Government policy is to encourage greater participation in HE and also to try and reduce student withdrawal from courses for non-academic reasons. Significant funding has therefore been made available to institutions to provide access to hardship funds and bursaries, fee waivers, hardship loans and opportunity bursaries. This funding, which totalled £91 million in 2002/03, is allocated to HEIs by HEFCE on behalf of the DfES and comprised the elements shown in Table 3.8.

A further £2.3 million was provided to help meet the costs of administering these funds at HEI level.

Table 3.8   Student support funding, 2002/03

Element	£ million
Hardship and bursary fund	66
Fee-waiver fund	14
Opportunity bursary fund	11
Total	91

Source: HEFCE 02/12, student support funding for higher education institutions 2002–03

The theme of facilitating the HE and FE interface for the benefits of widening student participation in HE and FE was emphasised in 2002/03 funding by the provision, by the DfES, of £5.4 million to provide support in FE colleges to students undertaking HE courses.

HEFCE has set up systems for monitoring the use of such funds and in 2002/03 any unspent balances have to be repaid.

Moderation

To ensure that HEIs are able to manage any significant changes in their funding, HEFCE operates a 'moderation' system which acts as a 'shock absorber' to limit large funding changes between years. For 2003/04 this was set at a cash increase of 2.25 per cent, equivalent to a zero percentage real change on 2002/03, but moderation was only provided where it amounted to over £100,000.

The Secretary of State's letter covering the period to 2005/06

This letter to the chair of HEFCE regarding 2003/04 and the years up to 2005/06, was groundbreaking in that it openly stated that HE was inadequately funded to meet the objectives it was expected to deliver. The objectives can be summarised as:

- improvements in quality of research and teaching;
- expansion in student numbers;
- increased knowledge transfer to business and the wider community.

The letter claims a 19 per cent increase in funding by 2005/06 over that previously planned for 2003/04, although many in the HE sector believe that this calculation is based on an unrealistic view of actual inflation against the Government's assumptions.

However, the letter admits that this funding growth is insufficient and introduces the concept of HEIs levying variable tuition fees of up to £3,000 from 2006/07 to increase total funding available.

It is instructive to compare the allocations being made by HEFCE in 2003/04 to see how closely they match the priority areas in the Secretary of State's letter. His major paragraphs are headed:

- research and science;
- support for research;
- capital for research; links with business and the community;
- teaching quality and standards;
- strategic development – £7 million made available in 2003/03 increasing to £13.5 million in 2005/06. This can be used, for example, to support strategic alliances, mergers and collaboration with FE innovative programmes of study such as two-year degrees;
- widening participation;
- foundation degrees;
- credit systems;
- partnerships with FE;
- student numbers;
- HE workforce developments;
- student support and tuition fees;
- capital initiatives – including 'investing for innovation' and capital funding for students with disabilities and special educational needs;
- other issues – this includes a section on the appointment of a voluntary independent adjudicator to hear student complaints.

It is evident that HEFCE allocations follow this guidance very closely.

TTA allocations

The TTA funding to HEIs covers primarily initial teacher training (ITT) which lead to a professional teaching qualification, with a far smaller element being for in-service training (INSET) for teachers who are already qualified.

The mainstream ITT funding allocation methodology (£208.5 million in 2003–04) is highly targeted, with allocations being provided to HEIs for registering set numbers of students in specific subject categories. The basis of the formula is the number of FTE training places multiplied by the unit of funding (price tariff). In 2003–04 this ranged from £3,428 to £5,286 per FTE. The precise unit of funding depends on the phase/subject studied, the level/mode of study and the type of provider. The weighting index for different training places ranges from 1.0 to 1.54224. Many of these student numbers in ITT will be in 'shortage' subject categories where there is a national shortage of teachers.

The TTA operates a very elaborate scheme for recovering funds for unfilled places, known as 'holdback'. Different amounts on sliding scales can be recovered by the TTA depending on the different schemes which apply which are:

- additional secondary mathematics and science new entrant scheme (see TTA circular letter 03/QAF/0068);

- secondary vocational subject scheme (see TTA circular letter 03/QAF/0051);
- the original scheme (see TTA circular letter 03/QAF/0049).

For readers with a particular interest in TTA allocations, further detail on allocations for 2003–04 can be found in TTA circular letter 03/QAF/0049.

LSC allocations

There are three main types of HEI which deliver FE provision and which, therefore, receive funding allocations from the LSC (the successor to the FEFC):

- many former polytechnics were significant providers of further education and on obtaining HEI status continued to deliver FE provision;
- some former specialist FECs have transferred to HE status but continue to deliver large-scale FE provision;
- there have also been a number of cases of merger of HEIs and FE colleges which have resulted in the merged organisation (a HEI) delivering FE provision.

The funding methodology of the LSC differs from that of HEFCE, but a number of key elements of the funding methodology are similar. The methodology comprises:

- a 'national base rate' – reflecting the length of the learning year and the basic cost of delivery, with 25 per cent being assured fee income and based on 10 per cent achievement;
- programme weighting to reflect differential costs;
- an uplift for disadvantaged student – 'to support widening' participation;
- an adjustment for area costs to allow e.g. for higher costs in London.

HE funding allocations to FE colleges

A significant proportion of HE provision is delivered not in HEIs but in FECs. Although the level of HE provision in most FECs is a small part of their total activity (and nil in some cases), in a significant number of FECs, the level of HE activity (in terms of registered students) will be in excess of 20 per cent of total activity. The HE provision delivered in FECs is varied and can include HNDs/HNCs, foundation degrees, full degrees, and so on.

There are two distinct approaches to the funding of HE provision in FECs:

Direct funding from HEFCE

Certain FECs receive funding for HE provision directly from HEFCE in a manner similar to HEIs. The teaching allocation methodology set out earlier in this chapter applies equally to HE taught in FE colleges (FECs), and in 2003/04, 171 FECs were expected to receive direct funding from HEFCE.

Franchised provision

Under this approach, an HEI will franchise-out some of its HE provision to an FEC. Students will be registered as students of the HEI but most (if not all) of their teaching will be undertaken by FEC staff in the FEC itself. Examinations will be set and moderated by the HEI but examination papers are likely to be marked by FEC staff. The HEI will receive funding from HEFCE for the HE provision involved but will pass a proportion of that funding to the FEC in recognition of the major role it plays in HE provision. Usually, the FEC also collects and retains student fees.

The most controversial financial issue under franchising concerns the proportion of HEFCE funding which is retained by the HEI. In general terms, the following comments are appropriate:

- the percentage of funding retained by the HEI, under a franchising arrangement, varies enormously. We have seen variations between 15 per cent and 60 per cent being applied;
- it is not clear that the percentage of funding retained by the HEI is, in any way, related to the costs it incurs in operating a franchised arrangement;
- it is not clear that the percentage of funding retained by the HEI is linked to the level of services (e.g., staff development) provided by the HEI to the FEC.

Overall, there is usually a lack of transparency in the financial arrangements surrounding franchising and both HEIs and FECs complain that they are 'losing money' in undertaking franchised provision.

There has also been considerable encouragement for HEIs and FECs to form consortia to develop services, and funding has been provided by HEFCE to assist such developments. For 2003/04 a £8.7 million fund, of which £3 million was earmarked for capital, was available to FECs to develop HE in such consortia arrangements and to help them raise their quality standards. The consortia arrangements have objectives of increasing access to teaching and learning, aiding staff development, encouraging cross-institutional co-ordination and improving employability levels.

Strengths and weaknesses of the current approach

No resource allocation system will ever be perfect, but a workable system needs to be acceptable to a clear majority of the participants. This is probably the case with the T methodology but possibly not so with the R and special funding elements.

Strengths of the current methodology

The strengths of the T resource allocation methodology include:

- relative simplicity with a limited number of price bands;
- outwardly transparent and enables HEIs to assess likely consequences of their own decisions (however, the outcome can be influenced by changes of student numbers in other institutions);
- within the T allocation HEIs have flexibility in deciding internal resource allocations, that is they do not have to follow through the HEFCE weightings in internal resource allocation models;
- in view of the +/− 5 per cent funding tolerance band the system is relatively stable with limited changes not affecting core HEFCE teaching funding unless HEIs are close to either end of the tolerance band;
- the methodology also incorporates a 'moderation' factor. This ensures that even if the funding methodology indicates that a significant reduction in funding is necessary, a short-term delay is applied by limiting the funding reduction in the first year. This is to enable HEI management to introduce measures necessary to cope with reduced T funding. The moderation limit for 2003/04 has been set at a cash increase of 2.25 per cent, the GDP inflation allowance provided by HEFCE, with a *de minimus* amount of £100,000. Therefore no HEI will receive moderation funding of over 2.25, and HEIs with significant T deficits need to fully justify their action plans for correcting their situations;
- the system, when introduced was subject to extensive consultation which included regional consultation meetings.

The R methodology was again initially clearly set out, although inevitably far more subjective in nature. It has, however, been less predictable in its out-turn than the T methodology. However it can be argued that a strength is that funding is directed to the highest quality research.

The special funding and other elements which complete the funding methodology, can be argued, in principle, to be simple to follow, and result in the allocation of the total available funding being transparent.

Weaknesses of the current methodology

Looking first at the T methodology, the weaknesses are in many instances the mirror image of the strengths.

- the limitation of four price groups has inevitably meant that subjects with very different levels of resource inputs have been squeezed into this limited number of price groups. Prior to the current model, HEFCE used a T methodology which used 11 AUCFs, or average units of council funding to allocate funds to HEIs. This provided greater funding differentiation between different academic subject categories (ASCs) and the concept of the +/− 5 per cent tolerance band did not exist;

- the existence of HEFCE price bands can influence internal HEI resource allocation. The strict market argument would be to provide each subject with funds directly related to its funding category (plus tuition fees). This could result in changes in internal resource allocations, directly related to the external funding being received. A number of HEIs do use internal resource allocation methodologies which mirror external ones, while others use internally derived formulae. The source of the costing data behind the price groups is arguably a major weakness in the current (2003/04) T system. The price groups have been developed using HESA (Higher Education Statistical Agency) data. This organisation was established in 1992 to collect and publish HE statistics for the UK. It produces an annual finance statistics Return (FSR) which is the main source of financial information on HEIs. It has also produced detailed information on costs of academic departments from which much of the current T methodology has been derived. (The 2003/04 methodology used nearly 40 academic cost centres.) However, there are doubts about the consistency of data submitted to HESA, as, particularly in the past, HEIs were not consistent in the way they interpreted data requirements. It is also not clear from published data, how overhead elements such as estate costs, have been incorporated differentially into the weightings used. Therefore an outwardly robust system may have been built on dubious cost data;
- another weakness in a supposedly 'uniform' system is the special adjustments for specialist institutions, small institutions and old and historic buildings. Is a T methodology fair to all HEIs, which requires such specific support to certain HEIs to enable them to function?
- inevitably the T system works within a closed envelope of funding and changes in recruitment patterns throughout HE can therefore influence projections/plans of individual HEIs. The introduction of student tuition fees in 1998/99 resulted in student recruitment in more prestigious HEIs generally increasing at the expense of that in the newer HEIs, a number of which experienced a significant loss of grant income with consequential financial difficulties;
- a final point to note is that the existing T methodology does not take 'quality' into account. Separate mechanisms exist for assessing the quality of academic provision, but this is not linking into the T funding methodology. This is marked contrast to the R methodology in which, as previously described, volume and quality are key drivers.

Turning to the R funding methodology, the fundamental weakness has been the inability of HEIs to assess the outcome for their institutions, and hence to plan effectively. This has been caused by the general improvements in assessments research quality in the RAE with a more-or-less fixed envelope of funding. The net result has been a destabilising effect in the sector, particularly in those HEIs which had been encouraged to improve research performance from a low historical funding base. In retrospect it can be argued that the policy of encouraging all HEIs to undertake research might have been mis-guided. Was it realistic to expect an economic return from those developing their research capability? But on the other hand how much fruitless expenditure on research is there in a number of the well-established research universities? The weakness in the special funding allocations is the questionable need for many of them, particularly when inflation funding has not been meeting inflation costs in recent years. Given the overall financial pressures, is this the best use of scarce resources?

The bidding processes integral to a number of the special funding allocations have been unpopular as significant managerial effort has been necessary to try to obtain such funding. In a number of instances, bidding has resulted in only a relatively small number of HEIs being successful.

Alternative approaches and likely developments

Both the overall direction of HE policy, which is considered further in Chapter 12, and HEFCE's strategic plan for 2003/08 will influence future resource allocation methodology for both teaching and research as will a number of one-off studies and reports.

Teaching (T) funding

In August 2003 HEFCE issued a consultation document, Ref 2003/42, entitled 'Developing the funding method for teaching from 2004–05: consultation'. The changes proposed were generally developments of the existing methodology although they were likely to have significant effects on a number of HEIs.

Consultation took place on a number of issues, the most significant being in relation to price groups. Earlier in this chapter, written before the consultation document was prepared, weaknesses in the pre-2004–05 teaching methodology were identified as the data used in the methodology and the manner in which overheads were treated in the price groups calculations. HEFCE reviewed its FTE cost centre data for the period 1999–2002 and concluded that cost variations between cost centres were not as great as in the weightings they were using. Reasons suggested for this were the wider use of computers irrespective of discipline and the treatment of central overheads. Although HEFCE felt that there may well have been some narrowing of the cost base it is also felt likely that elements in the pre-2004–05 methodology, may disproportionately have favoured the higher cost areas. HEFCE therefore proposed to realign, as appropriate, nearly 40 different academic cost centres into its price groups. HEFCE also found that price group B had clearly identifiable higher- and lower-cost elements and proposed a sub-division of this price group into B1 (higher cost) and B2 (lower cost) categories.

In December 2003, following this consultation on teaching funding methodology, the HEFCE Board reached decisions which included the following:

- four price groups to remain, with no sub-division of band B;
- interim decisions on price groups for media studies and sports science, pending reviews for 2005–06, with psychology and computer software engineering included in band C, combined with reviews of certain criteria;
- band C funding for all year-out sandwich students;
- weightings for 2004–05 to be:
  - Price Band A: Weighting = 4.0;
  - Price Band B: Weighting = 1.7;
  - Price Band C: Weighting = 1.3;
  - Price Band D: Weighting = 1.0;

HEFCE anticipated that band D funding would increase by about 20 per cent, to £3,400 per student FTE.

- various fee assumptions to be included in the funding calculation for 2004–05 for undergraduate and post-graduate students, in particular that fees for part-time and full-time undergraduates(per FTE) are the same;
- a 10 per cent premium on unweighted FTE numbers for part-time and foundation course students.

The above changes can significantly affect the position of an individual HEI *vis-à-vis* the +/− 5 per cent funding tolerance band and HEFCE stated that for those taken outside the tolerance band, initially, the HEI's premium would be reviewed with subsequent adjustments being through changes in student numbers, either up or down, as appropriate.

Research (R) funding

In May 2003 Sir Gareth Roberts, President of Wolfson College, Oxford, produced a major report for the UK Funding Bodies entitled 'Review of research assessment'. This report contained 16 recommendations, on which the UK Funding Bodies decided to consult on nine and on part of a tenth. The other recommendations covered funding, administration and process and the Funding Bodies agreed to consider these matters individually.

The recommendations generally were about process:

- peer groups, with modifications, to remain the main assessment mechanism;
- six year cycle with next RAE in 2007/08 and light-touch monitoring midway through the process;
- assessment of each HEI's research competency about two years before the main RAE;

- one-, two- and three-star ratings to provide quality profile, with indication beforehand of anticipated proportions in each category;
- UoAs reduced from 68 to 20/25 with 60 sub-units; moderation between overlapping panels to ensure consistency;
- clarification of amount of research that can be submitted per researcher, submission by groups, staff eligibility;
- development of performance indicators and HEIs advised of their relative performance;
- strategy statements at research unit level from HEIs.

In addition to the above, and perhaps the most contentious recommendation, was the proposal that there should be multi-track assessments with HEIs with low research intensity not being considered in the main RAE exercise. Less time-consuming methods would be used in such cases. The Report pointed out that in 2002/03 in 40 out of 132 English HEIs R funding came to under 2 per cent of combined R+T funding. The conclusion had already been arrived at by some sections of the education media, before consultation closed, that nine new universities and 28 HE colleges were unlikely to receive any RAE funding in the future as they would be excluded from the next RAE. If this were the outcome, these HEIs could suffer serious financial consequences in terms both of direct funding and reputation, and small high-calibre research units in such HEIs could feel very aggrieved at this situation.

In August 2003, while consultation on the Roberts Report was underway, HEFCE put out for consultation a paper entitled 'Review of research funding methodology' (Ref. 2003/38).The proposals made were in the context of the Government's White Paper, HEFCE's own strategic plan for 2003–08 and the Roberts Report.

In December 2003, following this consultation exercise, the HEFCE Board reached decisions on research funding methodology which included the following:

- in 2004–05 departments rated 5* for the first time in the 2001 RAE would qualify for additional resources if research staff numbers for the 2001 RAE had been at least maintained since 1996 (In 2003–04 it was necessary to be rated at 5* in both RAEs.);
- in 2004–05 an extra £8 million of capital to be allocated as part of SRIF to the four HEIs with the largest SRIF allocations;
- from 2005/06, funding for post-graduate researchers through one funding mechanism;
- as requested by the Secretary of State, the January 2004 meeting of the HEFCE Board would review funding levels for 5*, 5 and 4-rated departments.

Vigorous debate will continue on the question of research funding methodology in view of the financial benefits arising from research funding and of the importance of 'research' in defining what constitutes a 'university'.

Chapter 4

Strategic business planning
The financial dimension

Introduction

Overview

This chapter is concerned with strategic planning in HEIs and the role and contribution of finance to that process. Strategic planning is undertaken in most medium to large organisations in both public and private sectors but a broad distinction can be drawn between two main types of strategic planning which indicates a major difference in approach between them.

- **Type 1**: Strategic planning in public sector organisations such as local authorities and the NHS is largely concerned with how to best use a fixed pool of resources in such a way as to meet the needs of service users in the most effective and efficient way. Thus it involves assessing the needs of service users and identifying the most effective and efficient means of delivering services with fixed resources.
- **Type 2**: Strategic planning in private sector commercial or quasi-commercial organisations is concerned more with the identification of markets and products, the achievement of competitive advantage and the maintenance of financial viability. We refer to this form of strategic planning as **strategic business planning**.

Constitutionally HEIs are private sector organisations which operate in a manner akin to many commercial organisations in that they have to attract students in a competitive market and win research and other contracts to achieve financial viability. HEIs do not have to make dividend payments to shareholders and so they have similarities to 'not for profit' organisations. This is something of a misnomer since such organisations do actually make profits but all of the profits will ultimately be reinvested back into the business as opposed to being distributed to shareholders. Likewise, HEIs will need to make financial surpluses for reinvestment back into the organisation.

The terms 'strategy' and 'strategic planning' are, possibly among the most mis-used words in the English language and there is usually considerable confusion as to what is meant by strategy. Like most aspects of management, the essence of organisational strategy is very simple and is concerned with answering three main questions in relation to the organisation:

1. Where are we now?
2. Where do we wish to get to **in the longer term?**
3. How do we get where we want to be?

These three questions can be regarded as being in increasing order of difficulty to answer. It is **relatively** easy, although time consuming, for an organisation to establish its current situation and where it stands in relation to its external working environment. It is more difficult for it to establish where it wishes to be to in the longer term as regards its size, its range of activities, its priorities, and so on. However, the most difficult aspect of strategy is establishing how the organisation is to get from where it is now to where it wants to be in the future. Achieving this can often require significant and radical change in an organisation and the management of such change is often difficult particularly in the conservative culture of many HEIs.

Finance has a key role to play in strategic planning and this chapter is primarily about the financial role in strategic planning and the contribution that can be made by the finance function to this process.

The main stages of strategic business planning

The classical approach to strategic business planning has a number of inter-related stages which are shown in Figure 4.1.

These various stages can be linked and summarised in terms of the three key questions already identified:

- **Where are we now?** – SWOT analysis incorporating
  - internal appraisal of the organisation;
  - external appraisal of the environment.
- **Where do we wish to get to in the longer term?**
  - mission statement;
  - strategic objectives.
- **How do we get there?**
  - strategy development and evaluation;
  - risk analysis;
  - implementation plan.

Why prepare strategic business plans

There are a number of reasons why organisations, including HEIs, need to prepare strategic business plans:

- **Avoiding failure** Such failure can result from a number of causes including: inadequate market research, inability to recruit key members of staff, and

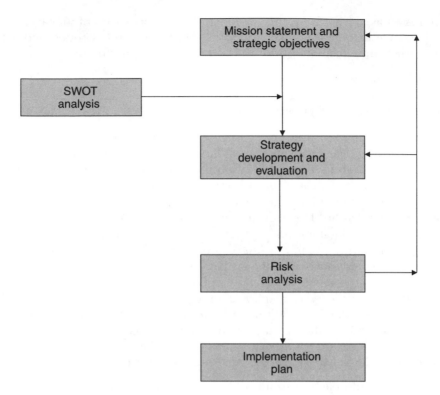

Figure 4.1   *Stages in business planning*

so on. Although there is no guarantee against failure, sound strategic business planning minimises the risk of failure.

- **Achieving success** Not synonymous with avoiding failure but more to do with such matters as achieving growth and improving service standards. Precise indicators of success will be identified by the mission statement and strategic objectives of the organisation (discussed later in this chapter). Again, strategic business planning can assist an organisation in achieving success.

- **Oganisational co-ordination** Although strategic business planning can take place at the organisational level, individual departments frequently prepare their own plans to ensure they have a viable business unit with a viable strategy. Where the organisation has decentralised a large amount of authority to individual departments, the strategic business planning process can be used as a channel for co-ordination and as a means of ironing out any potential confusion, duplication and disfunctionality between such decentralised plans.

- **Gaining internal commitment** A vital ingredient of an effective organisation is its staff's commitment to the mission and objectives of the organisation. This can be a lengthy and difficult task but the approach employed in preparing a strategic business plan can contribute towards achieving this commitment. Too often, strategic business plans are written by senior managers to be read by other senior managers with many middle/junior managers and front-line staff having little or no involvement in the process. It is important that all staff are involved in the strategic business planning process to help to internalise and work towards the organisation's overall objectives and to ensure that all views are considered.

- **Raising finance** A request to a bank, or other funding agency, for a large loan is likely to be met with a counter-request for a business plan in justification. The business plan must underpin the content of the business case for undertaking, in particular, capital projects.
- **Statutory requirements** Where organisations are part of the public sector or obtain large amounts of public funds (e.g., HEIs) the preparation of business plans is often a statutory requirement.

Strategic business planning in HEIs

In this section we consider approaches to strategic business planning in HEIs.

Strategic context

As HEIs are independent private sector organisations it is incumbent on them to develop strategies which ensure the ongoing viability of the institution and enable it to meet its longer-term aspirations. However, a number of additional points also need to be recognised:

- HEIs in the UK compete with one another for students and research funds in a manner akin to commercial organisations. Thus their strategic business plan must have a strong commercial emphasis.
- Each HEI forms part of the overall UK HE sector and the development of the HE sector is a key component of public policy. Hence, in preparing a strategic business plan, an HEI cannot ignore the public policy and the strategic aims of the Government and funding councils.
- To a lesser or greater degree HEIs in the UK can be considered as forming part of the global HE sector and thus can be considered as competing with HEIs in other countries both in terms of winning research funds and in attracting students. Thus, in preparing a strategic business plan, HEIs also need an awareness of trends in the global HE market.

Mission statement and strategic objectives

For an HEI, this involves defining the longer-term strategic aspirations of the organisation through the derivation of a mission statement. Although the HE sector is, officially, a unified sector with all HEIs being regarded as being of equal status and calibre, in reality there are significant differences in activities and resource base between the world-class research-intensive universities and the other HEIs. Not surprisingly, therefore, significant differences will exist between overall missions of individual HEIs. These differences will concern a number of issues including:

- **Teaching and research** The leading research universities will have a mission which is strongly focused on world-class research and which places research at least equal to or possibly of greater importance than teaching. Other HEIs will have a much more teaching-oriented mission with research, if undertaken at all, being a subsidiary activity undertaken, primarily, in support of teaching. Between these extremes will be HEIs with differing balances between teaching and research activity.
- **Geographic focus** The older and more research-intensive universities are more likely to be serious players on an international stage and their mission will reflect this. Other HEIs will operate nationally while yet others will have a more local or regional focus.
- **Third stream activity** HEIs may differ as to the extent they wish to move away from traditional areas of teaching and research into various aspects of what is often referred to as 'third stream activity'. Although the recent HE White Paper and the subsequent Lambert Report emphasises the need for better links between academia and business it is likely that HEIs will differ as to the priority they place on such third stream activities. Some will see third stream income as a financial necessity while in others the emphasis will probably remain on the pursuit of funds for teaching and research.

The development of strategic objectives will involve fleshing out the mission statement into precise and quantifiable elements and such objectives provide the foundation for outlining what the HEIs aims for in *the longer term*. An HEI strategic business plan should have a series of strategic objectives which will be institutionally specific, but a number of over-arching objectives also exist which should apply to all HEIs and should be incorporated into their plan.

- **Viability** The plan needs to ensure viability, and particularly financial viability, for the organisation. It is not sufficient for the HEI to plan to, merely, break even financially or to make a small financial surpluses, since an unexpected event could endanger the viability of the organisation if it has no financial 'cushion' to absorb the shock.
- **Sustainability** The plan needs to ensure that the HEI will be sustainable in the longer term given that it operates in a competitive environment

both for students and for research funding. HEIs will, therefore, have to remain competitive in the HE market (be this a domestic market or an international market) and must ensure that they identify (and provide funds for) future investment in physical resources (e.g., buildings, equipment, IT) and human resources (skills, knowledge, etc). The HEI which does not plan for such investment will, over time, probably become less competitive and this could endanger its sustainability.

- **Acceptability** Perhaps the key resource in any HEI is its academic staff and such staff work in HE for specific reasons. Therefore, it is of vital importance that the strategic business plan of the HEI is acceptable to the academic body. Looking externally, where an HEI has strong links to the local community or region then the strategic business plan needs to be acceptable to local stakeholders such as the local authority and the RDA. Finally, where an HEI is a large receiver of Government funds from funding councils it is important that its strategic plan is acceptable to Government and supports Government policies in relation to HE. However, where an HEI is less reliant on funding council revenues then this may be a less important issue.

If we turn to specific strategic objectives, an HEI could have any of those shown in Figure 4.2.

These examples are illustrative and not exhaustive. However, it is vitally important that strategic objectives should be capable of quantification and measurement.

Teaching and learning objectives	Research objectives
• Growth in student numbers • Improvement in student retention rates • Widening of participation • Improved teaching quality • Improved student satisfaction • Improved student employment	• Improved research ratings via RAE • Increased research contract/grant activity • Increased global research • Increased research for local/regional organisations
Third stream objectives	**Objectives regarding HEI resources**
• Increased links with local and regional business organisations • Increased links with multi-national companies based in the UK • Increased links with economic development agencies	• Reduced staff turnover • More flexible labour force • Improved visual appearance of the campus

Figure 4.2 *Possible HEI strategic objectives*

SWOT analysis

Strategic business planning must be undertaken with a full understanding of one's position and what the future may hold. A key element is a SWOT (strengths, weaknesses, opportunities, threats) analysis which comprises two distinct but related parts:

Internal appraisal: strengths and weaknesses

It is essential that any internal assessment of the HEI is both systematic and honest. Experience has shown that many organisations overstate their strengths and understate their weaknesses because they find it uncomfortable to face up to reality. Examples of areas to be covered in this internal review include:

- **Academic staff quality** – good researchers will be needed for research purposes while good teachers will be required if it is wished to expand teaching and learning.
- **Equipment** – good-quality scientific equipment will be needed to promote research capabilities but also good IT facilities will be needed for all strands of activity.
- **Student residences** – any HEI will require reasonable student accommodation if it wishes to attract students, this factor being particularly important in relation to overseas recruitment.
- **Campus appearance and layout** – the visual appearance and layout of the campus may influence student choices.
- **Financial position** – an HEI with substantial financial reserves has the capacity for investment whereas an HEI with low reserves and poor financial performance will find it difficult to obtain investment funds.

External appraisal: opportunities and threats

This aims to review the business environment in which the HEI operates in order to identify opportunities to seize and threats to avoid or negate. It is important to realise that some factors can represent an opportunity or a threat depending on circumstances. A number of opportunities and threats may present themselves to an HEI preparing a strategic business plan and these matters should be taken account of in the plan. Some examples include the following:

- **Demographic and social trends** – demographic changes in the local population (particularly the numbers of residents in the 18–25 age group) can have implications for HEI planning of local recruitment. Also, national demographic changes can have implications for changes in the size of the population served, its structure in terms of age, sex and social class and its attitudes.

- **Competitor trends** – for attracting students, the HEI will have other HEIs as competitors but also competition may come from local FECs who are also delivering HE provision. For research, the main competitors will be other HEIs but for third stream activities, potential competitors will be a wide range of commercial organisations as well as HEIs.
- **Technological trends** – developments in teaching and learning technology are likely to impact on the HEI and should be considered.
- **Business trends** – trends in the local and national economy can provide both opportunities and threats to HEIs. Positive economic developments such as new factory developments can provide potential sources of new business for HEIs but also an economic downturn might provide opportunities for recruiting greater numbers of students seeking retraining.

Strategy development

Within an HEI a variety of different strategies might be identified as there are usually several different routes to any destination. HEI strategies can be viewed as a series of strands which meet to provide an overall corporate strategic plan for the HEI. Some of these strands are concerned with the business activities of the HEI and some with the resources it utilises. This is illustrated in Figure 4.3.

In reality these separate strategies are best viewed as components of an overall and integrated strategic business plan, hence our reference to them as strands. Thus within the overall strategic business plan there will be a series of

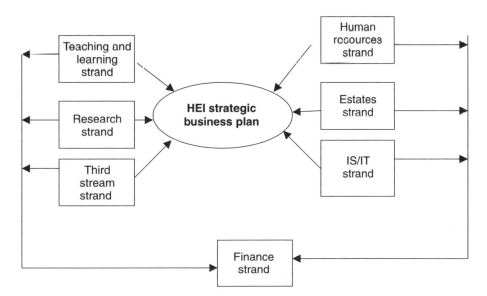

Figure 4.3 *Strategic development strands*

business strands concerned with teaching/learning, research and other third stream activities and also a number of resource strands concerned with HR, estates and IS/IT. Binding all of these together will be the financial strand. In the absence of a robust financial strand an HEI cannot be confident that its overall strategic business plan can be afforded or that it will be able to meet its financial objectives concerning surplus/deficit, cash flow, capital financing, and so on.

Regarding the business strands, the formulation of strategy within an HEI will be primarily be concerned with the following issues:

- **Strand size** – what is the desired overall magnitude of each of these strands? For example, what is the student number target and how big does the HEI aim to be? It is often automatically assumed that an HEI should always aim to grow in size but this is not always true. Although larger size may improve competitiveness and provide economies of scale, negative points may be associated with growth. For example, growth in size may mean that an HEI loses its caring and comfortable image for some students.
- **Strand balance** – although all HEIs will pursue all of these strands to some extent, the process should consider the overall balance between them and whether this needs to change. For example, one HEI may wish to give increased focus to teaching at the expense of research, whereas another may wish to increase its focus on working with industry.
- **Strand configuration and diversity** – within each of the strands, the HEI strategy will need to address the diversity of activities undertaken and the detailed configuration of those activities.

In more detail, various aspects of the strands might comprise the following.

Teaching and learning strand

- **Mix of students** – it will need to identify the balance to be placed on the recruitment of students with regard to:
  - source of students (e.g., domestic, overseas);
  - mode of student (FT, PT, distance learning);
  - level of student (UG, PG, CPD).
- **Curriculum content** – basically, in response to market forces, an HEI could decide to do one (or a combination) of three things:
  - Maintain its current range of curricular activities.
  - Enlarge its range of curricular activities. This could involve the HEI moving into completely new curriculum areas but this might require substantial investment in physical and human resources. It is more likely that curriculum developments will take place at the margins of existing activities with new developments involving refocusing of existing activities, or the development of combinations of existing activities,

for example, the development of environmental sciences from the core disciplines of geography and biology.
- Contract its range of curricular activities by eliminating less popular activities in certain subject areas or by eliminating complete subject areas. In recent years a number of HEIs have reduced engineering and science curriculum activities. However, in many HEIs, there is likely to be strong academic resistance to such actions.
- **Curriculum delivery methods** – the strategy will need to identify the balance to be placed on different curriculum delivery methods including:
  - traditional campus-based learning;
  - direct outreach provision;
  - franchising of HE provision in FE colleges;
  - distance learning;
  - e-learning.

Obviously the costs, risks and potential returns from each of these approaches will vary substantially.

Research strand

The HEI may decide to adopt one or a mix of strategies including:

- strengthening research activity in all subject areas or alternatively just focusing on its stronger areas;
- promoting greater multi-disciplinary and collaborative research;
- attempting to improve the profitability of its contract research.

Third stream strand

The HEI may decide to:

- improve its focus on CPD activities;
- set up a consultancy business, possibly by means of a wholly owned company;
- try to better exploit its intellectual property as a source of income.

Resource strands

Figure 4.3 shows the various resource strands that make up the strategy, namely: human resources, estates, IS/IT and finance. In developing a resource strategy a number of issues will need to be addressed including the following:

- what should be the balance between full time, temporary and hourly paid staff;
- what staff remuneration mechanisms should be introduced;
- on how many campuses should the HEI operate;

- what should be the balance between purchase and lease of equipment;
- what role should IS/IT play in teaching and learning;
- what is an appropriate balance between fixed costs and variable costs for the organisation?

Strategy evaluation

Having identified and developed possible strategies, each must be evaluated to establish the best way forward. There are two essential matters to consider:

- is the strategy feasible – will it enable the strategic objectives to be achieved?
- is the strategy resource feasible in terms of the availability, to the organisation, of key resources?

Both of these are important and necessary conditions as it is possible to develop strategies which are feasible regarding strategic objectives but not feasible in resource terms. The opposite may also be true and strategies which are resource feasible should not necessarily be followed. Commercial organisations frequently sell off profitable and well-resourced activities, simply because they do not fit in with the strategic objectives of the organisation.

Assessing strategic feasibility

This involves identifying that strategy which has the best chance of success in terms of attaining the HEI's strategic objectives. Three different evaluation approaches are summarised here:

- *Identify competitive advantage*: suitable where an organisation/HEI is in competition with others to provide some of all or its range of products and services. Evaluation of the possible business strategies will be in terms of whether they can give the organisation a competitive advantage over the other providers. This competitive advantage could be through lower costs, by product differentiation (e.g., better quality), or by specialisation (niche market).
- *Undertake a strategic appraisal*: this approach involves evaluating the various strategies proposed against the results of the SWOT analysis. If for example a particular strategy utilises one of the existing strengths of the organisation then this would be a plus point for that strategy. However, if the strategy required pursuit of an activity in an area where the organisation was weak, for example, with poorly skilled staff, then it would have to choose between not pursuing that particular strategy, or taking action to reduce or eradicate the weakness, possibly through significant investment. Each of the strategies identified are judged as to whether it involves building on internal strengths or weaknesses or whether it involves

building on areas identified as 'opportunities' or 'threats'. Thus for each strategy a scorecard is compiled which assists the HEI in making an informed judgement about which is the best strategic option.

- *Portfolio analysis*: this approach involves evaluating strategies according to their risk/return profile. In reality different activities generate different rates of return and also have different risk profiles. Furthermore, in the 'real' world high return is usually associated with high risk. Different business strategies could be evaluated by a consideration of their risk/return profiles usually referred to as portfolio analysis. The various aspects of risk and return can be considered in relation to the mix of activities undertaken and the mix of resources needed to undertake those activities. There is no correct combination of risk and return and it is for each HEI to choose a strategy that it judges to be most appropriate.

It is important to emphasise that these three approaches to evaluating strategies are not mutually exclusive but can be applied individually or in combination.

Assessing resource feasibility

Strategies must be feasible both in terms of achieving strategic objectives and in resource terms, the latter including: human resources, fixed assets, specialist supplies and finance. Some factors which may result in a strategy not being resource feasible are:

- unavailability of certain human resources;
- fixed assets and specialist supplies are unobtainable;
- the whole strategy is financially unsound;
- redundant resources cannot be disposed of.

Although finance is not the only resource which must be considered it is perhaps the most critical. This aspect of resource feasibility is discussed further in a later section.

Strategic business planning and risk

Any strategic business plan should consider the potential risks faced by the organisation and the possible ways of dealing with those risks. Such risks may have implications in a number of areas including:

- student perceptions;
- research council perceptions;
- public perceptions;
- staff perceptions;
- financial performance.

Issues of uncertainty and risk should be addressed systematically according to the following stages:

- **Risk identification** – identify possible sources and causes of risk. This must be undertaken thoroughly and will require considerable thought, brainstorming and critical evaluation. Some examples of such risks might include:
  - poor teaching quality assessment;
  - poor research assessment;
  - loss of key staff;
  - failure of key equipment;
  - IT failures;
  - late completion of a new building;
  - shortfall in student recruitment;
  - rise in interest rates.
- **Risk analysis** – the various risks should be analysed to assess:
  - the probability of the risk occurring;
  - the implications of the risk occurring including possible financial implications.

These tasks must be done thoroughly and objectively since there is much evidence (see the *Economist* 24–30 January 2004) to show that people have an inherent tendency to misjudge both probabilities and implications of risks.

- **Risk prioritisation** – from the above analysis, tabulate the risks identified in terms of order of priority to be addressed.
- **Risk handling strategies** – in the strategic business plan, the HEI has to consider how to respond to the risks it faces. Broadly, there are only four possible actions in relation to each risk factor:
  Minimise risk – actions could be taken to minimise the risks faced by, for example, replacing an ineffective manager or an unreliable piece of equipment, providing staff training or developing new procedures or protocols.
  Transfer/share risk – risks could be transferred to or shared with another organization, for example, by the sub-contracting of certain activities such as IT management to a third party which would assume many of the IT risks involved.
  Avoid risk – the level of risk associated with certain activities may be unacceptably high and the HEI might decide to avoid such risks by not undertaking a particular activity or undertaking it in a very different way. An example might the avoidance of certain overseas ventures where the HEI might face an unacceptable degree of risk due to currency fluctuations or insecurity of payment.
  Retain risk – not all risks can be transferred or completely eliminated. Thus the HEI must be clear about what level of risk it is prepared to retain and accept.

- **Risk coping practices** – in view of the residual risks which are inevitably retained within the organisation, it is important to have in place established practices and procedures for coping with such risks should they materialise. This could involve effective early-warning monitoring of known risk factors and having in place contingency plans to deal with the impact of retained risks which actually manifest themselves. These could be arrangements to hire contract personnel to replace the loss of specialist staff or arrangements to lease buildings or equipment to replace those lost through breakdown or sabotage. Also it would involve putting in place financial contingency measures and financial provisions to deal with the impact of risks that might occur.

Implementation planning

Strategic business plans need a comprehensive and detailed implementation plan to ensure that the planned events actually occur. In reality the large size of many such plans is frequently due to the need to describe the large number of tasks that need to be undertaken to put the business plan into action. Such a plan will have a number of key parts including:

- tasks that need to be performed;
- individual responsibilities for ensuring they are performed;
- timetable for completing tasks;
- resources needed.

The implementation of a strategic business plan may well require substantial changes in the organisational arrangements and operational practices within the HEI. Such changes are often so radical that they may generate fierce opposition and resistance to change within the organisation and successful implementation may depend on overcoming such resistance to change. Hence, as part of its implementation plan, the organisation needs to develop a suitable change management programme and commit sufficient resources to that programme.

Monitoring of business plans

Few implementations go completely according to plan. Hence it is important that the implementation of a plan is monitored robustly. In practice this means having suitable project management arrangements to ensure that:

- adequate information is available about the progress being made in implementing the plan and the impacts of that implementation;
- the implementation progress is constantly reviewed and updated;
- immediate action is taken where the implementation deviates seriously from plan.

The financial contribution to HEI strategic business planning

In any HEI the finance function has important roles to play in the development of strategic business plans and can make important contributions in a number of areas.

Setting of financial objectives

Along with other planning objectives, the HEI needs to have some clear financial objectives. For example, funding councils have, in the past, suggested that HEIs should aim, as a minimum, to generate a financial surplus equal to 3 per cent of turnover, but in today's climate of equal importance will be issues concerning cash flow and the generation of usable funds for investment purposes.

Financial analysis of existing activities

An analysis can be provided of the financial performance of existing activities to identify the level of surplus/deficit being generated by each activity. At a basic level this would involve identifying the overall performance of individual departments and within that the separate financial performance of teaching, research and other activities. Beyond this an analysis might be provided of the financial performance of individual courses and research projects. Such an analysis will enable the HEI to see the levels of cross-subsidy within its existing portfolio of activities and to plan accordingly for the future. Comparisons can be made of the costs of undertaking various activities in the HEI compared to other HEIs or other organisations. The technique of benchmarking, which is discussed below, will facilitate this task.

Resource forecasting

This essentially involves forecasting the likely level of resources available to the organisation over a strategic period of several years and will need to assess:

- the impact of the Government's public expenditure plans on overall public sector funding;
- the impact of public policy trends on different parts of the public sector and individual HEIs;
- the impact of possible changes in the mechanisms of resource allocation;
- the impact of inflation on the organisation;
- the impact of variable student top-up fees on income levels;
- the potential for generating income through the recruitment of overseas students;
- the potential for generating third stream income.

Given the level of uncertainty and risk involved it will be necessary to prepare several different resource scenarios based on differing sets of assumptions and upon which different strategic planning scenarios can be built. Financial modelling is an essential tool and will be discussed further below.

Financial evaluation of strategic options

In preparing strategic business plans, HEIs must develop and evaluate a number of different strategic options and undertake an evaluation of the financial implications of those options. Options which might be evaluated include the following:

- reconfiguration of the range and/or volume of service provision;
- rationalisation/amendment of methods of delivering service;
- rationalisation/reconfiguration of estates options.

None of these changes can be achieved in one year and thus there must be a multi-year strategy. Longer-term financial plans will be needed to support strategic planning and it is completely inadequate to rely on an annual financial plan. HEIs need to develop a multi-year financial plan covering at least a 3–5 year period and, possibly longer. Such plans should incorporate the following:

- **Income and expenditure account** – this will show the forecast financial performance, in terms of surplus or deficit, for each year in question and will enable the organisation to assess the rate of return it is likely to achieve on its assets.
- **Balance sheet** – this will show the forecast financial position at the end of each financial year in terms of assets and liabilities and, most critically, the forecast cash position.
- **Capital programme** – this will indicate the planned pattern of capital expenditure of the organisation over the strategic period which will influence the income and expenditure account, in terms of depreciation, and the balance sheet in terms of fixed assets.
- **Cash flow statement** – this will show the pattern of cash inflow and outflow over the strategic period covering both revenue and capital items.

Again, in all of the above situations it would be beneficial if HEIs could develop a financial planning model (or models).

Project appraisal

Often a strategic business plan will incorporate a number of specific projects such as new buildings, new staff, new income generation activities which will need to be appraised from a number of different standpoints, a key one being the financial appraisal.

Case study 4.1   *Financial evaluation of strategic options*

Sandilands University is a multi-campus post-1992 university which has been encountering severe financial difficulties in recent years due to problems of student recruitment. The university plans to embark on an ambitious programme of change which will incorporate:

- changes in the pattern of courses and curriculum content in a number of departments;
- expansion of certain third stream activities;
- rationalisation of 25 academic departments to eight schools;
- rationalisation of its campuses from three down to one;
- substantial changes in administrative practices and procedures.

These changes will also take place over the period when variable top-up fees are due to be introduced.

The changes taken together will have significant implications for income, capital costs and running costs.

At the present time the university does not possess financial models which are sophisticated enough to accurately and quickly identify the financial implications of proposed changes. Hence the strategic planning process is being delayed. The university has decided to commission the development of such financial models which will facilitate quicker and better evaluation of the various options being considered.

Funding strategies

To implement its strategic business plan, the HEI will need demonstrate how it can fund its investment programme. Possible sources include:

- borrowing;
- grants;
- internal funds;
- partnership arrangements with a third party;
- leasing.

Its funding strategy will need to show the sources of funds it intends to utilise to finance its future developments and the different levels of risk attached to the differing sources. For example, borrowing may run the risk of increased costs due to increased interest rates whereas grants are basically risk free. Thus in developing a financing strategy the HEI will need to take account of the risks associated with each financing source and the overall impact on its balance sheet structure.

Financial techniques and HEI strategic business plans

In the remaining section of this chapter, we discuss some particular financial techniques which can be of relevance to the financial aspects of HEI strategic business plans:

- cost and income benchmarking;
- financial modelling;
- investment appraisal.

Cost and income benchmarking

Benchmarking is a technique which can help assess the current performance of activities in the HEI. For example an HEI might attempt to compare its costs and income levels against benchmarks derived from costs and income of other HEIs and/or other organisations. Inferences could then be made about those activities.

Although the thrust would relate to the benchmarking of costs and income, for the process to be useful a wide range of information would need to be collected including:

- cost information;
- income information;
- information about volume of activity/workload to establish unit costs;
- organisational arrangements;
- process descriptions.

In this section we explore the potential use of benchmarking in more detail.

Internal benchmarks

For activities generic to departments within HEIs a series of internal benchmarks could be developed including the following:

- average class contact hours per member of academic staff;
- average number of research publications per member of academic staff;
- average income earned per member of academic staff.

Clearly differences between subject areas will need to be taken account of when making comparisons against the benchmarks.

HE sector benchmarks

Another approach might be to benchmark activities in one HEI against that in other UK HEIs. This could be done in two distinct ways:

- using benchmarks derived from all HEIs;

- using benchmarks derived from a cohort of comparable HEIs (e.g., Russell Group universities or a group of 'new universities').

The necessary information could also be obtained in two ways:

- **Using publicly available information** – performance could be compared against other HEIs by using information which is in the public domain such as:
  - HESA statistics;
  - Annual accounts;
  - HE Yearbook;
  - Professional associations.

  Although some interesting comparisons can be made using this information, two key factors limit its usefulness. These are:
  - the information is usually at too high a level of aggregation to make meaningful comparisons at an individual functional level;
  - considerable concern exists about the degree of consistency, between HEIs, in the methods they use to record publicly available information. This undermines the confidence in any such comparisons that may be made.

- **Undertaking a special exercise** – the alternative to using publicly available information is to undertake a special exercise to collect information from other HEIs. The advantage of this approach is that one can define, specifically, the type of information one wishes to collect. The major disadvantage is that experience has shown that it is often very difficult to get cooperation from other institutions in terms of sharing information. The term 'commercially confidential' is often used as a reason for not sharing information. However, the following approaches might help to increase the level of cooperation:
  - an offer could be made to the other institutions to share the findings of the study on a non-attributable basis;
  - an attempt could be made to undertake the exercise collaboratively with each institution sharing the costs of the exercise and sharing the results;
  - the information might be collected by a third party which keeps the results of individual institutions confidential;
  - information might be collected through face to face interviews rather than questionnaires. However, this approach is time consuming.

  Although this approach to benchmarking is obviously attractive the difficulties of getting comparable information should not be underestimated.

External benchmarks

Current performance at an HEI might be compared against that for a range of other organisations. This is particularly relevant for those functions which are generic and non-HE specific such as: payroll, payments and personnel administration. Comparisons might be made against any of the following:

- overseas HEIs;
- UK public sector organisations such as: NHS Trusts, local authorities;
- UK private sector organisations operating in similar business areas (e.g., private training organisations or private research organisations);
- other UK private sector organizations (e.g., credit-rating comparisons).

A wide range of information is publicly available through trade associations, professional bodies and so on. However, most of the organisations involved will be considerably different from HEIs in terms of organisation, business profile, cultural background, level of technology and so on, so the comparisons should be used with caution.

Financial modelling

A financial model will aim to demonstrate the financial effects of possible changes in real world situations. Clearly, the real world situation will differ between different types of organisation and the 'real world' of an HEI is very different from that of say a hospital or a manufacturing company. Thus any model will be constructed to incorporate the essential and significant features of the real world situation in which the organisation operates. While important features of the real world must be included in the model, other features can safely be ignored as their impact will be insignificant.

Strategic financial planning in HEIs can be greatly assisted by the development and use of computerised financial planning models as in undertaking strategic financial planning one is not looking for precision but rather looking to evaluate and compare broad strategic options. This will involve looking for the broad-brush financial implications of these options and the degree of significance, in financial terms, between options.

Types of financial model

Different types of financial planning model, can be developed and used for different strategic financial planning purposes. The following classification of such models is suggested:

- **Costing models** – in an earlier section it was noted that a key element of a SWOT analysis would be the production of information on the current financial performance of various HEI activities. It will therefore be necessary to establish the costs (and income) of those various activities and the development of a costing model can help with this. Such a model would apportion central department costs to academic departments using certain pre-determined cost drivers (e.g., staff numbers, space) and then would disaggregate each element of department costs over individual activities in accordance with previously agreed principles. The impact of changes in assumptions about cost attribution or in levels of cost and/or activity can easily be seen using such a model.

- **Option appraisal models** – where an HEI is considering any form of development then a model can be developed to financially appraise the various options involved. Take for example a campus expansion where options might include:
  - expansion on existing campus;
  - development on a greenfield site;
  - city centre development.

  A model can be developed to calculate the cost and income streams associated with each of the options, based on inputs such as increased student numbers, increased staff numbers, capital expenditure, and to financially appraise the outcomes of each option. Similarly models could be used to financially appraise various options concerned with a PFI or PPP development by a HEI.

- **Resource allocation models** – as discussed in Chapter 5, many HEIs have developed and used resource allocation models as a means of distributing financial resources to their academic schools and departments. The two key aspects of such a model would be:
  - mechanisms for distributing the various income sources (e.g., HEFCE funds, student fees, research councils grants) between academic schools and departments based on the level of activity undertaken by each school/department in relation to the different activities involved;
  - mechanisms for recharging the costs of central support services (e.g., finance, registry) to academic schools/departments which will usually be recharged using a series of drivers such as staff numbers, student numbers, space.

  As well as using such models to make actual allocations of funds and costs to academic departments, such models may also be used as crude forms of financial planning models.

- **Financial planning models** – to improve the financial analysis of their strategic business plans, in future, it will probably be necessary for HEIs to develop more sophisticated financial planning models than used previously. Such financial models can assess the financial implications of a large number of different planning scenarios by answering *what if* questions. In evaluating strategic business plans, such models can take account of diverse factors and planning assumptions and assess their financial implications. Having been constructed, such financial planning models could be used to assess the financial impact of changes in planning assumptions such as the following:
  - growth/contraction in student numbers in specific subject areas and price bands;
  - change in student mix (e.g., overseas, non-traditional);
  - change in mode of course delivery (e.g., FT/PT/distance learning);
  - changes in student fee levels;

- changes in the mix of academic staff employment (employed, hourly paid);
- different approaches to teaching and learning;
- different levels of capital expenditure in new buildings and equipment;
- increased/decreased volume and profitability of research contracts;
- increased/decreased volume of third stream income;
- changes in the levels of support costs.

Such financial models can identify any major shortfalls between the resources available and the resources needed to implement a particular strategic option, but for the model to provide a realistic representation of the real world the following factors must also be incorporated into the model:

- **Cost and cost driver relationships** – within the model, it is necessary to establish and define which cost drivers influence which types of cost. For example, within an academic department teaching and learning costs may be driven by departmental student numbers (FTE), but student assessment costs may be driven by a combination of numbers of modules and numbers of students. Also, whereas departmental costs might be driven by departmental student numbers, central costs will be driven by total HEI student numbers. Thus it is will be important to identify relevant drivers and the links between changes in the drivers and changes in related costs so that they can be built into the model.
- **Cost profiles** – within the model, profiles will need to be developed to establish the link between changes in the level of the cost driver and changes in levels of cost. Such profiles will need to recognise that in relation to changes in the levels of the cost diver some costs are fixed, some directly variable and some semi-variable. In many cases, HEIs will have an unclear picture of these profiles and will need to test out different types of profile between driver levels and costs. In future, it is likely that greater precision will be needed and rough and ready calculations assuming linearity will not suffice.
- **Resource capacity constraints** – for a planned expansion of activity (e.g., increased student numbers) HEIs will sometimes be capable of, largely, absorbing additional students on the basis of current resource levels while sometimes additional growth will require additional resources. Hence the model should include capacity measures for different types of resources (e.g., staff, lecture rooms) which will indicate when it can absorb student growth without additional costs.

Good practice in developing financial models

A number of good practice issues should be considered and applied when developing financial models:

- **Degree of complexity** – Models must provide a realistic representation of the 'real' world and although simplicity is desirable, the model should not be so over-simplistic as to be naïve. As already mentioned, some HEIs use their existing resource allocation models for financial planning purposes but most of these imply a linear relationship between activity levels and cost and so do not provide for realistic financial planning. Hence, to facilitate realistic financial planning, some degree of complexity is probably inherent in all but the crudest financial modelling.

- **Output driven** – Models must be 'fit for purpose' and deliver the outputs needed. Models must be driven by business needs, *not* availability of data. Where the required data is not immediately available then specific exercises may be required to collect that data. Failing that, assumptions may have to be made which will then comprise factors of uncertainty to be considered when undertaking a sensitivity analysis.
- **Design principles** – financial models should incorporate certain procedures designed to facilitate good practice, such as:
    - within the model architecture, identify separate areas for input, output and calculations. Mixing them up will be a source of confusion and error;
    - models must be capable of being audited and validated by a third party;
    - models must be reasonably user friendly;
    - good model documentation must be available.

Capital investment appraisal

A key aspect of a strategic business plan concerns the level and type of capital investment to be undertaken. Like most organisations in the private sector, HEIs undertake a wide range of capital investment in new buildings, new equipment and vehicles. Such capital investment can be for a variety of purposes, such as teaching, research, student accommodation or student services, and requires careful consideration and evaluation for a number of reasons including the following:

- *Large-scale expenditure* – frequently capital projects involve considerable expenditure.
- *Longer-term implications* – capital investment usually has implications for many years ahead.
- *Irreversibility* – many capital projects, once undertaken, cannot be reversed without significant additional cost.
- *Incremental revenue costs* – although some forms of capital investment can lead to lower overall revenue costs (e.g., energy conservation), many forms of capital investment, such as a campus expansion, can lead to higher revenue costs.

Effective decisions about capital investment will be critical to achieving strategic objectives and erroneous decisions can jeopardise achievement of those objectives. Hence, it is important that decisions about capital investment are rigorously appraised both in terms of the range and quality of services to be delivered and the likely financial outcomes.

Financial aspects of investment appraisal

In an HEI, capital investment might be undertaken for a number of reasons such as improved profile, achievement of government policy etc and although projects should be appraised with these aims in mind it is essential that such projects be subject to a thorough financial appraisal. This will focus on three issues:

- economic viability;
- affordability;
- funding viability.

Economic viability

At the outset, it is important to appraise the overall economic viability of a proposed capital development. There are various commercial approaches to capital investment appraisal such as payback (which merely involves calculating how many years it will take for the returns from a project to repay the initial investment) and accountants' rate of return, which are fairly simple in nature and are commonly used. However, the main weakness of these approaches is that the only issue considered is the size of the various cash flows associated with a project and they ignore what is termed the time value of money since the timing of the cash flows is not considered. Thus they assume that £100 received or paid in year 1 is equivalent to £100 received in year 2 and so on. However, economics teaches that money has a time value as well as a magnitude and argues that £100 received in year 1 has a greater value than £100 in year 2 (which has greater value than £100 in year 3, etc). Similarly, £100 spent in year 1 has a higher cost than £100 spent in year 2. This is for two main reasons:

- the future is uncertain and £100 receivable today is preferable to £100 in a year's time when one may no longer be able to enjoy the benefit of that £100;
- £100 today can be invested to produce a return which will be in excess of £100 in a year's time.

This basic principle of the time value of the money leads to the discounted cash flow (DCF) approach which takes account of both the magnitude and the timing of the cash flows involved when evaluating capital projects. It is this DCF approach which (under funding council guidance) must be used for the financial appraisal of projects in HEIs.

It is not possible here to give a full explanation of the DCF approach and the interested reader is referred to the many excellent books on the subject, but an attempt is made here to give a brief explanation of the rationale of the method.

Basic principles of DCF

With DCF, cash flows, whether they are inflows or outflows, in whatever time period they occur are converted to a common point of reference, namely a present value. Present value is essentially the converse of compound interest. Assuming an interest rate of 10 per cent, then if £100 has a future value of £110 in a year's time the converse is that £110 receivable in a year's time has a present value of £100. Similarly, £121 receivable in two years' time has a present value of £100. Thus all cash flows can be converted to a present value. When cash inflows and outflows are combined, the present value becomes a net present value (NPV).

Let us look at a simple practical example. An organisation is considering two possible projects involving investment in new equipment both of which have a capital cost of £100,000. The organisation can borrow money at 10 per cent to purchase the equipment. Both types of equipment have a four-year life and will be used to manufacture different products. There will be production costs associated with the manufacture of the products and revenues from the sales of the products. The financial implications are shown in Figure 4.4.

Three points should be noted about the results of the appraisal:

- in terms of total cash flow, project Y has a larger positive net cash flow than project X;
- but project X has a larger net present value of cash flows than project Y; this is because the larger positive cash flows in project X occur earlier in the lifespan of the project and thus generate higher present values than cash flows occurring later in the project;
- project X has a positive NPV whereas project Y has a negative NPV.

DCF techniques provide two decision rules for the financial appraisal of potential capital projects:

- in purely financial terms, projects which show a positive NPV should be undertaken while those which have negative NPVs should not be undertaken; in this case, project X should be undertaken but project Y should not;
- where several competing projects have positive NPVs but only one can be undertaken (e.g., because of limited investment funds available), the project with the highest positive NPV should be chosen.

The results of a DCF analysis will be significantly affected by the discount rate used in the analysis. In the above example, for simplicity, a discount

Basic data

	Project X			Project Y		
Year	Production costs	Sales revenue generated	Net cash flow	Production costs	Sales revenue generated	Net cash flow
	£	£	£	£	£	£
1	−20,000	+60,000	+40,000	−20,000	+38,000	+18,000
2	−30,000	+65,000	+35,000	−30,000	+65,000	+35,000
3	−30,000	+65,000	+35,000	−30,000	+65,000	+35,000
4	−20,000	+36,000	+16,000	−20,000	+60,000	+40,000

Results of DCF analysis

	Project X		
Year	Net cash flow	Discount factor = present value of £1 in the year	Present value of cash flow
	£		£
0	−100,000	1.00	−100,000
1	+40,000	0.91	+36,400
2	+35,000	0.83	+29,050
3	+35,000	0.75	+26,250
4	+16,000	0.68	+10,880
Total	+26,000	NPV =	+2,580

	Project Y		
Year	Net cash flow	Discount factor = present value of £1 in the year	Present value of cash flow
	£		£
0	−100,000	1.00	−100,000
1	+18,000	0.91	+16,380
2	+35,000	0.83	+29,050
3	+35,000	0.75	+26,250
4	+40,000	0.68	+27,200
Total	+28,000	NPV =	−1,120

Figure 4.4   *Using DCF for investment appraisal*

rate of 10 per cent was used. In practice, however, the following approaches will apply:

- In the public sector, organisations are usually required to use a discount rate of 3.5 per cent, as laid down by HM Treasury. The validity of this 3.5 per cent discount rate may be questioned but it is supposed to represent the marginal rate of return, in real terms, being achieved by the private sector of the economy.

● In the private sector, organisations will derive their own discount rate based on their cost of capital which is derived from the financing structure of the organisation.

Use of DCF in the HE sector

HEFCE guidance is available on the appraisal of capital investments in HEIs and this guidance incorporates a requirement to use NPV techniques to appraise capital projects. The guidance emphasise the following points:

● the potential projects should, usually, be appraised over a period of 25 years;
● the calculation of NPVs should be undertaken using the discount rate set out in HM Treasury guidance for public sector investments (3.5 per cent). This requirement may seem somewhat anomalous since HEIs are not public sector organisations and much of their capital investment will be financed from commercial rather than publicly funded sources. Thus their actual cost of capital may be somewhat different from that reflected in the Treasury rate.

Affordability

Any major investment project will have a number of financial implications including:

● capital expenditure;
● non-recurring costs;
● recurring costs;
● depreciation costs;
● income streams;
● receipt of capital grants;
● financing costs of loans;
● repayment of loans.

All of these items will have an impact on the future financial performance of the HEI as shown in its income and expenditure account. A project which is not properly financially appraised could have such a negative impact on the projected (I&E) financial performance that it cannot be regarded as affordable and the capital investment appraisal should therefore involve projecting the impact on the I&E account of undertaking the proposed level of investment.

Funding viability

In many situations, HEIs undertaking major capital projects will have to incur significant borrowing to finance the project even though some grant finance

Case study 4.2   Investment appraisal

Burntwood University is considering undertaking a major investment in a second campus which will significantly increase its student numbers. The basic parameters of the project are as follows:

- capital expenditure;
- additional running costs;
- additional income streams.

Using the above figures, the university has conducted a DCF analysis and the project shows a small positive NPV.

However, the university has little access to capital grants and so most of the capital expenditure will have to be financed from commercial loans resulting in additional borrowings and additional financing costs.

In the light of this, the university has also forecast the likely impact of the project on its income and expenditure account and the results are as follows:

	Without project (£m)	With project (£m)
Income	29.7	36.8
Running costs	28.7	35.5
Additional financing costs	–	2.1
Surplus/deficit	1.0	(0.8)

The high level of additional financing costs associated with the project impacts on I&E performance in such a way as to make the project unaffordable, even though it generated a positive NPV.

may be available. However, the ability to borrow is not unlimited and will be constrained by HEFCE restrictions contained in the Financial Memorandum and the willingness of financial markets to provide capital finance. Thus the investment appraisal will need to consider the viability of the proposed funding strategy and the associated risks.

Chapter 5

Budgetary systems and budgetary management

Introduction

In any organisation of significant size, a system of budgeting is essential and all HEIs will operate some system of budgeting and budgetary control. However, a budgeting system should not just be seen as a narrow instrument of financial control operated by the finance director to constrain overall expenditure within set limits, but should also be seen as a key element of management which aims:

- to improve the overall performance of an organisation in terms of the quantity, quality and cost of services delivered;
- to show how plans for change are to be implemented.

This chapter considers the issue of budgets and budget management in an HEI context and is structured as follows:

- the main purposes and functions of a budget system;
- the different types of budget that can exist;
- an overview of the key elements making up a budget system;
- the use of resource allocation models (RAM) in HEIs and their link to the budget process;
- the role of budget setting in performance improvement;
- factors to be considered when establishing budgetary arrangements.

In each case the application and operation of budget systems within HEIs will be considered alongside general principles of budgeting.

Purpose of a budget system

As already noted, it is not the sole, nor even the most important, purpose of a budgeting system to contain expenditure within pre-defined limits. This can be achieved in any large organisation without a sophisticated budget system by means of a number of fairly crude measures such as:

- freezing staff vacancies;
- cutting back on buildings and equipment maintenance to the bare minimum;
- deferral of purchases to a later date.

However, these crude approaches can have serious longer-term consequences for the organisation and cannot be seen as an effective approach to resource management. Hence, a budgeting system is an essential managerial tool which needs to be operated for a number of reasons:

- **Delegation** – once organisations reach a certain size they become too large and complex for one individual to manage. Delegating certain decisions to lower levels of management is one way of resolving this problem and this can be aided by utilising a system of budgets. Giving a subordinate manager a budget delegates the authority to incur expenditure up to the budget level without the need to refer the expenditure decision to higher authority. Thus in an HEI, certain budgets may be delegated from the centre to the faculty, from the faculty to the department level and even further delegated to a particular section or curriculum area within a department. There is a strong argument for saying that delegation should improve the speed of decision making, since subordinate managers do not need to obtain higher authority to implement a decision. It can also be argued that such budget delegation may also lead to better decisions because the lower level manager is closer to the point of action and therefore better informed about what needs to be done.
- **Planning** – budgeting is an important element in the planning process of an organisation. Periodically an organisation will usually need to prepare a plan which outlines the activities to be undertaken over the next few years and the resources to be used. Typically such a plan will be for several years duration with the first year being firmer than the later years. Thus the budget of the organisation will then be the expression of that plan in financial terms.
- **Resource allocation** – linked to the planning function is the function of internal resource allocation. The overall resources available to the organisation are limited and must be shared among competing activities in the organisation. The budget system is the usual mechanism for doing this. The use of resource allocation models is commonplace in HEIs and will be discussed later in this chapter.
- **Financial control** – having set a plan and allocated resources accordingly, it is important that the plan is achieved. This is also true in financial terms and one key role of a budgeting system is to exert managerial control over spending to ensure that actual expenditure does not deviate too far from what was planned in the budget both in terms of individual budgets and the organisation as a whole. This is usually referred to as budgetary

control and involves periodically reporting to budget managers their actual spending in a period compared to that planned so that corrective action can be taken where needed.

- **Motivation** – finally and perhaps the most neglected function is that of motivation. Much evidence exists to show that budgetary systems are not behaviourally neutral. The way in which budgets are set and budgetary control operated can have a considerable impact on the managerial performance of an individual manager.

Types of budget

Within any large organisation, including an HEI, a number of different types of budget will exist. The main ones are as follows:

Income budgets

HEIs need to generate income to fund expenditure and undertake activities. In HEIs, income is received from a variety of different sources and, therefore, the HEI will have a range of income budgets which reflect targets for generating income from those different sources. These income budgets will need to be carefully monitored since shortfalls in such income budgets could cause severe problems in the organisation. Within an HEI, there will be income budgets relating to a number of different income sources such as:

- domestic student fees;
- overseas student fees;
- funding council's income;
- research contract income;
- consultancy fees;
- catering and residential charges.

Such income budgets may be retained and monitored centrally in the HEI and not distributed to individual departments. Alternatively they may be delegated to academic or support departments in the organisation and monitored at the lower level. In the HE sector there is no consistent pattern and different HEIs will have different arrangements for dealing with income budgets, as shown below:

- Some HEIs have an overall income budget for domestic student fees with central monitoring of this budget, while in others the income budget for domestic student fees will be broken up with each academic school or department having its own income budget which it must monitor.
- In most HEIs, individual departments and schools will probably have an income budget for such activities as short courses and consultancy. However, in some HEIs, part of this income may be top-sliced and retained at the centre of the HEI while the rest of the income would accrue to the relevant department.

Expenditure budgets

Expenditure budgets in an HEI will be set for various departments and units within the organisation and may cover a range of items such as:

- permanent staffing costs;
- temporary staffing costs;
- consumables costs;
- travel expenses;
- equipment costs.

The annual expenditure budget of the HEI is set both globally and in terms of individual departments budgets, the former being set by reference to the total income available to the organisation from various sources. Also, the overall budget for the HEI must be approved by the Governors and this duty cannot be delegated to lower levels.

Capital budgets

We have already seen that capital expenditure is concerned with expenditure on larger items which have a working life in excess of twelve months although the precise definition of what constitutes 'capital' will vary between HEIs. Within a HEI there will be a variety of capital expenditure budgets related to activities such as:

- purchase of teaching or research equipment;
- purchases of other equipment (e.g., estates related equipment);
- IT procurement;
- purchase of vehicles;
- buildings construction;
- buildings refurbishment.

Larger capital projects such as major building construction will take several years to complete, and whereas most income and expenditure budgets will be for a one year period, the capital budget for such a major construction project will be for the total cost of the project over the multi-year period. However, with such a multi-year projects it is still likely that there will be separate funding allocations for each year of the project.

Main elements of a budgetary system

Although the detailed aspects of a budgetary system will vary between different types of organisation, the fundamental features will remain unchanged. Any budget system has three main components namely: a budget framework, a budget setting mechanism and a budget reporting system. Such a framework will apply as much in an HEI as in any other type of organisation and each of these components is discussed in some detail below.

Budget framework

General principles

The role of the budget system as a means of delegation within an organisation has already been discussed, and a budget system must reflect the framework of responsibility and accountability in the organisation. This means answering the following questions:

- who are to be the budget holders in the organisation?
- what specific activities are they responsible for?
- what items of expenditure are to be included in their budgets?
- what items of income are to be included in their budget?
- what workload and performance standards are required from them?
- what powers of authority do they have in relation to their budgets. For example, are they able to switch funds between different budget categories or do they require higher approval to do this?

Answers are never clear cut and will vary from organisation to organisation. No two organisations will have the same organisational and managerial arrangements and consequently neither will they have the same budgetary framework. For example, in some HEIs buildings maintenance might be the responsibility of a central estates manager while in other organisations the budget might be delegated to individual operational managers. In the former the estates manager decides what work should be done while in the latter it is the operational managers who make the decision.

There is no one correct approach and organisations must implement the organisational arrangements which best meets their local needs. Selecting the most appropriate budget framework in an organisation is not purely an accounting matter. Budget responsibility is a corporate topic which has financial, commercial and managerial implications.

Furthermore, it must be recognised that many organisations, including some HEIs, do not have a rational and tidy budget framework along the lines described above. Quite often, one sees examples of individuals having responsibility for activities but having no control over resources or expenditure and with no nominated person responsible for controlling them. Thus the framework described above must be seen as something to be aimed for and not as something which already exists.

Typical HEI budget structures

As with any large organisation, there will, in most HEIs, be a large number of individual budget holders each controlling specific responsibilities and resources. Although the precise pattern of budget holders will vary, in most

HEIs, these can, in general, be classified into two main types:

Academic unit budget holders   There will be a series of budget holders with responsibility for academic units in the HEI be these schools, departments, research centres, and so on. As discussed in Chapter 1, there will be a wide variety of academic arrangements in HEIs. Two typical examples are shown in Figure 5.1.

In the first example, budgets will be delegated from the centre to faculties (and to support departments) although clearly some budget will be retained at the centre. In turn faculties will delegate budgets to academic departments but with considerable variation in the magnitude and range of income and expenditure so delegated. In some cases, faculties will retain only small budgets with most of the budgetary decisions being made in departments, while in other cases, faculties will retain large budgets and so have considerable budgetary decision-making powers. In the second example, budgets are delegated by the centre to schools although the centre may retain some of the roles and budgets that might have been delegated to faculties in the first example. Furthermore, even within an individual academic unit such as a department or school, there is likely to be further budgetary delegation with separate budget holders for different subjects or different courses. Again there is no standard model for this.

Support unit budget holders   These will be the heads of the various support departments in the organisation. Some will be responsible for academic support units such as student services and learning resources while others will be responsible for, largely, administrative departments such as finance or registry. However, it must be emphasised that this is a dynamic and not a static arrangement. Various technological, academic and organisational

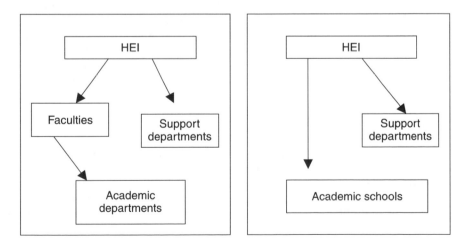

Figure 5.1   *Examples of academic budget structures in an HEI*

developments in the HEI can result in a constant flux in administrative arrangements with various departments being restructured, merged and so on with consequential changes in budgetary arrangements to reflect these organisational changes. Thus, for example, the increasing use of electronically based learning resources is commonly leading to mergers of departments (and budgets) of learning resources and IT. As with academic units, within an individual support unit there is likely to be further budgetary delegation with separate budget holders for different functions. Thus, for example, within the personnel department there may be separate budgets for recruitment, training and so on.

Patterns of budget responsibility in HEIs

Whatever the structure of budget holders there will be corresponding variations in their patterns of responsibility for income and expenditure. Some examples may illustrate this:

- as already noted, in some HEIs certain income budgets will be delegated to schools and departments while in other HEIs they will not;
- in some older HEIs, staff budgets may be retained at the centre and not delegated to individual departments, however, this is a declining practice;

Case study 5.1   Budgetary arrangements

The Oakland College of Higher Education has traditionally operated a centralised system of budgetary control whereby most items of expenditure are the responsibility of assistant principals in the college. The only budgets delegated to the heads of academic departments are those for such items as stationery, postage and travel. The college has been considering the further delegation of budgets to academic heads, most notably the budgets for staffing. Although there are potential advantages in undertaking such delegation, the college has decided against this course of action for the time being because:

- it is not felt that academic heads will, effectively, manage budgets and so the college could incur a substantial overspend;
- the current financial systems are not capable of providing the required financial information and the small finance department cannot provide sufficient support;
- the college is undertaking a process of substantial strategic change and it is felt that delegation of budgets will inhibit rather than facilitate this change.

The college will revisit this issue in three years time.

- in some HEIs, buildings and equipment maintenance budgets will be held in the central estates department while in other HEIs they will be delegated to departments who will commission and pay for maintenance work.

Budget-setting process

Whatever budget framework is adopted there will be some process or mechanism for setting expenditure budgets for individual departments. Budgets will usually be set for a twelve-month period, but, as noted earlier, in some HEIs budgets may be prepared for several years' duration with the first year being firmer than the later years. This would operate as a rolling process with the outline budget for year 2 being converted into a firm budget the following year.

The budget setting process will need to cover the various types of budget.

Income budgets

Income budgets will need to be estimated for the various sources of income that the HEI expects to receive, and responsibility for these income budgets needs to be allocated to individuals in the HEI. Some examples of income budgets and their method of forecasting are as shown below:

- **Funding councils income** – forecasts will be made of the level of funding council grants likely to be receivable by the HEI during the year. For teaching, this will be based on the projected numbers of domestic students, the funding council resource allocation mechanism and the total funds available to the sector. For research, the level of income receivable each year is likely to be reasonably stable except when there is the impact of a Research Assessment Exercise (RAE) to consider. In this situation, changes resulting from the RAE can have a significant effect on the HEI's income projections.
- **Student fees** – forecasts will be made by reference to the projected numbers of students in each category (e.g., UG, PG, overseas) and the planned fee rate for each type of student. In future, the introduction of variable top-up fees for domestic UG students will make this a more complex task since HEIs will need to assess the impact of different fee levels on student demand.
- **Research contract income** – forecasts will be derived of the projected level of research contracts that each department anticipates earning during the year.
- **Residential income** – forecasts will be based on such factors as projected occupancy rates (term-time and vacation) and the likely price levels that can be achieved. Consideration will need to be taken of the possible impact on demand of price increases.

- **Catering income** – forecasts will be made based on projected throughput of catering activities and anticipated price levels. Consideration will need to be taken of the possible impact on demand of price increases.

Expenditure budgets

HEIs need mechanisms or approaches to setting expenditure budgets for departments and for the institution as a whole. Detailed budget setting will vary considerably from HEI to HEI but a number of general approaches can be identified, as below.

Incremental budgeting

The main determinant of the expenditure budget of a department will be the previous year's expenditure budget. Thus the starting point for the 2003/04 budget being that for 2002/03. Adjustments will be made for; the effects of inflation, new developments, changes at the margin or the need to generate an efficiency improvement. However, the budget of the department is not linked to its projected workload nor is any attempt made to justify the historic level of the budget. Consider the simple example in Figure 5.2 of a buildings maintenance budget in an HEI.

The weakness of this approach is that the base budget is not queried for appropriateness and relevance and no link exists with the overall workload, only with marginal changes in workload. Such budgets are effectively fixed budgets since they will not usually be changed in-year in response to changing workload demands placed on the department.

Workload based budgets

With some budgets, or parts of budget, the budgeted level of expenditure can be linked to the planned level of workload in the department. Take for

	£000
Budget (2002/03)	500
deduct efficiency target on existing services (2%)	<u>−10</u>
	490
add cost of pay awards (4%)	<u>20</u>
	510
increased workload (estimated 6% growth in repairs)	<u>30</u>
Budget 2003/04	540

Figure 5.2   *Example of an incremental budgeting approach*

example a catering budget in an HEI:

- projected number of meals for the year   240,000
- standard cost of provisions per meal   75p
- provisions budget   £180,000

The standard cost of provisions is a target cost which will apply throughout the year but which will clearly vary from meal to meal. Budgets such as these are termed flexible budgets since the overall budget level will be flexed in accordance with the numbers of meals actually produced.

However, a pre-requisite for setting workload-based budgets is the availability of credible measures of workload on which those budgets can be based. In many areas such workload measures do not yet exist and so workload-based budgets cannot be developed. For example, consider the difficulty of identifying suitable workload measures (which could be used for budget setting) for academic departments, registry, student services, finance, and so on.

Zero-based budgeting (ZBB)/priority-based budgeting (PBB)

These approaches were developed to overcome the weaknesses of the incremental approach of failing to look at the base budget of a department. They are particularly applicable to central support departments in an HEI rather than to academic departments. PBB is essentially a simpler and more pragmatic version of ZBB but the thrust is the same in both cases. Under ZBB/PBB, no budget is automatically rolled forward as is the case in the incremental approach. Expenditure budgets must be scrutinised and budget managers must indicate:

- the specific and discrete activities they undertake in their departments;
- the costs attaching to each of those activities;
- the benefits and priority of undertaking each of those activities.

Senior management can then scrutinise all departments in the organisation, compare the costs with the benefits and priorities attaching to each activity, and where appropriate make adjustments to individual base budgets in line with overall corporate priorities.

Whatever the merits of ZBB/PBB in principle, there are some clear practical problems. The procedures are cumbersome and time consuming and it will probably be difficult to switch resources between areas of activity without retraining staff and/or making redundancies.

Mixed approaches

These three approaches to expenditure budget setting are not mutually exclusive. For example, the provisions element of a catering budget might be a flexible or workload-based budget while the catering staffing budget might be a fixed budget established by the incremental or PBB method.

Moderation of expenditure budgets

By whatever method they are set, the sum of the departmental expenditure budgets must, at all times, be reconcilable to the total of income budgets less any funds being held as reserves, for contingencies or for planned surpluses. Figure 5.3 illustrates this using a simple example.

However, income budgets do not necessarily remain stable and, unlike expenditure budgets, are to a certain degree outside the direct control of the HEI. Hence, the HEI will periodically need to review its income budgets and, if necessary, amend its expenditure budgets or reserves in the light of planned changes in income.

An important example of this concerns student numbers. Early in the academic year HEIs will need to compare actual student enrolments against the planned enrolments on which the original income budgets were based. This is because significant shortfall in student numbers and income streams may lead to a combination of reductions in financial reserves, planned surpluses or reductions in expenditure budgets.

Where an individual department has a delegated income budget, the achievement of that income budget will also determine its overall expenditure budget. Any shortfall in income – for example, from short courses, might lead to a reduction in an expenditure budget or depletion of accumulated reserves. However, in extreme cases it may not be possible, in the short term, for the department to reduce its expenditure budgets to the required level without damaging its operational capability. In these circumstances, financial assistance will be required from the centre over an interim period.

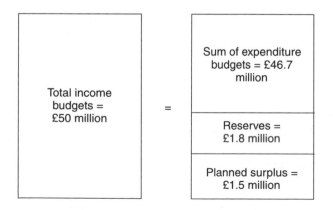

Figure 5.3   *Moderation of budgets*

Capital budgets

As noted previously, capital budgets will usually be prepared on a project basis. Estimates of capital expenditure on building works, engineering works and equipment will be prepared by technical specialists such as architects and engineers. Where the project extends over several years, estimates of expenditure will usually be prepared for each year based on the likely level of capital works to be undertaken in that year.

Budgetary reporting mechanisms

General approaches

To manage their budgets effectively, budget managers need to be provided with information showing their progress against their budgets, be they income, expenditure or capital budgets. Thus the provision of budgetary information must be a clear part of the information and IT strategy of any organisation. Although the precise configuration of information systems will vary considerably between organisations, a number of common themes can be identified which are applicable to all budgetary information systems:

- *Relevance* – budget managers need relevant information. This relates to issues of responsibility and control as managers require information on those items of expenditure over which they have responsibility and can exert control.
- *Frequency and timeliness* – in many organisations budget managers may receive monthly budget reports within a few days of the end of the month, but with decentralised information systems managers can often obtain such information at any time via computer terminals within their department. However, even where such decentralised budget information systems exist, the timeliness of the information contained will be conditioned by how frequently the budget system has been updated by the main financial feeder systems such as payroll, payments and income.
- *Format* – the precise format of a budget report will vary, but will usually show the following information:
  - total budget for the year;
  - budget for the month, which may be a simple twelfth of the annual budget or is adjusted to reflect seasonal variations in some type of expenditure such as heating costs;
  - expenditure for the month;
  - variance for the month;
  - cumulative budget for the year to date;
  - cumulative expenditure for the year to date;
  - year end estimated expenditure;
  - variance for the year to date.

- *Accuracy and content* – the information on actual expenditure included in budget reports can be of three main types:
  - cash payments actually made;
  - accruals of creditors, being expenditure on goods and services received but not yet paid for;
  - commitments, being goods and services ordered for which an expenditure commitment exists but which have not yet been received.

  Budget reports usually include accruals of creditors but they may not include commitments, although this is becoming more common. Budget managers obviously need to be aware of any additional expenditure commitments not included on their budget reports.
- *Support* – support and advice on the content of budget reports is needed by budget managers. In some cases, departments or directorates might have their own decentralised finance officer while in other cases support will be given by a central finance department. Provision of such support is a key role of the finance function.

Enhancements to budget reporting mechanisms

A number of enhancements to basic budget models can be identified and may be applied in some HEIs.

Profiling of budgets

In simpler budget systems the monthly expenditure for individual budget headings is compared with one twelfth of the annual budget and variances are reported. Clearly in some instances this approach is bound to produce misleading information. Consider the following:

- heating costs – comparing actual expenditure with twelfths of the budget will result in budgetary overspends in winter months and underspends in summer months;
- grass cutting costs – comparing actual expenditure with twelfths of the budget will result in budgetary overspends in summer months and underspends in winter months.

These are extreme examples of seasonal variations in expenditure but there are many examples where expenditure is not incurred evenly throughout the year. Hence more advanced budget systems try to profile budgets to reflect expected expenditure for the months in question. Variations from budget can then be regarded as real and not seasonal variations. This is particularly relevant in HEIs since students only attend the institution for about 8–9 months of the year and so costs will be affected accordingly.

Budgetary variance analysis

As noted above, a typical budgetary control report might show the variation between actual expenditure and planned budget both for the month and the cumulative position for the year. In practice, variations from budget may occur for a large number of reasons such as workload pressures, price increases or poor expenditure management. A simple budget variance does not indicate the reasons why expenditure has deviated from budget. The technique of budget variance analysis was developed in industry many years ago as a means of explaining the reasons why expenditure has deviated from budget. It has practical application in an HEI as is outlined below.

Let us first continue with the example of the catering budget in the earlier section. The relevant data is shown in Figure 5.4.

A standard budgetary control system would merely show that the catering department had exceeded its budgets by £2,000 but even a cursory analysis would show that there are two factors at work here, namely:

- the volume of meals produced exceeds the plan;
- the unit cost per meal is less than planned.

Basic data

	PLANNED	ACTUAL	VARIANCE
Numbers of meals	240,000	260,000	+ 20,000
Expenditure	£180,000	£182,000	+ £2,000
Cost per meal	75p	70p	– 5p

Variance analysis

Volume Variance = (planned volume – actual volume) × standard cost

$$= (240,000 - 260,000) \times £0.75$$

$$= -£15,000 \text{ unfavourable}$$

Cost Variance = (standard cost – actual cost) × actual volume

$$= (£0.75 - £0.70) \times 260,000$$

$$= +£13,000 \text{ favourable}$$

Figure 5.4 *Example of budgetary variance analysis*

Variance analysis uses this information to disaggregate the causes of an expenditure variance and reveals the following:

- an unfavourable overall expenditure variance of £2,000 disguises an unfavourable volume variance of £15,000, partially offset by a favourable cost variance of £13,000;
- responsibility for these two variances rests with different people. The cost variance is the responsibility of the catering department, the volume variance probably rests with someone such as the student admissions department. Variance analysis focuses responsibility for the different causes of an expenditure variance.

Shown above is a very simple two-part variance analysis. In practice more complex variance analyses can be prepared.

Resource allocation models (RAM) and the budgetary process in HEIs

Introduction to RAMs

In some HEIs the budgets of individual departments are primarily expenditure budgets with little or no delegation of income budgets. Thus the HEI having estimated the likely level of income receivable from all sources will set an overall expenditure budget for the institution as a whole. The budget setting process then involves setting expenditure budgets for individual departments (using one or more of the approaches outlined above) such that the total of expenditure budgets does not exceed the total expenditure budget for the HEI as a whole.

The alternative approach adopted by many HEIs is to develop and use a resource allocation model or RAM. Such models will, in effect, share out the projected income of the HEI (on some suitable basis) among departments, the latter being free to set their own budgets within the total delegated income figure. Many HEIs consider an appropriate RAM essential to the management of the institution as its use facilitates a devolved approach to management which:

- enhances institutional decision making;
- offers incentives to academic units to contribute to the institution's overall strategic and financial objectives.

Furthermore, they will argue that the absence of such a mechanism can create a vacuum in which senior managers and academic staff are unable to fully analyse the impact of both internally and externally made strategic decisions. This can lead to decisions being made on narrow departmental criteria which do not benefit the institution as a whole and which do not facilitate the achievement of corporate objectives.

Types of RAM

For HEIs considering the development or enhancement of any RAM, its credibility within the academic community is a key issue. Heads of departments and staff must be able to easily understand and trust the underlying methodology of any proposed model if it is to be utilised to its full potential. It should be both fair and transparent, with any strategic contributions or subsidies openly identified. Therefore, it is essential that a balance is struck between ease of use by academic managers and the need for the model to reflect all key variables.

Different types of RAM can be developed but in broad terms a resource allocation model could be one of three types as illustrated below.

Type A

With this model (Figure 5.5) the first stage would be to set the budgets for central support departments using one or more of the methods described above. The total HEI income would then be top-sliced, to finance the budgeted costs of these support departments and the remaining income would then be distributed among academic departments which would establish their own budgets on the basis of the total income delegated to them.

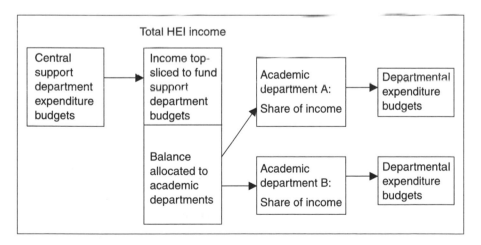

Figure 5.5   *Resource allocation model: Type A*

Type B

With this model (Figure 5.6) the total HEI income would be distributed among academic departments without any top-slicing. Support department budgets would be established as previously but the costs of these support departments would then be apportioned over the academic departments on some suitable basis. Finally, academic departments would establish their own budgets on the basis of the total income delegated to them less the costs of support services recharged to them.

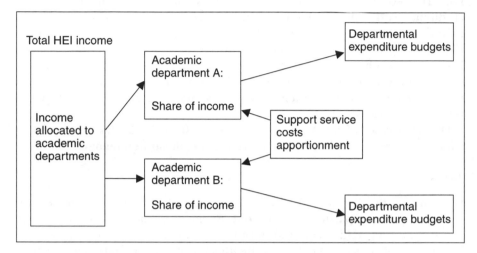

Figure 5.6   *Resource allocation model: Type B*

Type C

This approach (Figure 5.7) is the same as for type B but with one important difference concerning the central support department costs. With a type B

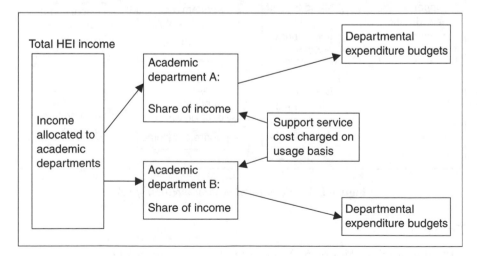

Figure 5.7   *Resource allocation model: Type C*

approach the costs of central support departments are apportioned over academic departments irrespective of the use made by those departments of central support services. Under a type C approach, central support departments would establish a service level agreement (SLA) with each central support department which would define:

- the services to be provided by those departments;
- the quality standards to be achieved;
- the costs of providing those services.

The recharge of central support costs to academic departments would be based on the actual level of services provided by the support department in accordance with the SLA.

Under such an approach, the support departments have, effectively, to mirror academic departments in having to pay their own way through the delivery of services to client departments. Such approaches have not been widespread in the HE sector although they have been developed in sectors such as local government and the NHS so there are no insurmountable problems. We consider model C as an example of good practice and would anticipate further development. However, we recognise that the careless introduction of such a model could easily destabilise an HEI if academic departments continued using university funds to purchase such services externally while the same services were still being provided in-house.

Operation of a RAM in practice

The operation of a RAM will require the following actions:

- prior to the commencement of the financial year:
  - allocation to departments of budgeted income;
  - setting of expenditure budgets for departments based on that income;
  - reconciliation between budgeted income and expenditure for each department;
- during the financial year:
  - monitoring by departments of actual income received compared with budget;
  - monitoring of actual expenditure incurred by departments compared with budget;
  - monitoring of variations between actual income and actual expenditure and the implementation of remedial action where such variations are significant.

Many individual academic departments have accumulated financial reserves over the years and any financial surpluses or deficits generated in a particular year will increase or decrease those reserves.

Case study 5.2 Resource Allocation Models (RAM)

Underwood University operates an RAM for budgetary and financial management purposes. For 2002/03 the Business Studies Department at the University received a total income allocation (from all sources) of £3.80 million. The department set total budgets of £3.75 million aiming to create a surplus of £50,000 which would be added to its accrued reserves.

Part way through the year the department realised the level of income it was generating through overseas students was substantially less than budget. It took action to reduce expenditure to bring it in line with budget. Since recharges from central support departments could not be influenced the savings had to come from reductions in hourly paid teaching staff.

In the event the amount of expenditure reductions proved insufficient to meet the shortfall in budget and the department generated a deficit of £25,000. This deficit was deducted from the reserves of the department.

Detailed aspects of a RAM

The various types of RAM described above require HEIs to undertake specific actions as outlined below:

- **Top-slicing of income** – this may be achieved, for example, by deducting a common percentage from all income sources or by applying different percentages to different types of income. The latter approach might avoid dis-incentivising academic staff from undertaking income generation activities by applying a lower percentage top-slice to entrepreneurial income.
- **Distribution of income to academic departments** – again a number of different approaches will be applied, the usual practice being:
  - HEFCE (T) income – the HEI's total (T) income would be distributed, after any top-slicing, to academic departments pro-rata to domestic student numbers (FTE) using a weighting for different subject areas. The weightings applied may be the HEFCE price band weightings or the HEI's locally determined weightings;
  - HEFCE (R) income – the HEI's total (R) income would be attributed, after any top-slicing, to academic departments in accordance with the research ratings of departments as obtained via the RAE;
  - undergraduate student fee income – this would be allocated to departments, after any top-slicing, pro-rata to UG student numbers (FTE);
  - post-graduate student fee income – this would be allocated to departments, after any top-slicing, pro-rata to the PG fee income earned by the department;

- research contract income – this would be allocated to departments, after any top-slicing, on the basis of the income earned by the department;
- consultancy/short course income – the amounts attributed to departments would be based on actual earnings by the department after any top-slicing.

- **Setting of departmental budgets** – once a department has an income allocation it will need to set individual budgets which equal the total funds available. In doing this it will utilise one or more of the approaches outlined above.
- **Apportionment of central support costs** – various approaches will be used to apportion central support costs to individual academic departments. Typical approaches would be:
  - estates maintenance costs: pro-rata to the space occupied by each department;
  - registry costs: pro-rata to students enrolled by each department;
  - personnel costs: pro-rata to staff numbers in each department;
  - student services costs: pro-rata to full time equivalent student numbers in each department.
- **Establishment of SLAs** – where a type C approach is adopted it will be necessary to establish SLAs (including financial aspects) between academic and support departments. Broadly, the financial aspects of the SLA could be on one of three bases:
  - Block basis: the client academic department pays a monthly sum for a defined block of services (e.g., the provision of financial advice from the finance department).
  - Unit basis: the client academic department pays for each unit of service delivered. Examples could include: a charge per student admitted by the admissions department, a charge per invoice paid by the finance department, a range of charges for specific jobs undertaken by the estates maintenance department.
  - Combined basis: a combination of the above with a fixed sum for an initial level of service and a unit amount for each subsequent unit of service.

Budget setting and performance improvement

In many organisations, including HEIs, the budget setting process might provide a key means of implementing improvements in the quality, costs and efficiency of service delivery. In the example of estates maintenance shown earlier, a targeted efficiency improvement can form part of the budget setting process. The simplest approach is to apply 'across the board' targets to all budget heads which, although relatively simple to undertake, has the great danger of creating a non-optimal solution since efficient and non-efficient departments are given the same target. Also, there is the danger that unsustainable cuts may be applied to certain departments which may result in additional expenditure being incurred some time in the future. An alternative approach is to set differential targets in particular areas.

There are clearly many ways in which such performance improvements might be identified but the key ones are :

- **Improved staff productivity** – approaches such as better management, better remuneration systems or better workflows could be evaluated to obtain the same level of workload with lower staffing levels.
- **Remuneration costs** – although, in theory, HEIs are free to set their own terms and conditions of employment, in practice few have deviated greatly from national agreements. Nevertheless, an alternative remuneration structure, possibly coupled with lower staffing levels, might generate cost improvements. This approach can only be undertaken organisation-wide and not on an individual departmental basis.
- **Process improvements** – much of the activity in organisations is based on tradition and precedent. A root and branch review of the various academic and non-academic processes might lead to simplification which in turn could provide an unchanged service at lower cost. In this context business process re-engineering (BPR) may have great relevance in HEIs. Much of BPR involves the use of improved information systems and hence BPR needs to be considered in the context of IT investment.
- **Organisational arrangements** – consideration must be given to whether the current organisational model is the optimum one. One aspect of this is the balance between centralised and decentralised provision of support services. Although the emphasis in recent years has been on the decentralisation of services (e.g., finance), pressures also exist in some areas of activity for some degree of re-centralisation. These should be considered, since it may be the only way to realise substantial cost savings on support services.
- **Information systems and technology** – in many support services, processes can be improved and substantial cost savings can be realised through changes to the configuration of information systems and technology. In the field of finance and procurement, for example, new systems involving increased user interfaces can result in savings in administrative costs. However, such technology is usually expensive (and may not be affordable) and implementation difficulties are often substantial.
- **Outsourcing services** – this involves obtaining services traditionally provided in-house from an external source such as payroll, maintenance or even registry. It can produce lower costs because the external agency is dealing with higher volumes of activity and can consequently achieve lower unit costs. Outsourcing can use formal market testing or some form of deal with another organisation to share the costs of service provision.

Overlaying all of these approaches will be the issue of change management as it likely that the realisation of substantial performance improvements will involve a considerable degree of organisational change which in turn could necessitate a combination of changed working practices and changed attitudes. Thus, in parallel with process review will be a need to consider how organisational change is to be promoted and managed in order to realise the benefits of the changed processes.

Variations in HEI budgetary arrangements

From the above it will be evident that within the HE sector are numerous variations and permutations relating to different aspects of budgetary systems. For example, there will be variations with regard to the:

- degree of delegation of income budgets;
- degree of delegation of expenditure budgets;
- structure of budget managers;
- budgetary powers given to those managers;
- mechanisms for setting budgets;
- budget reporting arrangements.

The view is sometimes (incorrectly) expressed that since all HEIs are in the same line of business there should be some standard budgetary arrangement which will be optimal and will apply to all HEIs. Unfortunately, life is never that simple and HEIs will differ between one another in terms of history, culture, mission, organization, and so on. Hence, what is an appropriate budgetary arrangement for one HEI will not be appropriate for another. Take, for example, the issue of delegation of budgets. It is often assumed that delegation of budgets is 'good' and non-delegation is 'bad'. However, a moment's thought will make one realise that delegation of large budgets to a group of managers who have limited skills in managing those budgets could prove disastrous and so should be approached with caution. Hence budgetary arrangements must be contingent on a number of factors and it is for each HEI to decide the best arrangements for itself. Also those arrangements should not be 'set in concrete' but should be kept under review. What is optimal today may not be so in three years' time.

Thus in considering budgetary arrangements, an HEI should take account of a number of issues including:

- the overall managerial culture of the organisation: if the organisation is centrally managed, a delegated system of budgeting will prove difficult to operate and vice-versa;
- the potential improvements in the speed and quality of decision making achievable through greater delegation of budgets;

- the risks of loss of financial control through delegation to staff not competent to manage budgets;
- the costs of implementing financial systems needed to support delegated budgetary arrangements;
- the capability of the finance department to provide support to budget holders;
- the potential loss of flexibility and efficiency caused by fragmenting budgets over a larger number of persons.

However, one common point which applies in all HEIs is that **the Governing Body must approve the annual budgets of the institution and this responsibility cannot be delegated**. This point is referred to again in Chapter 8 on financial control.

Chapter 6

Costing and costing systems

Introduction

In any organisation, cost information can be used for a variety of reasons and in recent years the subject of costing (and the related issue of pricing) of activities has become very topical within the HE sector. In this chapter we consider costing in HEIs and in the next chapter move on to consider pricing and the role costing plays in pricing decisions. However, at the outset it should be noted that there is often confusion in some HEIs about the difference between costs and prices. The distinction between costs and prices is important and can be summarised:

- *Cost* – this a financial expression of the resources committed by an organisation to a particular activity or product. Thus, when we say a particular item, such as a short course, costs £1,545.23 this means that the manpower, material and other resources, including overheads, committed to developing and delivering that course are estimated in monetary terms to be equivalent to £1,545.23.
- *Price* – a price is the amount of money that a purchaser or consumer is prepared to pay to receive a particular good or service and the income a provider finds acceptable. The key thing to note is that a price relates to the market and not the supplying organisation. It therefore follows that a price of a commodity can be in excess of its cost (implying a surplus), can be equal to cost, or can be below cost (implying a deficit). Thus the short course referred to above could be priced at £2,000 thus generating a clear surplus.

This distinction should be kept in mind throughout the remainder of this and the next chapter.

Uses of cost information in HEIs

We summarise below are what are probably the main uses of cost information in an HEI.

Budget reporting

In Chapter 5 the topics of budget management and budgetary control were discussed in depth. It will be clear that a key component of budgetary control is the availability of actual cost information to be compared with budgeted cost. In most budgetary systems this involves the provision of period cost information, which shows the income and expenditure of each school, department or faculty for a particular month in question.

Activity analysis

HEIs will, typically, produce routine information on the overall costs incurred (and income received) by the various schools and departments in the organisation. However, the information available is often not sufficient to enable an analysis to be undertaken of the financial performance of the various activities (e.g. research, teaching, consultancy) of the school/department. This is particularly important if the school/department is generating an overall financial deficit and the HEI wishes to know the main causes of that deficit. Alternatively, the HEI may wish to know which areas of activity are profitable and are a strength to be built on. In either case, an analysis will be needed of the costs (and income) attributed to discrete activities of the school/department.

Case study 6.1   Activity cost analysis

Within Redwood University, the biological sciences department is seen as a research active school but its research performance is believed to have declined in recent years. This is a concern given the impact this might have in the next RAE. However, the financial reports for the first six months of the year 2002/03 indicate that, overall, the department is generating a deficit of some £0.5 million and this comes on top of a deficit of £0.9 million in the previous year. The university undertakes an activity costing analysis which shows the following picture:

	Surplus/(Deficit) (£m)
Undergraduate courses	(0.1)
Post-graduate courses	(1.2)
Research	0.8
Total	(0.5)

In the light of this information the university undertakes a major review of the organisation and pricing of post-graduate courses and of the resources it is committing to research activity in the light of the subsidy research is proving to teaching.

Pricing

Clearly costs are an important input into pricing decisions but are not the sole, or even the most important input. This will be discussed further in the next chapter.

Project appraisal

Within an HEI, project developments under consideration often include:

- the development of new courses;
- the initiation of new research projects;
- the planned construction of new buildings, and so on.

Before any of these projects are initiated good practice will require a full project appraisal and cost information will be needed to undertake the financial aspects of that appraisal.

Benchmarking

It is common practice for HEIs to try and compare their performance against that of other comparable HEIs as a means of identifying potential improvements in performance. Thus it is quite common for an HEI to compare its

---

Case study 6.2   Cost benchmarking

Winterwood University prides itself on its international outlook and consequently its School of Modern Languages offers a wide range of courses in seven different languages. Unfortunately, over the last three years the School has been generating six-figure deficits, each year, and has accumulated deficits of almost £0.75 million. The School has undertaken an activity cost analysis which indicates that the bulk of the deficit is generated by two of the seven language areas. The School has subsequently undertaken a benchmarking exercise in collaboration with six comparable HEIs. This exercise involved sharing information on activity levels and costs in the modern language field. The exercise has concluded that a substantial proportion of the deficits generated in the two 'problem' languages are the consequence of unsustainable staffing levels. Hence there are two outcomes to this study:

- The School will take action to reduce its staffing levels and costs in the two 'problem' areas;
- The university, by recognising the importance of modern languages to its wider mission statement, intends to channel an increased level of funding to the School of Modern Languages in the knowledge that the School will be operating in an efficient manner.

financial performance (e.g., cost per student, cost per book issued, cost per invoice paid) against that of other HEIs and to do this it is necessary to have cost information about one's own organisation.

Principles of costing

In considering the issue of costing in HEIs it is important to first outline some general principles of costing. These include:

- product and period costs;
- direct and indirect costs;
- fixed and variable costs;
- total and marginal costs.

Product and period costs

These need to be clearly distinguished. Product costing is concerned with the costs of each of the organisation's products, while period costs are concerned with the costs incurred by different parts of the organisation during a discrete time period. In an HEI, product cost information would imply information about the organisation's goods and services such as: research contracts, long courses, short courses and consultancy projects. Period costing in an HEI would involve identifying the monthly costs of, for example, academic departments, the learning resources department, the marketing department, and so on.

Traditionally product costing in HEIs was limited but, for various reasons, HEIs have recently become more sophisticated in their approach, which will necessarily involve them in undertaking the following:

- identify their main product lines;
- identify the main cost elements associated with the delivery of each of those products;
- develop suitable approaches to attribute each cost element to each product.

Direct costs and indirect costs

There is a commonly held view that the cost of a particular product or activity is a unique figure. This is not the case. Cost data are derived by means of a series of costing approaches and assumptions and differing approaches and assumptions will give different costs for the same activity or product. Thus when examining the costs associated with a particular product or activity it is vital to understand the costing approaches applied to establish that cost and the assumptions underlying the approach adopted. It is therefore essential to understand the concepts of cost centres, and direct and indirect costs associated with those cost centres.

The differentiation between direct costs and indirect costs is fundamental to cost accounting practice but is frequently misunderstood, even by some accountants. Often the direct/indirect distinction is confused with the variable/fixed distinction (see below) with direct costs being seen as synonymous with variable costs and indirect costs being seen as synonymous with fixed costs. This is a misunderstanding since the two types of cost classification are based on different principles.

To understand the direct/indirect distinction it is first necessary to appreciate the role of the cost centre in cost accounting. A cost centre is essentially a component part of the organisation against which costs can be collected. Some examples of cost centres in a factory would be a department, a machine or a product line and in an HEI would be an academic department, a support department, a curriculum area or an individual research project.

The distinction between direct and indirect costs relates to the different ways in which costs are recorded against cost centres. Consider the factory based example in Figure 6.1.

In this factory there are three machines, representing our cost centres, and management needs to know the total costs of running each of the machines. Certain costs, such as labour and materials, are referred to as direct costs since the information systems in the factory will identify where each of different costs have been incurred. Timesheets will record the labour hours/costs incurred on each machine and the stores issue system will show the materials

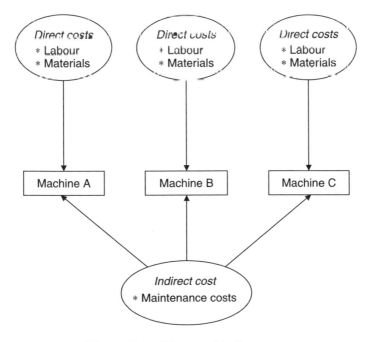

Figure 6.1 *Direct and indirect costs*

costs consumed by each machine so these direct costs can be **allocated** to each machine. When looking at the costs of the maintenance department, no record is available of the maintenance time spent on each machine and so it is not possible to **allocate** maintenance as a direct cost to each machine. To obtain the total running cost for each machine it is necessary to **apportion** or spread the total costs of the maintenance department over each of the machines in a reasonable manner. The key phrase here is 'in a reasonable manner' and the basis chosen must be regarded as a proxy for the maintenance requirements of each of the machines. For this example we can state the following:

- **Reasonable basis for apportionment**
  - running hours of each machine;
  - age of each machine (in years);
  - product output of each machine.
- **Unreasonable basis for apportionment**
  - age (in years) of the machine operator;
  - height of each machine;
  - original cost of each machine, and so on.

Thus the total costs of running each of the machines will depend on the method of apportionment chosen for maintenance costs and different methods of apportionment will produce different total cost figures.

Let us now apply this same model to an HEI using the example shown in Figure 6.2.

The cost centre used is an individual academic department. In an HEI, academic staff salaries will be easily attributed to an individual academic department through available information systems. Hence, this cost can be regarded as a direct cost and is **allocated** to the department. Energy costs are also a cost of running the department but usually the only information available concerns the energy costs of the HEI as a whole. Hence, to obtain the total

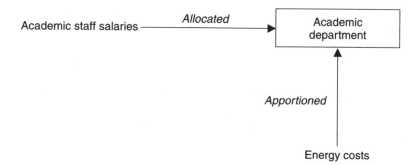

Figure 6.2 *Allocations and apportionments in an HEI*

running costs of the department it is necessary to **apportion** the total HEI energy costs over departments using an appropriate method, which might for example, be related to the floor area or volume of each building involved. Thus the figure for the total running costs of the department will depend on the apportionment bases chosen for indirect costs such as energy. Similar issues will apply to other indirect costs.

A number of points should be emphasised regarding the above example:

- *Mix of allocation and apportionment* – there is no single correct total cost attributable to a particular cost centre. Total costs are derived from a combination of direct costs which are directly allocated and indirect costs which are apportioned in some way. Different approaches and assumptions will give different results. Consider the simple example in Figure 6.3.

  Both situations are identical. However, in the second situation, the department might actually have energy meters fitted and so can identify the exact amount of energy consumption of the department. Thus, energy can be regarded as a direct cost which is allocated to the cost centre. Directly allocating a cost instead of apportioning it produces a different result and hence a different total cost.

Situation A		Situation B	
£		£	
Academic salaries (allocated)	50	Academic salaries (allocated)	50
Energy (apportioned)	20	Energy (allocated)	40
Total costs	70	Total costs	90

Figure 6.3 *Impact of different accounting methods*

- *Basis of apportionment* – where cost apportionment is applied it is important to realise that there is no single correct basis of cost apportionment. As long as a particular basis of apportionment is 'reasonable' in specific circumstances then it may be used to derive total costs.

There is no single 'correct' or 'accurate' cost. The end result of a costing exercise is dependent upon the balance between allocation and apportionment of costs and the method of cost apportionment actually used. Two different costing methods will give two different results both of which are reasonable. A number of important managerial issues flow from this.

- The degree of accuracy of the cost information produced depends on the extent to which costs can be directly allocated rather than being apportioned. What determines whether a cost can be directly allocated or indirectly apportioned is the sophistication of the organisation's information systems. However, the more sophisticated the information systems the higher would be the costs of producing costing information.

- The degree of costing accuracy needed by the organisation will depend on issues such as: the type of organisation, its geographic location, its current efficiency level, the degree of competition it faces in the market, and so on. There is no simple answer to this question. For example, an HEI facing little competition will probably have less need for accurate cost information than an HEI facing tough competition.

Thus, in designing a costing system there is always a balance to be struck between the need for accuracy of cost information and the cost of obtaining that information. Hence an HEI must evaluate both the benefits and the costs of costing. Furthermore, although some commonality of structure is possible **no** standard costing system can be defined for all HEIs. HEIs vary considerably in their needs for financial information, the degree of accuracy required, and the resources they can devote to providing that information. Hence each HEI must make its own judgement on this matter.

Fixed costs and variable costs

The distinction between a fixed cost and a variable cost is simple in principle but difficult to draw in practice. It is essentially concerned with the way in which the magnitude of a particular cost varies in relation to the activity or throughput level of the organisation. Three different types of cost behaviour can be identified. These are illustrated graphically in Figure 6.4.

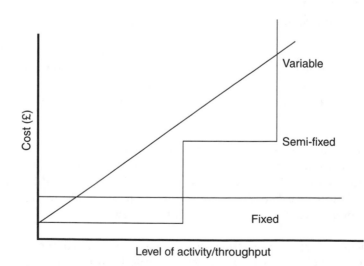

Figure 6.4   *Fixed and variable costs*

- *Variable costs* – the level of cost varies directly with the level of activity in the organisation. In a factory setting, direct materials may be regarded as a cost, which varies directly with the level of production.
- *Fixed costs* – the magnitude of cost is unaffected by the level of activity in the organisation. In a factory setting, the factory rent would usually be fixed and would not vary whatever the level of factory production.
- *Semi-fixed costs* – the above two examples are basically extremes and in practice most cost types will be neither totally fixed nor completely variable.

The distinction between a variable, fixed and semi-variable cost is not precise and judgements often have to be made. However, Figure 6.5 considers the likely situation in an HEI, using student numbers as the measure of activity, and gives some examples of possible cost behaviour in an HEI.

However, a word of warning about such a simplified approach to cost classification is needed. The type of cost behaviour encountered may not always be clear and may depend on the way in which the organisation procures goods and services. For example, in Figure 6.5 it has been suggested that lecturing staff pay is a semi-fixed cost in relation to student numbers. This is because small changes in student numbers will not result in changes to the lecturing staff numbers (and hence pay) although larger changes will take place for larger movements in student numbers. However, where the HEI employs large numbers of hourly paid lecturing staff then lecturing staff pay may becomes increasingly a variable cost since increases or decreases in student numbers may lead to an immediate increase/decrease in the numbers of hourly paid lecturing staff employed.

Type of cost	Cost behaviour	Comments
Grounds maintenance	Fixed	Unlikely to change in relation to student numbers.
Catering consumable	Variable	Assumes changes in student numbers will impact on numbers of meals sold.
Lecturing staff	Semi-fixed	Assumes that changes in student numbers beyond a certain point might necessitate a stepped change in lecturing staff numbers and hence costs.
Management	Fixed	Unlikely to change in relation to student numbers.
Photocopying	Variable	Assumes changes in student numbers will impact on numbers of photocopies made.
Equipment maintenance	Semi-fixed	Assumes that increases in student numbers beyond a certain point will increase wear and tear and hence maintenance requirements.

Figure 6.5 *Types of cost behaviour in an HEI*

Total costs and marginal costs

Total cost implies inclusion of all the costs associated with a particular activity. This will incorporate both the direct costs of an activity and a share of the indirect costs apportioned to that activity. This is illustrated by the following simple example concerned with the costs of manufacturing a product.

Volume of production = 1,000 units		
Costs of production:		
	Total costs	Unit cost
	£	£p
Materials	2,500	2.50
Labour	7,500	7.50
Variable overhead	2,000	2.00
Fixed overhead	1,000	1.00
Total	13,000	13.00

Thus the total cost of producing one unit of the product is £13.

The marginal costs are the incremental costs of producing additional units of the product and will differ from the total cost because of the issues of fixed and variable costs referred to above. If production is increased, some costs will increase while others will remain unchanged.

Using the above example, consider the impact on cost of increasing production by 50 units (i.e., 5 per cent). The following situation is likely to apply:

- *Materials* – producing 50 additional units of product will result in an incremental or marginal cost of £125 being incurred (i.e., 50 × £2.50).
- *Variable overhead* – since this overhead is defined as variable it will vary directly with the level of production. Thus increasing production by 50 units will result in an incremental or marginal cost of £100 being incurred (50 × £2).
- *Fixed overhead* – by definition this overhead cost is fixed and will not change with increases in production. Thus the marginal cost in this area is nil.
- *Labour* – this is the most problematic area since it is not clear what impact an increase in production of 5 per cent will have on labour costs. Three scenarios are possible:
  - the increase in production can be absorbed by the existing labour force and thus the marginal cost will be nil;
  - to cope with the increase in production employees will need to work overtime at a premium, thus, the marginal costs of increasing production will depend on the overtime hours required and the overtime premium paid;

– to cope with the increase in production additional employees will need to be recruited. Thus the marginal costs of increasing production will depend on the numbers and pay of additional employees needed.

For simplicity, in this example we have assumed that the increased production can be met by the existing labour force.

Thus the differences between marginal and total costs can be summarised as follows:

Costs of an additional 50 units of production based on total costs

= increased units × total unit cost
= 50 × £13.00
= **£650**

Costs of an additional 50 units of production based on marginal costs

= Materials + labour + variable overhead + fixed overhead
= £125 + nil + £100 + nil
= **£225**

This distinction between total and marginal costs is an important one and must be fully appreciated. The relevance of this distinction to HEIs is demonstrated in the following examples:

- **Financial forecasting** – HEIs will need to forecast the financial effect of changes in future activity levels and to do so will need to distinguish between fixed costs, variable costs and semi-fixed costs. For example, if an HEI planning a short-course programme, estimated likely incremental costs using total average costs, it would probably overestimate them since the total average cost would include a proportion of costs such as buildings maintenance, heat and light, and so on that would not increase if the short courses were undertaken. Furthermore, some HEI resources may have slack capacity and increased workload can be absorbed without any cost increases. For example, slack capacity in teaching accommodation might mean that additional students can be recruited without providing additional teaching space. Hence the HEI needs to analyse each cost and identify those costs, which will vary if additional students are recruited for, say, a ten-week period.
- **Pricing decisions** – the distinction between marginal and total costs is important for pricing purposes. Although the general rule is that prices should be set by reference to total costs, circumstances arise where they can be set by reference to marginal costs. This is discussed in the next chapter under marginal cost pricing.

Activity-based costing

Activity based costing (ABC) is an approach to costing which was developed in the USA and became popular in this country in the 1990s. ABC was developed by manufacturing industry, which recognised that over a 40–50 year period, the composition of product costs had altered substantially.

The main reasons were:

- *Direct labour* – through the introduction of automation and IT the direct labour element of product costs had fallen dramatically.
- *Direct materials* – the direct materials element of product costs had remained largely unchanged.
- *Overheads* – overhead functions, such as materials handling, quality assurance and marketing, had grown substantially and the element of product cost they represented had grown to match the fall in direct labour costs.

As seen earlier, traditional approaches to costing involved the allocation of direct labour and materials costs while overhead costs were usually apportioned using an appropriate basis. The advocates of ABC recognised that applying such crude approaches to the treatment of overhead costs, which were such a high proportion of cost, was severely distorting total product costs. ABC uses more sophisticated approaches to apportion overhead costs involving identifying what activities in the organisation actually 'drive' the level of particular types of cost rather than a statistical share. It therefore eliminates much of the distortion.

Using material stores costs as an example, the traditional crude approach would be to apportion the total material store costs over products pro-rata to the volume or value of the products involved. ABC recognises that material store costs have three different elements and that a different activity drives the level of cost in each case. This is illustrated in Figure 6.6.

ABC would analyse the numbers of batches of materials received relating to the different products and apportion materials receipt costs pro-rata to the numbers of batches in each case. Different calculations would be needed for materials storage and materials issue.

ABC could have great potential in HEIs as it can be used to identify the activities, which drive the delivery of particular services. This is illustrated in Figure 6.7 using course costs as an example.

Activity	Cost driver
Materials receipt	Number of batches received
Materials storage	Volume of space occupied
Materials issue	Number of batches issued

Figure 6.6   *Activity drivers: stores*

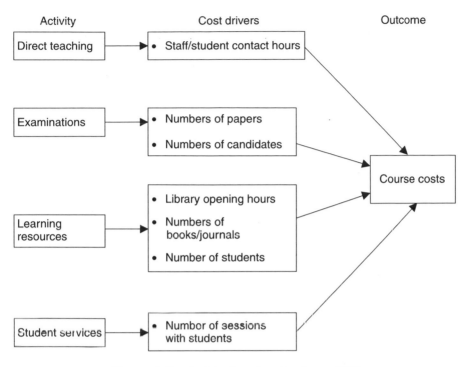

Figure 6.7 *Activity based costing in an HEI*

ABC may assist in getting a better understanding of how HEI costs behave but two common problems can arise:

- the lack of suitable data on activities to establish bases for cost attribution;
- the relatively high costs associated with setting up an ABC system.

HEI costing systems

Approaches to costing in HEIs have varied substantially; traditional approaches to costing in many HEIs could probably be summarised as follows:

- the direct revenue costs (pay and non-pay) of departments were identified to individual departments but no (or limited) sub-analysis, down to course or project level within a department, was available;
- support service costs were attributed to individual departments using a broad-based method of apportionment;
- limited information was available on the costs of any specific and material development projects;
- information on depreciation costs was limited and such costs were not attributed to individual departments or activities.

Clearly this implied that the range and quality of cost information in HEIs was somewhat limited. In recent years things have started to change. Financial pressures in the HE sector have necessitated a better and more comprehensive range of costing information and this has led HEIs to develop more sophisticated costing systems. Also, but probably to a lesser degree, the reporting requirements of the Transparency Review (see below) have required them to enhance their existing costing systems. However, the degree of sophistication employed will vary between institutions.

Figure 6.8 illustrates a typical costing approach in an HEI. The lines indicate cost-flows.

Each of these stages is considered in turn.

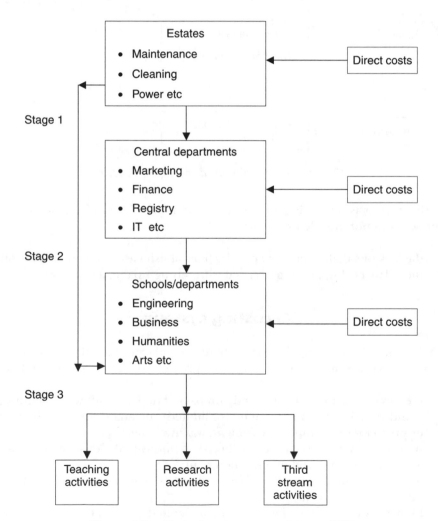

Figure 6.8   *Typical costing approach in an HEI*

Stage 1: Attribution of estates costs

The various estates costs will be attributed, by allocation or apportionment, to the various units including both academic schools/departments and central departments. A common basis used is the floor area occupied after redistributing common areas.

Stage 2: Attribution of central department costs

This stage will involve attributing, by allocation or apportionment (mainly apportionment), the costs of each central department over individual schools/departments. Some examples of possible approaches are shown in Figure 6.9.

More complex approaches are possible involving:

- one-way transfers of cost between central department (e.g., finance to registry) and also to academic units;
- reciprocal transfers of cost between central departments to reflect the support that central departments also provide to one another (e.g., finance to personnel and personnel to finance).

However, in examining these more sophisticated approaches, consideration must be given to the costs of costing. Enhancements to existing costing systems will have costs in terms of staff time, computer software and so on which must be offset against the potential benefits arising from more, and more accurate, cost information.

Stage 3: Attribution of school/department costs

The total costs of a school or department now comprise its own direct costs (e.g. academic staff costs) plus the proportion of central department overheads which have been attributed to the school/department via stage 2. These school/department costs now need to be analysed over the broad categories of activity within an academic department, namely, teaching, research and third stream activity. The major cost element is likely to relate to academic

Central cost	Driver for departmental apportionment
Estates	Floor area of each department
Registry	Numbers of students registered from each school/department
Personnel	Staff numbers in each department
Finance	Direct expenditure of departments

Figure 6.9 *Possible approaches to the attribution of central department costs*

staff salaries and thus a key driver is the division of academic staff time between teaching, research and other activities.

These matters will be discussed further in the section concerned with the future design of HEI costing systems.

Transparent approach to costing (TRAC)

No discussion of costing in the HE sector would be complete without a discussion of the TRAC, introduced through the Transparency Review (TR), and which is one of the driving forces for the development of improved costing systems in HEIs. The TR was established owing to government concerns (expressed during the first CSR of the 1997 Labour Government) about the lack of any reconciliation between research funding and research expenditure in HE. The level and sources of research funding to HEIs was clearly known and is summarised thus:

- **HE funding councils** – comprises a block grant funding from the funding councils which is provided for 'the cost of salaries of permanent staff, premises and central computing costs; support for basic research; and a contribution to the costs of research training'. Institutions are free to distribute this internally at their own discretion as long as it is used to support teaching, research and related activities.
- **Other sources of funding** – research funding also comes from a variety of public and private sources, including research councils, EU and private industry.

However, although the level of research funding was known, HEIs could not indicate what proportion of their total expenditure was undertaken on research, how this expenditure related to total research funding for the HE sector, and whether any cross-subsidisation occurred between teaching and research. This was because HEIs did not have the costing systems needed to disaggregate their expenditure between teaching, research and other activities. Hence the TR resulted in the approach to costing known as the TRAC.

Using a fairly standardised methodology the TRAC requires all HEIs to produce information on the full costs of their teaching and research activities, and then requires them each year to produce an analysis of these expenditures over specified categories. However, a spin-off from this mandatory requirement is that HEIs may have developed costing systems which can be used for internal management purposes in the institution.

The TRAC methodology can be considered in two parts:

- cost disaggregation;
- cost adjustments.

Cost disaggregation

Cost disaggregation involves taking the total costs of the HEI (per the annual accounts) and disaggregating those costs over five activity categories:

- publicly financed teaching (PFT);
- non-publicly financed teaching (NPFT);
- publicly financed research (PFR);
- non-publicly financed research (NPFR);
- other (O).

This process of disaggregating costs is carried out using a fairly standard approach defined in the TRAC methodology. In summary this is:

- **Academic staff costs** – the costs of staff totally dedicated to a specific activity (e.g. research associates working full time on a research council project) can be directly allocated to that project unless more than 10 per cent of their time is spent on other activities. However, the bulk of academic staff work on a range of teaching, research and other activities. Hence the TRAC methodology requires HEIs to collect information about the way in which academic staff distribute their time over the five categories. This is often done by getting each member of staff to fill in a questionnaire, indicating, in percentage terms, how they have used their time. These time allocations are aggregated and used as the basis for apportioning academic staff costs over the five categories.
- **Non-academic staff costs** – if identifiable to a specific activity (e.g., a research project) non-academic staff costs are directly charged to the activity. Otherwise they are apportioned over the five categories using a suitable proxy such as the proportions of academic staff time.
- **Departmental non-staff costs** – if identifiable to a specific activity the costs are directly charged to the activity. Otherwise they are apportioned over the five categories using a suitable proxy.
- **Central department costs** – staff within central departments are not required to account for their time in the same way as academic staff which does seem inconsistent. Instead all central costs (excluding trading activities such as residences and catering which are treated as 'Other' activities) are apportioned over academic departments using a minimum of four cost drivers. Some examples of these were shown in Figure 6.9. In practice, individual HEIs may use a more sophisticated range of cost drivers (e.g., weighted space costs allocated on the use of each room) to apportion costs over the five categories and may use many more than four drivers.

Cost adjustments

In addition to disaggregating the costs shown in the annual accounts of the HEI, the TRAC requires a series of cost adjustments which reflect the long run economic costs of the institution. It is argued that these economic adjustments are necessary as conventional accounting practices fail to fully reflect economic costs facing HEIs. To ensure that pricing decisions reflect long-term economic costs, and thereby contribute towards sustainability, the adjustments made ensure that the organisation has made financial provision to:

- maintain its operational capability;
- be capable of replacing assets when they wear out;
- be capable of acquiring new and additional assets to meet future business needs.

The cost adjustments made are described below:

Infrastructure adjustment

Accounting practice requires that organisations measure their financial performance (surplus/deficit) over a period by comparing income earned with total costs incurred. The total costs must include *all* costs including the costs associated with capital depletion as a consequence of wear and tear on buildings and equipment. The latter is done by charging depreciation on fixed assets to the income and expenditure account to reflect the wear and tear on fixed assets and the depletion of capital that has occurred. In practice, most organisations charge depreciation in their statutory accounts calculated on the basis of the historic (or purchase) cost of the fixed assets involved. However, to ensure that the organisation has maintained its capital in terms of its productive operational capacity, accounting theory requires that the costs of capital depletion (i.e., depreciation) should be based on the current cost of the assets involved and not its historic cost. Thus the infrastructure adjustment in TRAC is designed to reflect the shortfall between current cost depreciation and historic cost depreciation.

The logic of the infrastructure adjustment suggests that it should be calculated by reference to both buildings and equipment in HEIs. In practice the adjustment is only made in relation to buildings. The approach applied is that all buildings assets are valued using insurance valuations based on current cost depreciation valuations. The infrastructure adjustment is the difference between this depreciation figure and the figure incorporated into the statutory accounts together with deductions made in relation to the cost of certain types of non-capitalised long-term maintenance. An absence of reliable information about the value of equipment in HEIs means that it is not possible to calculate the true magnitude of an infrastructure adjustment for equipment or even to establish whether it would be a material amount. Hence no such adjustment is made under TRAC.

The calculation of the infrastructure adjustment is summarised in Figure 6.10.

	2001/02 £m	2002/03 £m	Average £m
Buildings assets as shown in balance sheet	39.0	41.0	40.0

Depreciation as shown in the annual accounts for 2002/03 = £ 2.0 million

Depreciation rate = 2.0/40.0 × 100 = 5% (40 year depreciation period)

Current value of buildings (from insurance valuations) = £73.1 million

Depreciation at current cost = 5% × £73.1 million = £3.655 million

Depreciation at current cost	= £3.655 million
Less depreciation at historic cost	= £2.000 million
Less long term maintenance costs	= £0.150 million
Infrastructure adjustment	= £1.505 million

Figure 6.10 *Calculation of infrastructure adjustment*

Cost of capital adjustment (COCA)

The COCA is concerned with the level of financial surplus that HEIs should be generating. This need for HEIs to generate financial surpluses (excess of income over expenditure) can be considered from two standpoints:

- **Opportunity cost of capital** – HEIs have substantial portfolios of assets which have been financed from a variety of sources. In theory an HEI could sell off all of its existing assets and invest the proceeds in a different line of business which could produce a greater financial/economic return. This introduces the economic concept of opportunity cost, which means that by pursuing teaching, and research (and other activities) HEIs are forgoing other opportunities to use their capital in, possibly, a more profitable manner. The capital tied up in financing HEI assets has an opportunity cost and hence HEIs should be generating financial surpluses that reflect the opportunity costs of the capital tied up in the institution. However, this is very much a theoretical economic approach which has little practical applicability. In reality HEIs are not going to sell off their assets, either to reinvest the funds or to apply them to a different line of business. Hence, although this concept is a useful one which should be kept in mind, there are limitations to the extent to which it can be applied in practice.
- **Operational financial surpluses** – in most organisations, there will be a need to generate operational financial surpluses for a number of reasons. For example, a profit-making commercial company will need to generate operational financial surpluses to make dividend payments to shareholders. Although this may not happen every year, in the longer term, all shareholders will have an expectation of dividend receipts. However 'not-for-profit' organisations, which do not have shareholders (and do not need to pay dividends), also need to make operating financial surpluses.

HEIs are 'not-for-profit' organisations and need to generate operational financial surpluses for a number of reasons:

- Future investment in physical resources such as buildings and equipment in order that the HEI can continue to undertake teaching and research at a high level.
- Future investment in human capital, again in order that the HEI can continue to undertake teaching and research at a high level. Given that HEIs are a knowledge based industry this is at least as important as investment in physical resources.
- Financial provision for risk. HEIs will undertake a variety of activities with different levels of uncertainty and risk. Given that some of these cannot be completely avoided or controlled, prudence suggests that HEIs should plan to generate some degree of financial surplus to cushion effects which could result in a negative financial outcome.

These two standpoints underpin the need for HEIs to achieve a certain level of financial surplus which most are not, at present, achieving.

Under TRAC, the approach to calculating the COCA uses a percentage rate of return developed and applied (primarily) by the Ministry of Defence to commercial defence contractors. It is based on the risk-free rate of return allowed on non-competitive contracts issued by the Ministry. For each HEI, this standard percentage rate of return is applied to the average (over a two-year period) of the net asset value of the HEI as shown in its balance sheet (and defined as fixed assets plus current assets less current liabilities but excluding cash, investments, endowments without deducting provisions, deferred capital grants, etc). To this figure an abatement of 25 per cent is applied to reflect the fact that a proportion of HE assets are estimated to have been financed from Exchequer sources. This calculation is complex and is summarised in Figure 6.11.

	2001/02 £m	2002/03 £m	Average £m
Net asset value	49.0	51.0	50.0

Initial COCA = 11.40% × £50.0 million	= £5.70 million
Less abatement of 25 per cent	= £1.43 million
Gross COCA	= £4.27 million
Less surplus already in financial accounts	= £1.10 million
Net COCA	= £3.17 million

Note: The rate of 11.4% is applied in those HEIs where the fixed assets are valued on the basis of their historic cost. Where the fixed assets are valued on a current cost basis then a lower rate of 8.05% is applied.

Figure 6.11   *Calculation of cost of capital adjustment*

The COCA therefore represents the shortfall between the financial surplus the HEI has actually generated and the financial surplus it should have generated using the target rate of return. Under TRAC, this shortfall is then added to the expenditure of the HEI and apportioned over the five activity categories.

We would make the following comments about the use of the MOD rate as a basis for setting the cost of capital adjustment under the TRAC methodology:

- It could be argued that defence contractors have some degree of affinity with HEIs in that they undertake high levels of technological research and are in a knowledge-based industry.
- It is not clear that this risk-free rate of return allowed on non-competitive contracts is wholly applicable to HEIs who do undertake risk-based contracts and competitive contracts.
- Conventional accounting practice in the UK is based primarily around the historic cost convention (supplemented in a number of cases by revaluations) and thus the accounts of defence contractors would be a mix of these bases. Thus whereas HEIs (under the TRAC approach) make a separate infrastructure adjustment to reflect the difference between financial statement depreciation and replacement cost depreciation, no such adjustment would be made in the accounts of defence contractors. Therefore it could be assumed that the rate of return made by defence contractors incorporates what are effectively an infrastructure adjustment and a cost of capital adjustment.

Consequently, in the light of the above comments there must be some doubt that the MOD rate is a reasonable proxy for a reasonable rate of return for HEIs. Consequently, one might consider alternative approaches to establishing a rate of return for HEIs based upon the following premises:

- **Core and non-core rate of return** – the cost of capital adjustment could be considered as comprising two separate elements:
  - A core rate of return for all HEIs which would reflect the return to be generated by all HEIs given the similarity in their activities and the risks they face.
  - A non-core rate of return specific to each HEI designed to reflect significant variations in the risk profile of individual HEIs.
- **Core rate of return** – regarding the core rate of return, rather than using the MOD rate, consideration could be given to other approaches such as:
  - *Comparable sector rate of return*: An attempt could be made to identify a rate of return being earned by other comparable organisations working in similar sectors and business fields to HEIs. For simplicity we would suggest using other organisations undertaking both teaching and research and, ideally, to assist comparability, these should be

'not-for-profit' organisations. However, such organisations may not exist in the UK and overseas comparisons may be misleading.

- *HE specific rate of return:* As the main reason for including the COCA in the cost base of HEIs is to ensure that they generate sufficient operating surpluses for future investment purposes, the best approach might be to base the adjustment on the HEIs' future investment requirements in physical resources and human capital. Such a rate of return could be calculated on a sector-wide basis (and applied to all HEIs) or calculated on an institution-specific basis using appropriate estimates of the levels of investment required.

- **Non-core rate** – using a single rate for all HEIs would implicitly assume that all HEIs have the same level of business and financial risk. Clearly this cannot be correct although the magnitude of differences is unclear. Thus it may be appropriate to make adjustments to the core rate of return to reflect significantly different levels of business risk and financial risk between HEIs. This could be done, relatively simply, by assigning each HEI to one of (say) four risk categories each with a different variation from the core rate of return for each category. However, there would be costs associated with the identification and making of such an adjustment and it is not clear that the materiality of this factor would be significant enough to justify the costs involved.

Exceptional items adjustment

This adjustment is not an economic adjustment in the same way as the infrastructure and cost of capital adjustments but is about providing a better representation of the financial position of the HEI. The adjustment concerns the costs (or surpluses) of large, extraordinary or exceptional items such as the costs of a major restructuring of the HEI or the decommissioning costs for major facilities. Conventional accounting practice (as defined in FRS 3) requires that such costs be charged to the accounts of the organisation, in full, in the year in which they were incurred. However, it could be argued that such an approach distorts the financial performance of the HEI by charging large elements of cost in one year whereas the benefits of such expenditure will accrue over a period of years. Thus the exceptional items adjustment involves spreading those costs over a longer period of time (3 years) than is shown in the statutory accounts of the HEI.

However, it could be argued that conventional accounting practice is soundly based and that this adjustment is just a means of circumventing the constraints of that practice.

Format and interpretation of a TRAC return

Combining each of the above aspects of TRAC, a TRAC return for a hypothetical HEI would appear as in Figure 6.12.

	Total (£m)	PFT (£m)	NPFT (£m)	PFR (£m)	NPFR (£m)	O (£m)
Expenditure as per statutory accounts	66.555	31.552	4.864	12.404	7.863	9.872
Infrastructure adjustment	1.505	0.713	0.110	0.280	0.178	0.223
COCA	3.170	1.503	0.232	0.591	0.375	0.470
Exceptional items	0	0	0	0	0	0
Adjusted expenditure	71.230	33.768	5.206	13.275	8.415	10.565

Figure 6.12 *TRAC statements for an HEI*

Issues surrounding TRAC

A number of comments should be made about the TRAC methodology

- The TRAC methodology effectively involves minimum standards of costing which all HEIs should apply. In practice, many HEIs will go well beyond these standards and will have a much greater (than the five categories) level of disaggregation and much more sophisticated approaches to costing practice.
- Although there is a disaggregation of costs over the five categories, there is, within the methodology, no equivalent disaggregation of income. Thus the straight application of TRAC would not permit HEIs to evaluate overall financial performance on each of the five categories and assess if any cross-subsidisation exists between them. In practice, many HEIs will disaggregate their income.
- Whereas the statutory accounts of a HEI are subject to a full audit by the external auditors the TRAC results are not subject to such an audit. However, the internal auditors of the HEI may review the underlying processes on which the TRAC results are based. Inevitably, therefore, TRAC results do not have the same level of robustness and confidence as statutory accounts.
- Whereas the disaggregated accounting costs of the five categories reconcile to the total expenditure in the statutory accounts, the economic adjustments do not reconcile to anything and their reasonableness is not easily verifiable.
- The infrastructure adjustment is essentially incomplete since it does not incorporate any adjustment for equipment. However, this deficiency relates more to an absence of information on which to calculate the adjustment rather than any conceptual weakness.
- Although the COCA has conceptual validity, the current approach to calculating the adjustment must be regarded as dubious. Alternative approaches might be better.

- We have already noted that, currently, the COCA is abated by 25 per cent to reflect that a proportion of HEI assets have, **historically**, been financed from Exchequer sources. Given that the COCA is not about generating surpluses to replace the assets already owned (this is the role of the infrastructure adjustment) but is about the financing of **future** investment in new assets and human capital, it seems inappropriate to abate the COCA.

Future HE trends and their impact on costing

Looking ahead there could be significant changes in HEI costing and costing systems as a consequence of external factors. Figure 6.13 indicates some of the changes that could impact on HEI costing systems in the near future.

Strategic trends in HE

There would probably be a general consensus that higher education in the UK will undergo a substantial degree of change over the next 5–10 years even though there might be differing opinions about the extent of that change and its impact on different types of HEIs. Some examples of such trends are:

Teaching to learning

This is a trend, already heavily promoted in HE, which involves a substantial shift to independent learning by students. Possible implications are:

- the need to develop an extensive range of open learning materials;
- the need to invest, substantially, in learning technologies;

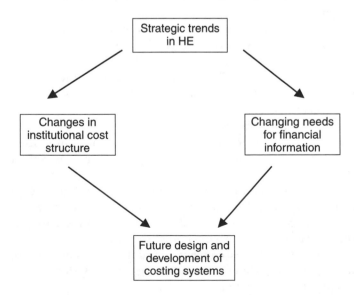

Figure 6.13 *Future HE trends and their impact on costing*

- the need to alter existing building layouts;
- changes in the magnitude and type of teaching staff workload.

E-learning

There is considerable discussion about the increased use of e-learning and the Internet to deliver curriculum activities and the development of the e-university. The extent to which this will impact is unclear but many HEIs are already active in this area.

HE funding changes

In future the financial burden of providing HE will fall to an increasingly on students through the use of variable top-up fees under which it is possible that, in future, students will be charged different fees by different universities, for the same or similar courses.

Collaborative research

Given the escalating costs of undertaking leading-edge research in science and technology, a trend towards the rationalisation of research together with increasing levels of collaborative research between HEIs is likely. The need for collaborative research has been emphasised in a number of quarters including the Roberts Review of research assessment in the HE sector. Such collaboration could result in increased sharing of fixed assets such as scientific equipment and the greater use of shared academic appointments.

Student population

The next 5–10 years will probably see substantial changes in the number and composition of the student population in HEIs. These could include increased student numbers (derived from Government policies envisaging an increase in HE participation rates) and increased diversity with increased overseas students, students undertaking foundation degrees and increased numbers of taught post-graduate students, and so on. These changes have implications for all aspects of HEI costs.

Changes in institutional cost structures

Organisational change

Substantial organisational change can be anticipated particularly in relation to support service departments. In line with trends in many other types of organisation, substantial investment in IT might be expected alongside a slimming down of staffing structures. This may be accompanied by greater delegation to academic departments although some HEIs may possibly move in the opposite direction and re-centralise certain support services. Central support services would have to operate on a 'trading basis' with academic departments for the provision of some services.

Impact on HEI cost structures

The above factors taken together will have a substantial impact on the cost structure of HEIs and thus their cost structure in five years time can be expected to have changed considerably. This is a critical point, the importance of which cannot be over-stated, although the overall pace of such change is unclear and will vary between institutions. Consequently, the pace of change in relation to cost structures will also vary considerably but the following general trends can be anticipated:

Capital costs

The level of capital related costs (e.g., depreciation, maintenance) can be expected to change in response to:

- increasing levels of capital investment in certain areas such as IT and specialist equipment;
- divestment of certain fixed assets such as campuses and buildings as a consequence of massive under-utilisation of the estate in some HEIs;
- an overall smaller fixed asset base for the HEI than at present.

Revenue costs

These can be expected to change in response to the following factors:

- substantial up-front revenue investment in the development of curriculum and learning materials;
- lower overall unit costs of teaching due to the shift from teaching to learning;
- increased expenditure on activities such as marketing and quality assurance in order to maintain market share;
- an increase in the level of costs shared with other institutions due to an increased level of collaborative research.

The overall effect of these changes **might** produce the following shifts in HEI cost structure:

- from revenue costs to capital related costs;
- from direct revenue costs to indirect revenue costs.

Changing needs for financial management information

Finance is a key resource of an HEI and hence good quality information on the costs and revenues of the HEI is a pre-requisite for effective decision-making.

Looking ahead, there are a number of areas where an improved range of financial information will be required. These include:

Financial strategy

The increasing pace of change and the degree of uncertainty will necessitate the development of robust corporate strategies in HEIs which will be supported by a number of resource strands including, of course, financial strands or strategies. Experience has shown that the main responsibility for the development and promulgation of such financial strategies will fall on senior finance personnel who will cascade the development of financial strategies throughout the HEI. To do this, they will need an increased range of financial information about the various activities of the HEI.

Internal resource allocation

There is strong evidence, in some HEIs, that teaching costs in some subject areas are significantly out of line with the (internal or external) tariff band for that subject. This could be due either to tariffs being inappropriate for the particular subject or to the costs being wrong. Thus improved cost information will be required to resolve this dilemma.

Intra-departmental activity analysis

While the costs of individual academic departments or schools are usually identified it is unusual for more detailed cost-information to be available. However, a number of pressures on HEIs suggest that a greater analysis of costs *within* departments will be required in the future.

Pricing decisions

The demands of the market-place for keen prices and the requirements of funding agencies (e.g., EU, MOD) for accurate cost information suggest a need for HEIs to improve the costing of their services. Moreover, in future years, students are required to pay an increasing proportion of HE fees HEIs will need robust information on the costs of their courses in order to inform pricing decisions on these mainstream activities.

Future design and development of costing systems

In the previous sections it was argued that the strategic trends affecting higher education will have a radical impact on the cost structure of HEIs. Changes in managerial information requirements will also influence the needs for cost information. Thus it is very pertinent to ask whether the current approach and current generation of costing systems in HE (as described above) will be adequate and appropriate. In particular we would highlight the following issues where development work will be required:

- central support service cost attribution;
- final cost centre structures;
- departmental cost attribution;
- cost behaviour classification.

Central support service cost attribution

The overall financial pressures on HEIs and the need for more accurate information on the costs of activities undertaken (including the requirements of the TR) will mean that more sophisticated arrangements are likely to be needed in future. There are a number of issues to consider:

- **Cost centre hierarchies** – in attributing support service costs to academic departments, it must be recognised that there is a degree of interdependence between support service departments and this can affect the treatment of such costs and the hierarchy of cost centres to be used. Two broad approaches can be applied which are illustrated in Figure 6.14.

    Model B is a simple model where the costs of each central support department are attributed to each academic department on some suitable

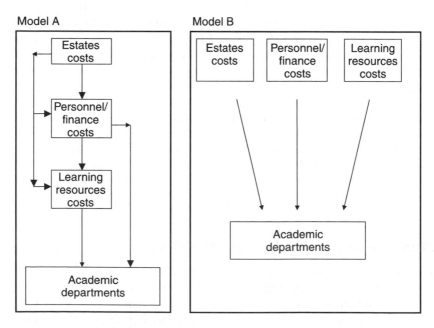

Figure 6.14   *Cost centre hierarchies*

basis. Model A is a more complex model which recognises that the various central support departments also service one another to some degree and the model reflects this by attributing costs between central support departments before attributing costs to academic departments. Clearly, model B is the simplest to operate and the temptation may be to always apply such a model. However, such a simple approach can introduce large distortions into the final cost results and therefore should be treated with caution.

- **Improved cost drivers** – an improvement to across-the-board cost apportionment would be to treat each cost-element of support services separately and to attach specific cost-drivers for apportioning such costs to individual departments. Using personnel costs as an example might lead to the following:
  - recruitment costs pro-rata to numbers of recruits;
  - training costs pro-rata to numbers of courses attended;
  - general personnel costs – pro-rata to numbers of employees.

There will be situations where a pool of support service costs can be attributed to departments using a number of different cost drivers but the driver actually used must be logically supportable as a basis for attributing costs. It might be that data on appropriate cost drivers are not available and the temptation might be to use some surrogate indicator (e.g., student numbers instead of space for estate costs). This must be treated with caution since experience has shown that the use of a surrogate cost driver can substantially impact on the distribution of cost. For example, using staff numbers instead of floor area to apportion premises costs can affect the total costs by as much as 6–7 per cent. Hence the use of such incorrect cost drivers should be resisted and where this is not possible the costing information produced needs to be given a clear 'health' warning.

In practice it might not be possible to get the required range of cost drivers at first attempt. Hence, the costing approach might need to be developed on an iterative basis as further information becomes available, which is acceptable provided it is recognised that the earlier cost information has accuracy limitations.

- **Service level agreements** – a further development might be the establishment of service level agreements (SLAs) between support service departments and academic departments which would define both the unit of service to be provided and the cost of that unit. Where it is considered applicable, an academic department would be charged according to the use made of the support department's services and the support departments would be expected to pay their way by providing services to internal as well as to external clients. Clearly a framework and rules are necessary as to how these SLAs operate and data will need to be captured on the use of support services by academic departments. If there is an option for departments to opt out of the SLA and purchase services externally, this would need to be managed carefully to avoid increasing overall HEI costs. Such approaches have been implemented in other organisations including, for example, parts of the NHS.

Final cost centre structures

Traditionally, the final cost centres in most HE costing systems are the individual schools/departments and current costing systems attribute direct and indirect costs to each department. Future management information needs will probably require a sub-analysis of departmental costs and Figure 6.15 illustrates some possible approaches and the relationships between each method of categorisation.

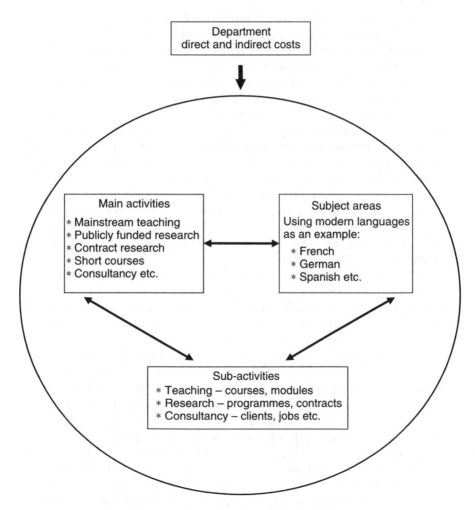

Figure 6.15   *Final cost centre structures*

Thus in developing costing systems a key task would be to identify an appropriate cost centre structure at the sub-departmental level which may well differ between departments.

Departmental cost attribution methods

In attributing departmental costs (direct and indirect) over the lower-level cost centres three substantial and material areas of cost exist for which reasonable methods of cost attribution will be required:

Academic staff time   The TRAC requires individual departments to obtain validated and verified assessments of academic staff time analysed over teaching, research and other. Within local government, many years' experience of apportioning central departmental overheads over service accounts suggest that it is difficult to obtain robust assessments of staff time by conventional methods. Although such approaches may be appropriate for the broad-brush requirements of the transparency exercise they are unlikely to be adequate as a means of producing accurate cost information for management decision purposes.

The need to provide intra-departmental analyses of costs will require a further sub-division of academic staff time beyond the categories of research and teaching. Thus, for modern languages, as well as the research/teaching distinction, it may be necessary to analyse staff time over different languages, different modules and different courses. These more sophisticated approaches to and methods of disaggregating such staff time may involve the use of programmed staff hours or experiments may need to be undertaken (as has been done in the NHS with health care professionals) of using technology such as portable data capture units (PDCUs) to obtain good quality data on the use of staff time.

A further issue concerns the amount of academic staff time (and other costs) devoted to development activities, be these new course developments and/or the development of learning materials for existing courses. Specific examples from the HE sector show that these development costs can be substantial. Some distance learning courses with examinations but no continuous assessment have ongoing teaching costs which are effectively nil while development costs may run into many hundreds of thousands of pounds. Thus it will be important to identify the costs of such development activities and, where appropriate, of capitalising such costs and writing them off, over a period of years, in the same way as research and development expenditure. In this way development costs can be matched against income receivable over a period of years.

Equipment   Particularly in scientific departments the costs associated with equipment (e.g., depreciation, maintenance) can be substantial. Similarly, the development of the e-university concept will substantially increase costs associated with IT. When such costs are a small proportion of total costs then broad-brush approaches will suffice, but when they are more significant crude approaches may introduce large distortions. Such costs will need to be attributed to specific activities reasonably accurately and methods of identifying and attributing such costs to different activities and of capturing the necessary data to undertake cost attribution exercises will need to be identified.

Other costs   It is often the case that apportionments are made on the basis of academic staff time committed to each of the activities. However, this can easily introduce distortions where the proportion of academic staff time associated with an activity is not a good proxy for the proportion of costs associated with the activity (e.g., IT costs). Hence it will be necessary to consider the following:

- the nature of each element of cost (direct and indirect);
- the likely driver of that cost in relation to activities;
- the availability of information to enable that cost driver to be applied.

Thus judgements will need to be made about the drivers to be used and the methods of cost apportionment to be applied. A degree of pragmatism must be coupled with a minimum level of accuracy if the final results are to be meaningful and where proxy cost drivers have to be applied great care must be taken to ensure that they do not distort the resulting costs.

Cost behaviour classification

Ultimately the costing information produced will be used by departmental and HEI management to manage the organisation and to make decisions. Thus the cost analysis should try and identify the various costs according to their behavioural type, namely:

- variable;
- semi-variable;
- fixed.

Such an analysis will inform managers when considering options and making decisions and although the distinction between these cost classifications may not always be clear cut it is important to attempt to try to classify them.

Developing costing systems: the way forward

There are a number of key stages, which should be followed in the development of effective approaches to costing in HEIs, as follows.

Costing strategies and policies

Before launching into any systems development, institutions need to give substantial consideration to the development of longer-term strategies and policies for costing in the HEI including:

- identifying longer-term needs for cost information;
- future costing systems architecture and cost flow structures;
- reviewing strengths and weaknesses of existing information systems (financial and non-financial) – existing systems may be adequate with some 'tweaking';
- likely resource availability – the amount available for costing systems development is inherently limited.

Costing systems development

HEIs will need to produce a costing systems development plan, which should include the following:

- identification of detailed information needs;
- development of detailed costing approaches and methods;
- enhancement of existing systems;
- selection of new systems;
- development of an implementation plan.

Training

Clearly, if the cost information produced through new systems is not fully utilised by academic and support managers the investment in such systems may have been wasteful. Hence it is vital to provide adequate training to all relevant staff about interpreting the cost information and how it can be used to improve decision-making.

In conclusion it can be confidently stated that the changes in the HE environment that will undoubtedly take place over the next few years will have a profound effect on the cost structure of institutions. This point must continue to be emphasised. In turn this will require new approaches to costing in HEIs over and above developments which may at present be taking place. Thus institutions should avoid the acquisition of new costing systems, at considerable expense, without first undertaking a strategic review of their requirements for cost information and the means of producing that cost information in the medium to longer term.

Chapter 7

Pricing

Introduction

Any organisation must set prices for the products and services that it delivers. Traditionally the pricing of goods and services has not been regarded as of great importance within HEIs but various trends within the HE sector have, in recent years, raised the profile of pricing and have indicated the need for improved pricing practices. Prime reasons for this include the following.

- **Introduction of top-up fees** – for many years, HEIs have needed to set prices locally for education-related activities such as fees for post-graduate students, overseas students and for short courses but fees for domestic undergraduate students have been fixed nationally. However, the introduction of variable top-up fees will create a market for undergraduate courses where the price of the course could be a major factor in the individual student's choice of HEI. This is a key issue for HEIs.
- **Income diversification** – financial pressures and the desire to diversify income streams have made increased external income generation an important objective and optimal pricing is a key aspect of this particularly in relation to:
  - research contracts;
  - consultancy contracts;
  - publications;
  - other services.
- **Increased fixed asset efficiency** – HEIs have a substantial range of expensive fixed assets including buildings, equipment and computers. It makes sense for the HEI to price activities in such a way as to maximise the use of this fixed asset base and hence improve its overall efficiency. This is sometimes referred to as 'sweating' the fixed asset base. Appropriate pricing can influence demand and hence the use made of these fixed assets.
- **Achievement of strategic financial objectives** – HEIs will have set themselves strategic objectives which will cover such matters as financial

---

Case study 7.1   Pricing and strategic objectives

Calderwood University has a strategic objective of widening access to its services and this is intended to apply to all of its activities and not just its undergraduate courses. The Health Studies School of the university runs a series of training programmes on health promotion issues for local organisations. The prices charged for these training programmes covers the full costs of the programme plus a profit element. The university has discovered that all of the places on these training programme are occupied by staff from the NHS and private sector providers of mental health services with no representatives from the voluntary sector. A substantial number of complaints have been received from local voluntary bodies stating that the price charged for places on the training programme is prohibitive. They claim that the university is failing to pursue its declared objective of widening access in this area of activity.

---

performance, market share and widening access. However, an ineffective approach to pricing can be a major contributor to an institution failing to achieve its strategic objectives as:
- costs may not be fully covered;
- income may not be maximised;
- strategic objectives may not be achieved;
- institutional profiles may suffer;
- financial deficits may occur.

The structure of pricing decisions

The structure of pricing decisions is illustrated in Figure 7.1 with the arrows highlighting the inter-relationships between the various factors.

There is a distinction between pricing strategy and pricing tactics. Pricing strategy means having a longer-term view of the pricing of services and products being delivered by the HEI. It should provide guidelines for pricing against which individual pricing decisions should be assessed while recognising that individual decisions will also be influenced by a series of shorter-term tactical considerations.

A strategic pricing policy will be determined by two main factors:

- the coordination of pricing strategy with the other elements of the marketing mix;
- strategic pricing factors.

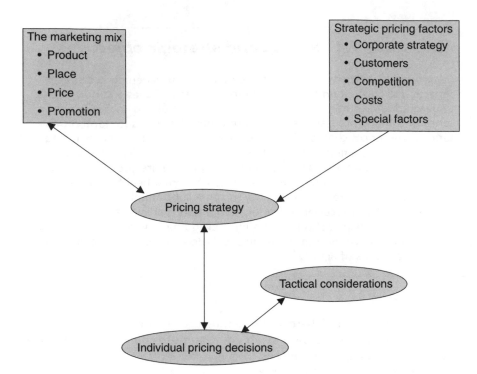

Figure 7.1   *The structure of pricing decisions*

Pricing and the marketing mix

In making pricing decisions any organisation must remember that pricing cannot be considered in isolation from other factors comprising the marketing mix.

Range of products and markets

In developing a marketing strategy, HEIs need to consider the wide range of services they offer and the relationship between these services and the markets in which they are sold. There will be existing long-established services and also newly developed services. Similarly there will be a combination of existing markets and new markets, which the HEI wishes to penetrate. Thus in terms of marketing the HEI can be faced with four possible options as follows:

• *Marketing existing products in existing markets* – continuing to market existing products to the existing customer base or to new customers within the same market segment. A strategy of market maintenance which for an HEI department implies the ongoing marketing task each year, of marketing the existing range of courses to the main market, such as the 18-year-old school leaver.

- *Marketing existing products in new markets* – this is often referred to as a strategy of market development. An HEI department might decide to market its existing range of educational activities in another country.
- *Marketing new products in existing markets* – a strategy of product development which involves 'selling-on' to existing customers. An HEI department which already provides a wide range of training courses to local employers might diversify and offer consultancy services to that same range of employers.
- *Marketing new products in new markets* – the most risky and probably most time-consuming approach but also the one which might give the greatest return. For example, an HEI department, which traditionally has focused its educational activities around full-time degrees and conducting national or international research, might decide to try and diversify into the marketing and delivery of research contract work (new product) to local employers (new market).

A pricing policy will need to take account of the nature of a particular service, the position in the market and the stage in the life cycle of the service being considered. If an HEI has just launched a new course or undertaken a new activity and it is able to set the price, then the need for growth and market penetration might be important enough to justify a low or even negative financial return resulting from a low sales price. As the project matures, sales growth might be seen as less important and so the price charged will be such as to produce high financial returns.

The above options are not mutually exclusive and HEIs might pursue several approaches simultaneously. The HEI will also need to consider, continually, its *competition*. For example, a market may be expanding and therefore competition may not be an important issue as demand is increasing with supply. However, in a static or shrinking market, competition must be considered as attempts to increase market share will be at the expense of others. Also, each option will require a differing degree of commitment to new product development and a differing approach to the other elements of the marketing mix.

Methods of service distribution

Marketing can be defined as the process of getting the *right goods and services* to the *right place* at the *right time*. This raises two key issues of:

- the location where goods and services should be made available to the customer;
- the logistics of distributing goods and services to the place where the customer can acquire them.

Case study 7.2   Pricing for market penetration

The business school of Burntwood University wishes to expand the range of consultancy services it provides to businesses in the local area. Although it feels it has the key resources required to deliver such services it has a very limited track record so lacks credibility with potential clients. Hence it has made a policy decision to price its consultancy services at a very low level such that it barely covers the marginal costs involved. By adopting this approach it hopes to attract business and thus build up its statement of experience. However, the director of finance of the university is very concerned about this approach. The DOF fears that once the policy is in place:

- potential clients will expect a continuation of this low pricing policy;
- university departments will also wish to continue with the pricing policy into the foreseeable future;
- the low price may be perceived as reflecting poor quality.

Hence the DOF has insisted that the low pricing policy be adopted initially for a nine-month period only. At the end of this period the pricing policy will be reviewed with the aim of moving towards a more realistic pricing policy.

Consider for example, the marketing (and purchase) of motor cycles, which may be through specialist shops, large retail chains, or by mail order or internet direct from the manufacturer. For the manufacturer each of these distribution options will have implications for sales volumes and revenues, costs and distribution processes. Hence each option must be fully evaluated.

Pricing policy needs to take account of distribution policy as the distribution channel chosen will influence the price that can be charged for a particular service. Such distribution considerations are relevant to HEIs since, for example, educational courses may be delivered in a number of different ways each with different logistical and cost implications:

- traditional attendance based courses;
- open learning courses;
- outreach courses;
- Internet based courses.

Sometimes, distribution methods are evaluated purely on the basis of cost. This is a mistake and a full financial evaluation needs to be undertaken which considers likely outcomes (for example, student take-up and revenues), as well as the costs related to each approach.

Promotion

Promotion concerns communicating information on products and services to potential and existing customers. It comprises four types of activity, which will have different degrees of applicability in HEIs in different situations. These are:

- *Advertising*: this could involve mass communication through various media (newspapers, TV, radio), which is paid for by the HEI undertaking the advertising. This may concern the HEI itself or focus on specific services or activities. The potential role of the Internet in marketing HEI services is important. Most HEIs have sophisticated web pages and many are moving to enrolling students online.
- *Sales promotion*: a number of disparate activities concerned with promoting the HEI as a whole and/or its services and activities. Examples might include:
  - exhibitions;
  - recruitment fairs – overseas and home;
  - displays;
  - mail shots;
  - HEI prospectus.
- *Public relations*: information which is presented to the audience, free of charge, through mass media communication such as newspapers and TV. It can involve editorial comments, news stories, or letters related to the HEIs. However, because the channel of communication is not paid for, the HEI has less control over the style, content and presentation of the message than when promoting through other means. The main purpose of public relations activity is to keep the HEI in the audience's mind and to present it always in the most positive manner. Most HEIs employ public relations/corporate affairs personnel who maintain relations with media, promote stories in the media and manage possible 'bad press' before it reaches the public domain.
- *HEI staff actions*: a commercial organisation will usually have a team of salespersons whose job it is to sell the company's products. Although HEIs will not usually employ salespersons as such, others undertake similar functions, for example staff employed in:
  - international office;
  - commercial liaison office;
  - schools liaison.

Also, there may be opportunities for other members of staff to 'sell' the HEI in various ways including during the student visit/interview process and through networking opportunities.

Pricing policy needs to be coordinated with promotion policy. Thus, if an organisation is launching a promotion initiative it may offer a special pricing package to support the thrust of the initiative.

Case study 7.3   Pricing and promotion

Blackrock College of Higher Education has a substantial amount of student accommodation on campus. Like most HEIs it wishes to market this accommodation to tourists, holidaymakers etc during the summer months. In recent years it has had some difficulty in achieving reasonable occupancy rates during July and August and needs to take some actions to alleviate the problem. Consequently it has entered into a partnership arrangement with a nearby theme park to market a joint package of college accommodation, meals and theme park entry. This package is to be heavily marketed in suitable magazines with a special offer of a reduced price for those who place a firm booking prior to the end of the year.

To summarise, in establishing prices for their services, HEIs must take account of the four elements of the marketing mix and ensure that they are properly coordinated with each other.

Strategic pricing factors

Although costs should be only one component of an effective pricing strategy, within HE the costs (however calculated) of a service have traditionally been the main determinant of its price. Basing pricing strategy decisions largely on the cost of provision implies an inward-looking organisation as pricing decisions also require an external perspective. Thus while HEIs may now have an improved understanding of their costs, to improve their pricing decisions many need to substantially improve their access to and understanding of market information. This means improving information on both customer needs and competitors.

There are a number of key factors, which, in combination, should be used to determine the HEI's pricing strategy for particular products.

Corporate strategy

In any organisation every decision taken should be in support of its overall strategy, and pricing methodology is no exception. An HEI's overall strategy should, therefore, govern the approach to pricing in practice. The HEI should have a long-term vision, which outlines its future direction, and what it is trying to achieve. HEIs are not in the world of setting simple 'bottom' line visions and it is likely that their vision will be characterised by an aspiration to improve quality, access, the learning experience of its students and development of its research capability. For example, an HEI may have, within its vision, an aspiration to increase the proportion of local ethnic minorities in its student population.

The corporate strategy sets out how the HEI will achieve its mission. It should be a detailed document, which contains measurable objectives over (typically) a three to five year period. Importantly, it is from this document that individual faculties and business units will be able to determine their own plans and priorities and, specifically, the pricing methods needed to achieve these.

In addition the HEI should have a pricing strategy which should emphasise that pricing decisions should not made in isolation of the 'big picture'. All staff involved in pricing decisions must understand the overall aims and direction of the HEI, so that these decisions do not conflict with but actually support the organisation in realising its objectives and mission. Often this potential conflict only materialises some time after the (incorrect) pricing decision has been made as it becomes evident that the HEI's ability to deliver a particular strategic objective is constrained.

Tensions between strategic objectives are always likely to exist and often become evident when a pricing strategy needs to be agreed. A particular issue concerns the relationship between financial and other corporate objectives. In establishing a strategic pricing policy there is often a trade-off between achieving financial objectives and achieving corporate objectives. The short-term financial return from a service will be heavily influenced by the price charged and, generally, the higher the price the higher the return and vice versa. However, the price charged will also impact on strategic objectives such as market share and rate of sales growth. Generally the lower the price the higher the rate of sales growth/market share and vice versa, although customers may pay a higher price if they perceive it buys them higher quality. The price charged must reflect the balance between financial and corporate objective, and in some cases the achievement of the corporate objectives might be paramount and justify a negative financial return – a loss-leader. For some HEIs, particularly the smaller colleges, the option of sustaining a loss-leader for other than a very short period may be impractical due to the scale of their operations.

This potential conflict in pricing strategy is illustrated well by the issue of undergraduate top-up fees which we anticipate will cause a dilemma in many HEIs about the fee-level to be charged. It may be that in a consideration of the markets for particular courses, the HEI's profile and the profiles of competitor HEIs will lead to an HEI setting fees at substantially less than the £3,000 limit. Setting the fee at a lower level might also facilitate the widening of access into HE. However, we anticipate that some will believe that the setting of fees at a level below that of competitors will send a negative signal to students about the nature and quality of the HEI itself and this will then act as a marketing disincentive.

There is no simple solution to resolving the tensions that may appear to exist between an HEI's various strategic objectives but there are important factors which should be taken into account in trying to reach a balance:

- all staff should be aware of the HEI's vision, mission and strategic aims and not just those which may have a direct impact on themselves or their department;
- strategic objectives do not all have to be implemented at the same time and pace; it may be necessary to balance a need to capture market share in a particular area in years one and two of the strategic plan with the need for a reasonable financial return from this activity which arises in years three to five of the plan;
- in order to ensure congruence between the HEI's strategic plan and pricing decisions, internal management arrangements must be sufficiently robust;
- wherever possible a pricing strategy should be prepared and adopted which should seek to translate the HEI's corporate strategy into pricing aims and objectives; this should reduce the risks of inappropriate pricing decisions being made.

Customers

Under this heading are two key issues:

Who are our customers?

An HEI's pricing decisions involve a wide range of its activities and in consequence involve many customer groups. Some examples, either current or prospective, are:

- home/EU undergraduate students;
- overseas undergraduate students;
- taught post-graduate students;
- research students;
- research sponsors (private, charitable, Government);
- commercial organisations (including SMEs and global corporations);
- individuals (e.g., purchasing books, digests or specific services).

However, the level of analysis may need to be greater than this. Consider an HEI developing a pricing strategy for domestic UG students in an environment of variable top-up fees. In developing a pricing strategy the HEI may need to disaggregate the market into a number of discrete groups and consider the likely levels of demand in each case. Issues to be considered are:

- **Location** – potential domestic UG students can be considered as follows:
  - part-time students from the local area;
  - full time or part time students recruited within the region;

- full time students recruited nationally;
- EU students.
- **Subject** – a further disaggregation by subject may be required since different subjects will have variable degrees of UG student demand.

Hence at the outset an HEI needs to undertake a certain degree of research about its actual or potential customer base. In doing this, it may make use of the following sources of information:

- Potential students:
  - student information systems;
  - UCAS;
  - Government organisations (e.g., British Council);
  - published commercial surveys;
  - information derived from commissioned market research surveys.
- Research sponsors:
  - annual reports;
  - media items;
  - networking at events.
- Commercial organisations:
  - local labour market intelligence;
  - business organisations (e.g., Chambers of Commerce);
  - annual reports;
  - information derived from commissioned market research surveys.

What factors influence customer purchasing decisions?

Within each of these broad customer groups will be a variety of factors that influence and determine any particular purchasing decision. Price is one of these elements, and so it is important to understand how customers may react to price levels and what other factors they will take into account. The key to understanding customer purchasing decisions is the comparison between price and the perceived future benefits which will arise from their purchases. For each purchasing option it is the combination of price and benefits, rather than the price alone, on which customers' buying decisions are made. Hence the importance of having some understanding of what customers are seeking, and the factors they take into account when making their choices. In many HEIs, a considerable time-delay often exists between knowledge about customers needs and a decision on a new course/product and in the absence of such information, incorrect assumptions are sometimes made.

Hence, HEIs need to gather information on what factors might influence the decisions of their actual or potential customers and Figure 7.2 summarises some of these.

Influencing factor	Possible sources of information
• Alternatives choices available to customers	• Advertising by other HEIs • Local knowledge and research • Survey of current/previous customers
• Key attributes that customers consider important when making their purchase	• Staff survey • Survey of current/previous customers
• The end-benefits that the customers desire	• Alumni – destinations of previous students • Survey of current/previous customers
• The price range that the customers consider fair	• Surveys • Local judgements

Figure 7.2   *Factors influencing customer purchasing decisions*

If an HEI is able to provide information in response to these issues, its understanding of its customers is considerably enhanced and its pricing strategy will, therefore, become more robust. This information can be analysed to address the following questions in relation to the goods and services offered by the HEI:

- who are our customers – current and prospective?
- what are their needs which might be met by purchasing our products or a similar product?
- what appear to be the main factors influencing their decision?
- how price sensitive is their purchasing decision?
- are customers' needs fully met by the offer? Are there gaps and what are the implications of addressing these?
- by what means can we influence their decision?
- are they potentially long-term customers of our institution?

Answers to these questions will influence the pricing strategy of the organisation.

Competitors

HEIs face competition from many sources including other HEIs (domestic and overseas), FE colleges and commercial organisations, and this competition is becoming increasingly complex and in many areas more intense. It is axiomatic that pricing decisions must take account of this competition. There are three aspects to this.

Understanding the market

Economic theory teaches that three main market structures exist In the context of the HE sector these can be considered as being:

- *Monopoly* – where one HEI or organisation effectively controls the market and therefore usually the price. An example here might be an HEI which has a patented research application.
- *Oligopoly* – where a small number of HEIs control the market. An example here might be the provision of degrees in veterinary medicine where there are only six UK providers.
- *Openly competitive* – in this situation there is extensive competition between HEIs and possibly other organisations. Take for example, undergraduate degree courses in business studies or computing where an HEI will be competing against hundreds of other HEIs and FE colleges.

Clearly an HEI can be faced with a number of different market scenarios and may be a monopolist in one market (specialised research), an oligopolist in another (specialist teaching) and face open competition in other markets (e.g., most undergraduate teaching). It is therefore important that an HEI has an understanding of its market position in relation to each of its products since this has implications for such matters as vulnerability, barriers to entry, and so on.

Analysing competitors

Within a particular market, competitors will probably exist and it is therefore essential that an HEI considers this issue and asks itself the following questions:

- What HEIs are we competing against?
- What other organisations are we competing against?
- What services do our competitors offer and how do they differ from ours?
- What is their financial position?
- What are their strengths and weaknesses?
- What are their prices/pricing strategy?
- Is this a key strategic market for them?

In many situations HEIs may be faced with many potential competitors, and gathering information on each would not be feasible. In these cases a judgement needs to be made on whether some broad assumptions can be made about competitors based on sampling techniques. As with all data collection, knowledge from the HEI's own staff should not be overlooked but should be welcomed as a potentially rich source of information. Sources of information for the identification of competitors can include:

- Key competitors
  - UCAS;
  - advertising by other organisations;
  - trade journals;
  - surveys of potential, current and previous customers;
  - staff knowledge.
- Market significance
  - targeted research;
  - analysis of financial statements, student numbers, strategic plans (if available);
  - intelligence from new staff.
- Prices
  - targeted research;
  - customer feedback;
  - staff knowledge.

Assessing market position

Once an analysis of competing organisations has been undertaken, an HEI should undertake a *full and frank evaluation* of how it ranks against them. This is partially, and necessarily, a subjective exercise and should be closely linked to the HEI's marketing strategy which should have identified its own strengths and weaknesses. A framework for analysing an HEI's market position *vis-à-vis* its competitors is set out below.

- *Market leaders* – these are the acknowledged dominant organisations in a particular programme or market segment. Leadership could reflect size of market share or perceived quality.
- *Challengers* – these are 'second place' organisations, often characterised by an aspiration to become market leaders. These HEIs may well have ambitious plans for expansion.
- *Mainstream* – often the majority of organisations in a particular market. Characteristics can include difficulties in maintaining market share and perceived significant barriers to growth (e.g., if an HEI appears in the lower quartile of a national ranking).
- *Niche players* – organisations which may operate in a particular niche or specialist market which is not currently well served.

Information on competitors can be useful for a number of purposes and in relation to pricing should be used to help develop an informed judgement of the following:

- How might competitors react to potential pricing moves and with what consequences?

- What aims (e.g., market share, financial return) can the HEI reasonably set itself given the competitive environment in which it operates?
- How can the HEI best insulate itself from actual or potential competitive threats?
- Is it viable for the HEI to continue to operate in this market in the long term?

Costs

There are three aspects of costing which should be considered in relation to pricing strategy decisions.

Total cost pricing

A general rule when making pricing decisions, price should be set **by reference to** the total costs of the activity being considered which in an HEI, can be regarded as being the sum of:

- direct costs;
- a share of indirect costs.

Individual HEIs need to devise appropriate models for apportioning indirect costs to their activities, after considering their own strategy and the behaviours they want to encourage. Information generated from the Transparency Review may also help HEIs understand their cost structures better and therefore help them make more effective decisions. A useful practical principle is to limit the number of different overhead recovery rates as staff may then find pricing and costing confusing and may make mistakes.

However, whatever the approach the HEI uses to apportion indirect costs to activities, limitations are often laid down by the 'customer' regarding the overhead costs they are prepared to accept in the price. The argument is often made that HEI overhead costs are already financed by public funds and so should not be paid for a second time. Thus although the HEI may seek the customer's agreement to a particular price, the customer may wish to examine the proposed costs and may limit the amount of overheads they are prepared to pay. This applies particularly to the pricing of research contracts; Table 7.1 summarises the contributions to overheads that sponsors are currently willing to accept in their prices.

Individual sponsors may be willing to accept specific, rather than general, contributions to overheads, for example, 10 hours of personnel time for every job created, 10 hours of library time for every PhD student, plus any capital equipment required. To this extent, prices for research grants funded by the Research Councils and the European Union, as well as teaching company schemes, are sponsor-determined, with little discretion open to the HEI to justify higher overhead contributions on the basis of actual costs. The results are also usually audited by the sponsor, with clawback possible if costs are not in line with budget.

Table 7.1 Limitations on overhead contribution rates

Sponsor	Overhead contribution from sponsors
Research grants funded by research councils	46% direct staff costs[a]
Research grants funded by the European Union	Circa 20% of all direct costs
Teaching company schemes	Typically 46% of 60% of staff costs
Charities and voluntary organizations	No indirect costs allowed in pricing

Note:
a But see Appendix regarding fEC.

Before making its pricing decision, it is essential for the HEI to ensure that all relevant costs are taken into account. Often, staff are conscious only of the direct costs and fail to understand the importance of incorporating a proportion of the indirect costs to ensure that the income generated will contribute to indirect costs and surplus. However, saying that price should relate to total costs does not mean that price must equate to total cost, and three scenarios are possible:

- **Price is greater than total cost** – this implies the generation of a surplus on the activity which will be available to fund future development activities of the HEI. The amount by which price should exceed cost (and hence the element of surplus) must be set by reference to the HEI's financial strategy and the overall financial surplus the HEI wishes to achieve.
- **Price is less than total cost** – this implies a planned deficit on the activity which is usually related to a deliberate 'loss-leader'. Again, the amount by which price should be set below total cost (and hence the element of subsidy) must be set by reference to other elements of the pricing decision such as competition and corporate objectives.
- **Price equals total cost** – in this case there is neither a surplus nor a subsidy.

However, the pricing decision may be more complex than this and variations in pricing may be applied differentially to types of customers and markets. Thus for one customer type the price may be set above total cost while for another customer, for strategic marketing reasons, the price may be set below total cost.

Marginal cost pricing

In specific circumstances it is appropriate and acceptable to base pricing decisions on the marginal costs rather than the total cost of that activity. The marginal costs of an activity are the additional costs that an HEI would actually incur if they undertook the activity. These are synonymous with variable costs but must not be viewed as synonymous with the direct costs of an activity. For example, teaching costs associated with a short course may, effectively, be fixed in nature even though they are directly attributable to the activity.

Case study 7.4   *Marginal cost pricing*

The print room of Oakdew University provides services to all departments in the university and generates 10 million units of work per annum. The following cost information is available about the unit:

Total costs of production

	Total costs (£)	Unit cost (p)
Materials	25,000	0.25
Labour	75,000	0.75
Variable overhead	20,000	0.20
Fixed overhead	10,000	0.10
Total	130,000	1.30

The unit has been asked by a private company to submit a tender for a once-off contract to undertake 300,000 units of work and has offered a fixed price of £2,800.

The total costs (including overheads) would amount to £3,900 (300,000 × 1.3p) which is well in excess of the price being offered for the contract. However, the head of the unit feels that since this is a fairly small (3 per cent of total workload) contract which is once-off, then it is appropriate to base the price on the marginal costs of production. These are calculated as follows:

Marginal costs of production

	Marginal costs per unit
Materials	0.25
Labour	nil
Variable overhead	0.20
Fixed overhead	nil
Total	0.45

Thus the marginal costs of undertaking this contract would amount to £1,360 (300,000 × 0.45p) and the price being offered is much greater than the marginal costs.

The following points should be noted:

- fixed overhead is by definition non-marginal;
- since there is slack capacity in the unit, it is assumed that the additional work can be undertaken by the existing staff and thus the marginal labour costs of this contract are nil. In other circumstances it might have been necessary for overtime to have been worked or temporary staff recruited and in this case there would have been a marginal labour cost.

Marginal cost pricing (the setting of prices by reference to the marginal costs of an activity) must be treated with caution. If all activities were priced on a marginal cost basis there would be a risk of generating insufficient revenues to finance the indirect costs of the organisation. Thus it should only be undertaken in the following circumstances:

- the proposed activity is for a once-off contract fairly short-term in nature. Thus it is not applicable to ongoing activities;
- pricing the activity at marginal cost will not affect the price charged for the mainstream provision of the same activity; this implies that an activity might be provided in some other geographic location;
- the proposed activity is a fairly small proportion of the existing workload of the department.

The excess of price over marginal cost is referred to as 'contribution' and it is important that the activity does make some contribution towards the fixed costs of the HEI. A judgement must be made about the size of that contribution.

Break-even analysis

The concept of contribution and break-even analysis is important in making pricing decisions. It recognises that pricing decisions are dynamic and must recognise the relationship between demand for a product and its price. Thus where there is a high volume of service provision by the HEI, the price may be set by reference to the maximum total contribution to be achieved.

However, since demand is inextricably linked to price different price levels will generate different levels of demand and, therefore, different levels of contribution. Figure 7.3 illustrates this using the example of a HEI producing and selling a publication.

Break-even analysis aims to identify the point at which a particular activity will financially break even and in Figure 7.3 it can be seen that the break-even point will be achieved at a price of £10 per guidebook.

Price (£)	Sales volume (nos)	Sales revenue (£)	Unit variable costs (£)	Total variable costs (£)	Contribution (£)	Fixed costs (£)	Profit (£)
10	200	2,000	5	1,000	1,000	1,000	–
12	180	2,160	5	900	1,260	1,000	260
14	140	1,960	5	650	1,310	1,000	310
16	100	1,600	5	500	1,100	1,000	100
18	80	1,440	5	400	1,040	1,000	40

Figure 7.3   *Break-even analysis*

Sectoral factors

Beyond the specific factors described above there are likely to be a number of other sectoral-specific factors which may impinge on pricing decisions in HEIs. These factors are particularly relevant to public sector organisations or organisations which receive large amounts of public funding. Some examples of these factors are discussed below.

Avoidance of unfair competition

HEIs need to avoid any charges of unfair competition either through accusations of forming cartels with one another in breach of the anti-competition legislation or by making unilateral pricing decisions which might result in them being accused, by other organisations, of unfair competition through the use of their public subsidy.

Accountability for the use of public funds

Vice-Chancellors and Principals of HEIs are accountable to Parliament for the financial health of their HEI and for their use of public funds. Failure to so account can result in public and Parliamentary concerns being raised and, in extreme cases, in investigations by the National Audit Office and the Public Accounts Committee. In making pricing decisions HEIs need to ensure that they not planning to use public funds to subsidise the delivery of private goods and services and also that there is minimum risk to public funds should some problem arise in relation to the activities involved. Before embarking on a particular venture, HEIs need to conduct a thorough risk analysis and identify both means of minimising any related risks and of dealing with unforeseen events should they occur. The latter would include identifying appropriate funds to meet any potential financial short falls.

Equity of access

The pricing of particular goods and services may affect the degree of access available for different individuals or organisations. A price which is too high may inhibit access for certain individuals and organisations, for example:

- particular groups of individuals may be inhibited (e.g., the unwaged);
- types of organisation may be inhibited (e.g., charities);
- overseas countries may be inhibited (e.g., developing countries).

These considerations may be of little relevance to a commercial organisation but may be to an HEI which receives large amounts of public funds and has a high degree of public and political accountability. Any concerns in this area might lead to substantial public disquiet and bad publicity for the HEI involved.

The pricing policy of the HEI might need to take account the impact its prices have on access for different segments of the community. To ensure that a reasonable degree of access is provided across the customer base there might be tiered pricing arrangements, with differential prices being charged for different groups or individuals.

The HEI will need to review its pricing policy. It might be that a strategy exists of not targeting particular groups or individuals which the HEI will need to review, both in legal and public relations terms. Having considered these factors, reducing access to certain services may be a deliberate and valid part of the HEI's strategy.

Service delivery vehicle

In delivering goods and services to customers, HEIs may use a number of different delivery vehicles:

- direct delivery by the HEI itself;
- use of a HEI owned company;
- use of a HEI trust;
- partnership with other HEIs or other organisations.

These different delivery vehicles will have different commercial and taxation implications which might be influence the type of delivery vehicles actually used.

Individual pricing decisions: tactical considerations

So far we have considered broad pricing strategies that HEIs might wish to adopt in relation to particular markets and particular products. However, HEIs often have to make individual pricing decisions for specific activities (e.g., a research contract bid) and there may be specific factors that need to be taken into account as well as the overall pricing strategy. The danger, however, is that too often specific factors are allowed to distract from the strategy to the extent that strategic considerations no longer apply. The classic example of this is the argument that a particular bid should be submitted on a loss-leader basis since it might then generate future work and income streams. In this case the old adage 'loss-leaders lead to losses' should be borne in mind.

Thus it is important when making pricing decisions to strike a reasonable and realistic balance between strategic considerations and specific factors. Some examples of common pricing tactics that can be used, but only once the overall strategic pricing approach has been agreed and considered, are:

- Incidental charges – The introduction of incidental charges can sometimes generate income over and above the fixed price. For example, separating out staff travelling expenses or printing charges can be worth while if they are expressed as a percentage of the price ('plus travelling and subsistence expenses not exceeding 10 per cent of the total price' or 'design and printing costs estimated at 15 per cent of the total price'). This can be risky if the customer is a sophisticated buyer and would seek to clarify these 'grey' additional costs.

- Piecemeal pricing – rather than putting forward an overall price for a particular good or service, this would involve breaking up the activity into a series of discrete elements and offering a separate price for each element. Thus the client is in a position to pick and mix what they wish to purchase. They may still purchase the total package but the ability to do it in a series of sequential steps gives them more comfort about their purchasing decision.
- Loss leaders – This is a common technique designed to attract customers in the hope that they will then continue to buy from you (at a higher price) in the future. Entering any market with a price that is not viable in the long term does present risks and an HEI would need to feel very confident about future business to pursue this strategy. Under-pricing can also lead to similar moves by competitors.
- Premium pricing – setting the price above the competition is usually associated with the good or service being of perceived high quality and possibly of limited appeal. If used carefully this tactic can generate significant surplus and at the same time make the customer feel that he or she is benefiting. However, there is a thin line between being desirable and overpriced.
- Discounting – discounting needs to be considered very carefully and the rationale clearly understood. HEIs need to consider why they are discounting and what was wrong with the original price. However, some imagination is needed. Consider discounts in relation to top-up fees which need not apply solely around course fees. Instead, they could include first-year accommodation costs, access to IT equipment or cash support over and above bursaries.

In the real world the dynamics of any pricing situation are often more complex than the theory outlined above. However, these examples serve to demonstrate that there is a significant range of imaginative pricing techniques and tactics that HEIs can use. The important point is that these must be set in the context of an overall pricing strategy within the overall marketing plan which ultimately derives from the HEI's corporate strategy.

Chapter 8

Financial control and audit

Introduction

All HEIs obtain a significant proportion of their funding from 'public' sources and, as a result of this, are highly accountable for their actions. Ultimately, Parliament could call any HEI to account for expenditure from such funding. HEIs are also accountable for 'public' funding obtained from outside the UK, for example, from European sources, for which they are accountable ultimately to the European Parliament.

There are, therefore, a series of controls and regulations which govern the actions of all HEIs, irrespective of how they were established historically. In addition, all HEIs will be subject to a variety of types of audit and this is discussed later in this chapter.

Framework of financial controls

The framework of control in HEIs can be considered under five main headings:

- Statutes and legal powers establishing HEIs;
- The financial memoranda (FM) of HEIs;
- Standing orders of the HEI;
- Financial regulations of the HEI;
- Financial procedures of the HEI.

Statutes and legal powers establishing HEIs

HEIs can be broadly divided into pre-and post-1989 institutions. Immediately prior to 1 April 1989, HEIs comprised either independent universities from a variety of historical backgrounds, which received core Government funding through the University Grants Committee, or were polytechnics or colleges, funded through local education authorities. The Education Reform Act of 1988 set up the Polytechnics and Colleges as independent statutory corporations, with funding being routed from Government through a separate funding council, the PCFC (Polytechnic and Colleges Funding Council). The statutory framework of such HEIs set the overall objectives of this group of HEIs, comprising initially about 30 polytechnics and about 40 colleges of HE. Under Section 124 (1) and (2) of the Education Reform Act their objectives were:

- 'Section 124 (1) A higher education corporation shall have power –
  - (a) to provide higher education;
  - (b) to provide further education; and
  - (c) to carry out research and to publish the results of the research or any other material arising out of or connected with it in such manner as the corporation think fit.'

- 'Section 124 (2) – A higher education corporation shall also have power to do anything which appears to the corporation to be necessary or expedient for the purpose of or in connection with the exercise of any of the powers conferred on the corporation by subsection (1) above, including in particular power.' This sub-section then lists particular powers, for example, to acquire and dispose of land and property, to borrow, to invest etc.

Also, Section 125 (1) of the Act states – 'Any institution conducted by a higher education corporation shall be conducted in accordance with articles of government, to be made by the corporation with the approval of the Secretary of State.' (The approval of the articles is undertaken by the Privy Council.)

Therefore the post-1989 HEIs have a clearly laid out statutory framework within which they must operate.

The pre-1989 HEIs have a statutory framework derived from a variety of sources:

- ancient universities, for example Oxford and Cambridge, were founded in the twelfth and thirteenth centuries;
- nineteenth-century London and civic universities;
- twentieth-century universities, established before the 1960s;
- universities resulting from expansion of the sector, primarily in the 1960s.

There will be considerable detailed differences between the Charters of such HEIs but all will operate within a well-defined regulatory framework.

The consolidation of the sector in 1992 following the passing of The Further and Higher Education Act 1992 did not change the statutory framework but enabled Polytechnics which awarded their own degrees to take the title University. Following the 1992 Act, three new funding councils were formed:

- The Higher Education Funding Council (HEFCE).
- The Scottish Higher Education Funding Council (SHEFC).
- The Higher Education Funding Council for Wales (HEFCW).

Each of the new funding councils took over the funding responsibilities of the UGC (University Grants Committee) and the PCFC (Polytechnic and Colleges Funding Council) in the relevant country. The new funding councils were instrumental in setting out the financial control arrangements for their HEIs in the form of a financial memorandum.

The financial memorandum (FM) of HEIs

All English HEI's obtain funding from the HEFCE for their HE provision and some also obtain funding from the TTA (where teacher training is provided) and from the LSC (if FE level education is provided). The requirement for funding councils to produce a Financial Memorandum governing the relationship between an institution and itself is incorporated in the 1988 Education Reform Act. The TTA and the LSC both have their own FMs but the fundamental document for English HEIs is the FM produced by HEFCE. It is helpful to set out the accountability chain from Parliament to show where HEFCE and its FM fits into this chain. This is shown in Figure 8.1.

The latest Financial Memorandum issued by HEFCE is document 2003/54 which took effect on 1 October 2003. The HEFCE Financial Memorandum covers the following:

- Introduction – including application, scope and compliance with the FM.
- Responsibilities of the Council.
- Responsibilities of the Institution.
- Allocation and payment of funds.
- Monitoring of estate management and financial commitments.
- Costing and pricing of activities.
- Financial statements.
- Audit.
- Other matters.
- Signature of designated office holder – The designated office holder must sign that he/she has received the Financial Memorandum.

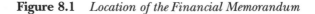

```
                    Parliament
                        |
                      DfES
                        |
                      HEFCE
                        |
                        | ---- The FM acts as the contract between the parties
                        |
                      HEIs
```

Figure 8.1 *Location of the Financial Memorandum*

The nature of the Financial Memorandum is clearly illustrated by this last bullet point. In addition to setting out the contractual framework within which an HEI operates, each year an HEI must sign Part II of the Financial Memorandum which is specific to each institution and sets out in detail the educational provision, in terms of student numbers and subjects, which the HEI must 'deliver' in order to obtain the contracted funding from HEFCE.

In Annex 2 to this chapter, we discuss some aspects of the FM in more detail and also consider recent changes.

Standing orders of the HEI

The statutory background covered above corresponds with the 'Memorandum' of a company established under the Companies Acts. The Financial Memorandum of the relevant funding council can be viewed as an externally imposed part of the Articles of a HEI which relates primarily to the publicly funded element of its activities. Each HEI will have its own Articles governing how it regulates its own affairs and its standing orders are a development/codification of these Articles. For example, the post-1989 HEI will have in place an 'Instrument and Articles of Government' which will cover such topics as:

- membership of the Board of Governors;
- number and appointment of members and their tenure of office;
- responsibilities of Board, Principal and Academic Board;
- delegation of functions and committees;
- appointment of clerk to the Board;
- procedures for meetings,
- appointment, conduct, promotion and supervision/dismissal of staff;
- grievance procedures;
- student related matters;
- financial matters;

The pre-1989 HEIs have standing orders which cover all the areas outlined above but the formats are likely to be more diverse than those of post-1989 HEIs. The 'rules' will set out the more detailed procedures and processes required to implement responsibilities incorporated in the Instrument and Articles of Government.

Financial regulations of the HEI

The Finance Section of the Articles sets out that the Board shall determine the policies relating to a number of financial matters, such as the determination of tuition fees, authority levels within the institution, purchasing procedures, banking and audit arrangements, and so on. Such financial regulations will be formally agreed by the Board in a set of Financial Regulations, normally drawn up by the Chief Financial Officer of the institution.

Such regulations are, therefore, a key element in the financial control framework of the institution. These financial regulations translate an institution's broad policies on financial control into practical guidance and in turn detailed financial procedures will be produced to ensure that the regulations can be effectively applied in an operational environment. It is, therefore, absolutely critical that the financial regulations are robust and comprehensive to ensure that all the HEI's financially related activities are included. The scope is well illustrated in the Chartered Institute of Public Finance's (CIPFA) document 'A Model Set of Financial Regulations for Further and Higher Education Institutions', published in a revised version in 2003. The main sections are:

- financial planning;
- financial control;
- accounting arrangements;
- audit requirements;
- treasury management;
- income;
- research grants and contracts;
- other income generating activity;
- intellectual property rights and general patents;
- expenditure;
- pay expenditure;
- assets;
- funds held on trust;
- other.

Fuller detail is set out in Annex 1 to this chapter.

The strength of the financial control in an HEI will depend ultimately not only on the strength of the Articles, Standing Orders and Financial Regulations but how those regulations are put into practice through the mechanism of the detailed financial procedures. The following paragraphs gives examples of two such procedures which demonstrate the level of detail they incorporate.

Financial procedures

These can vary greatly in detail, depending on the complexity of the process covered. The examples outlined in Figure 8.2 show the detailed processes concerning:

- the operation of a 'Supplier File' in relation to the purchase of goods and services and
- the wider processes covering the 'Investment of Surplus Funds'.

Supplier file

The purpose of these notes is to set up an authorised supplier on the institution's payments. The procedures can cover eight or so pages and include detailed images of screen layouts to assist staff with various processes. Headings covered will include:

- supplier name, short name, address, phone number, etc, discount terms, settlement terms, VAT treatment;
- how to enter this information into the system;
- control information;

These procedures should be detailed enough to enable any member of staff to complete the process unaided.

Investment of surplus funds

This procedure note includes sections on:

- cash flow forecasts (annual and ongoing) – how these relate to budgets, receipt of capital and revenue grants, payroll, taxation and creditor payment dates, etc;
- monthly monitoring – of previous month's out-turn and revision of forecasts;
- daily interrogation of bank accounts – detail on how to undertake;
- records of deals;
- reconciliations – bank and nominal ledger reconciliation;
- dealings – 'now' money, maturing loans;
- reporting procedures – for example; to Director of Finance, Vice-Chancellor, Board of Governors, etc;
- subsidiary company investments;
- list of approved Financial Institutions for investment purposes.

Figure 8.2   *Examples of financial procedures*

Some HEIs consolidate all their internally approved authorisation and spending limits into a single document known as an *Authorities Manual* which can be a valuable method of helping to spread good practice throughout the HEI.

Good practice guidance regarding financial control

Overview

In recent years much emphasis has been placed on training and developing staff and with increasing the competence of staff to manage increasingly large and complex HEIs. Many HE sector organisations, such as UUK, BUFDG, SCOP and the AOC have provided operational good practice guidance aimed at identifying exemplars in the sector and then disseminating that good practice in the sector.

Funding council guidance

The funding councils have also been active in assisting in such training and the HEFCE report of 1998 'Effective Financial Management in Higher Education' was a key document in this process. The HEFCE has used this document to ask institutions to review their own processes and the HEFCE's own internal audit function, when undertaking institutional audits, has reviewed institutions' own evaluations of their responses. The guide was aimed at the top level of governance, namely governors, heads of institutions and senior managers. The report asked institutions to answer a series of questions relating to their control processes which were grouped under 10 principles which were:

Governance

- Governing body responsible for direction and key decisions including strategic direction, stewardship of funds, and recruitment of the head and the 'Nolan' principles should be followed.
- Governing body responsible for the financial health and viability of the HEI.
- Clearly define, communicate, and regularly review the roles and responsibilities of the governing board, its committees and senior staff.
- Regularly review the competencies of governors and senior staff.

Strategic Planning

- Planning should be strategically developed around the mission statement and take into account external and internal influences and constraints.
- The corporate plan must incorporate a sound financial strategy.
- Realistic assessment and subsequent management should be applied to both risks and opportunities.

Process

- Information at all levels should be fit for purpose and timely.
- Clear communication structures must exist and be used.
- The principles above need to be underpinned by robust structures and processes.

Audit arrangements in HEIs

The role of audit

In a perfect world there would be no need for audit as all governance and operational management would be conducted according to accepted best principles. All decisions would be perfect and all processes would be performed with 100 per cent accuracy, using perfectly designed procedures.

The real world is not like this and audit, defined generally as 'a check or examination' is, therefore, necessary to reassure many different stakeholders that their diverse interests in an organisation or operation are being properly observed. There is always a balance, often in reality a tension, between the amount of 'auditing' and its cost, both in terms of the direct costs of running an 'audit operation' and the extra workload audit created for operating departments. Theoretically, there is a break-even level at which the marginal cost of additional audit is greater than the benefits it produces. The level of audit required will also differ depending on the type of organisation, its objectives and its sources of funding. For example, HEIs in the UK do not, in general, have shareholders and therefore external auditors of HEIs do not need to reassure shareholders that their interests are being safeguarded by proper financial reporting. In this last respect the well-publicised external audit failures in a number of US multinationals in recent years has highlighted the issue of 'who audits the auditors?' This topic is currently under review by many regulatory bodies.

Different stakeholders in HE will have different needs, and this immediately generates the fundamental division of audit between 'internal' and 'external'. Internal audit aims to provide reassurance for those governing and managing an institution that everything is in order internally and, whenever appropriate, also aims to assist management. This can be particularly important when management and other changes are taking place. In HE, external audit is aimed particularly at providing reassurance to external stakeholders that funding is being applied for the designated purposes. The funding councils are the key stakeholders as they are accountable to Government for the proper discharge of their responsibilities and all funding councils have, therefore, developed a strong 'Audit Code of Practice'. The HEFCE Audit Code of Practice is considered in greater detail in a later section, but before that it is helpful to outline the full range of auditing to which HEIs may be subject.

Audit bodies

Bodies which may have a right to audit HEIs are numerous and include:

- National Audit Office in England and Wales, Audit Scotland in Scotland;
- Funding Council Audit Service (e.g., HECFEAS for England);
- HM Customs and Excise – in respect of VAT investigations;
- Inland Revenue – both in respect of employment and general taxation matters;
- EU Audit – in respect of European Grants and funding; the terms of certain European funding will also enable to auditors of the head body to audit the records of other project members;
- Research Councils;
- Investment Management and Regulatory organizations;

- Statutory External Audit;
- Internal Audit.

The total resource spent on 'audit' from all of these sources is difficult to quantify but many practitioners in the sector believe that the total 'audit' demands interfere with efficient operations in the sector. Studies in the university sector have estimated that *direct* costs of audit are generally of the level shown in Table 8.1.

The level of information demanded by the different sets of auditors also varies significantly and at the most intrusive extreme, probably the European Union Auditors, can require the production of copy invoices supporting every item of expenditure on a project operating over many years. This may well conflict with the processing routines of an HEI.

Audit code of practice

Following the unification of the HE sector in 1992, audit codes of practice were produced covering all HEIs, the latest HEFCE version being issued in May 2002 (Ref HEFCE 2002/26). However, in December 2003 HEFCE issued a consultation document, 2003/60, with a final response date of 27 February 2004, which sought to update the May 2002 version. (Consultation was still in progress as this book was being completed.) The key proposed amendments reflected:

- the importance of corporate governance;
- a reduction in the audit burden and developments to increase self-regulation in the sector;
- a requirement for a statement on internal control to be included with the annual financial statements;
- risk management arrangements;
- making mandatory, rather than optional, the submission of internal audit annual reports;
- a requirement to provide separate providers for internal and external audit services.

Table 8.1   Costs of audit

Type of audit	Approximate expenditure per £100 million of turnover (£)	% of turnover
External audit	40,000	0.04
Internal audit	100,000 to 150,000	0.10 to 0.15

Source: Derived from BUFDG Audit Survey 2001/02

Once agreed, the updated code will apply from 1 August 2004.

Compliance with mandatory requirements of the code is a condition of grant under paragraph 74 of the HEFCE Financial Memorandum (HEFCE 2003/54) and mandatory requirements in the code are clearly listed in Annex A of the Code. Summarised these are as follows.

Mandatory requirements for HEIs

- governing body to take reasonable steps to ensure a sound system of internal control exists;
- effective audit committee which produces an annual report for the governing body and designated officer;
- normally audit committee members not to have executive authority or membership of finance committee;
- audit committee to satisfy itself that satisfactory arrangements are in place to promote the 3 Es – economy, efficiency and effectiveness;
- an effective internal audit function, reporting at least annually to governing body and designated officer;
- internal audit service must cover the whole internal control system;
- the head of the internal audit service must have direct access to the designated officer, the chairman of the audit committee and the chairman of the governing body, and unrestricted access to all records, assets, personnel and premises and so on; to be authorised to get all information and explanations considered necessary;
- fees to external auditors for non-audit services to be disclosed separately in the financial statements;
- HEFCEAS (HEFCE Audit Service) to have access to all records, information and assets, and so on; can require necessary explanation from any officer and have access to work of HEI's internal auditor and to that of external auditor;
- the governing body cannot accept restrictions of liability in respect of external audit of the financial statements;
- the following must be provided:
  - governing body to send audit committee's annual report to the HEFCE Chief Auditor;
  - governing body to send the HEFCE Chief Auditor, by 28 February, two copies of external auditor's management letter and management response;
  - designated officer to report serious weaknesses, significant frauds, major accounting breakdowns immediately to chairman of audit committee, chairman of the governing body, head of internal audit and the HEFCE Accounting Officer; internal and external auditors to report to them directly if designated officer will not act;
  - governing body to inform HEFCE Chief Auditor immediately on removal /resignation of external or internal auditors.

Other guidance in the audit code of practice

The Code provides much practical guidance to HEIs to help them establish sound audit arrangements. In particular helpful annexes are provided which provide model formats and guidance covering:

- *Model terms of reference for an audit committee.* The main body of the Code also states that members of audit committees should normally be provided with guidance on audit committees which have been produced by CIPFA, 'Handbook for audit committee members in further and higher education' and ICEAW (The Institute of Chartered Accountants in England and Wales), 'Audit committees: a framework for guidance'.
- *Procedures for testing externally both internal and external audit.* The Code recommends considering the market testing of external audit every seven years and also recommends that the lead partner on the audit should not hold that position for more than seven years on a continuous basis. It also recommends that consideration should be given every seven years to market testing the internal audit service and also states that at least every five years the HEFCE audit service (HEFCEAS) will review the audit services in place at an HEI by an assessment based on a professional peer review (HEFCEAS since renamed HEFCE Assurance Service).
- Model terms of reference for an internal audit service.
- Internal audit planning.
- Model engagement terms for external auditors.
- Suggested wording for the external audit report.
- Model format for the audit committee annual report.
- An annual audit return from HEIs. To be submitted with the audit committee annual report by the designated officer which has to provide information on governance, management and audit changes as these could affect the risk exposure of the HEI and hence the HEFCE's risk assessment of the HEI.

The Code also highlights the rights of HEFCEAS which is responsible by means of periodic reviews for evaluating and reporting on control and risk management arrangements in HEIs.

The TTA and LSC do not become involved directly in auditing in an HEI but may request that HEFCEAS undertakes specific audit work for their purposes.

Finally the importance of risk management, a constant theme throughout this book, is to the fore in the Code. The internal audit role in assessing the effectiveness of risk management processes is highlighted as is the technique of 'control self-assessment' (CSA) a technique by which an organisation seeks to undertake an internal review of risks and controls in order improve its effectiveness.

Internal audit

Most organisations would choose to have an internal audit service in view of the reassurance it provides and the HEFCE has made this a mandatory requirement in its audit code of practice. This requirement is linked to the need to provide the governing body, designated officers and other managers of the institution assurance on the adequacy and effectiveness of the internal control system, including risk management and governance.

Internal audit is not a substitute for managers accepting and undertaking full responsibility for acting within the regulations and procedures of an institution, including taking responsibility for risk management and ensuring that value for money is obtained. However, besides providing reassurance for governors and senior staff, internal audit can assist managers in undertaking their responsibilities. Specifically the HEFCE expects internal audit to monitor the whole internal control system and report on whether:

- institutional objectives are being achieved;
- resources are being used economically, effectively and efficiently;
- internal policies, procedures and external laws and regulations are complied with;
- assets and interests are being safeguarded;
- there is integrity of accounting and other information and records, as far as is possible.

In organisational terms, internal audit should have a direct right of access to the Chief Executive and the Head of Internal Audit should also have a direct right of access to the Chair of the Audit Committee and the Chair of the Board.

To plan and execute its work effectively, an internal audit function will develop an audit plan which must be approved by the institution's Audit Committee. This plan will have short-term (one year) and longer-term elements and demonstrate that the required level of audit work can be undertaken in an agreed planning period. The plan should cover aspects of all the institution's activities, not just those related to finance, although a significant part of an audit plan will be related to audits of the key financial systems, especially important being the payroll system. The HEFCE Audit Code of Practice advises that the 'overall plan should be based on an audit risk assessment and strategy which should be continually maintained and subject to periodic (normally annual) consideration and approval by the audit committee on behalf of the governing body'.

The internal audit plan should, therefore, comprise a Strategic Plan which might cover, say, four years and an Annual Plan covering the first year of the Strategic Plan. The plans will normally apportion total audit days available over the areas to be audited. Not all areas will be audited to the same extent each year, the objective in the Strategic Plan being to provide an adequate level of cover over the agreed planning period.

The 'plans' will be grouped in categories, for example main categories may be as shown below with more detail given in Annex 3:

- academic;
- support systems;
- student systems;
- estates;
- finance and purchasing;
- personnel;
- business developments;
- student union;
- investigations and contingency allowance.

There is no standard method of providing internal audit services in HEIs. Much will depend on the size of the institution and the quality of the staff it can attract. The range is, therefore, from an in-house service, through a consortium arrangement servicing a number of institutions, to provision by an external provider. The HEFCE would **not** normally expect an external provider to supply both internal and external audit services but if the audit committee decides that this arrangement should be used, HEFCE recommends that the audit committee should ensure that the two functions are clearly separated and that different sets of staff are used, particularly at partner and manager level.

External audit

Role of external auditors

The HEFCE Audit Code of Practice defines their role as follows:

> The primary role of external auditors is to report on the financial statements of institutions, and to carry out whatever examination of the statements and underlying records and control systems is necessary to reach their opinion on the statements. Their report should also state whether recurrent and specific grants and income from the HEFCE (and other bodies and restricted funds where appropriate) have been properly applied for the purposes provided and in accordance with the institution's Financial Memorandum with the Council.
>
> (Para 110 HEFCE Audit Code of Practice)

Specifically the external audit report, covering the annual financial statement, should state whether:

- 'the financial statements give a true and fair view of the institution's affairs and of its income and expenditure, recognised gains and losses and statement of cash flow for the year'. (Para 119 (a) Audit Code of Practice);

- funds for specific purposes have been properly managed, including HEFCE funds being used in accordance with the Financial Memorandum;
- financial statements have been drawn up in accordance with statutory requirements, including the SORP for Higher Education.

In addition to the formal external audit report which accompanies the financial statements, the external auditors should report on any significant management and control issues arising from the external audit by way of a management letter/report to the Audit Committee.

To undertake their task effectively, external auditors require unrestricted rights to access to both the institute's designated office holder and the chair of the audit committee. External auditors should also attend meetings of the audit committee.

External auditors, by their very nature, need to be as independent as possible and where they provide services in addition to the statutory audit, payments made for such services are required to be disclosed in a note to the financial statements. The Audit Committee will need to monitor the position if a considerable amount of non-audit work is undertaken to ensure that there is no conflict of interest.

In carrying out their duties, external auditors will normally liaise closely with the internal audit function and rely on work of the latter when preparing their external audit report. It is, therefore, normal for external audit to provide a view on the adequacy or otherwise of the internal audit service during the financial year and quite possibly for external audit to request that further internal audit work is undertaken where the internal audit plan has not been completed and high-risk areas not adequately covered.

External auditors must possess specified qualifications and institutions are expected, under the HEFCE Audit Code of Practice, to formally reappoint them every year after an assessment of their work by the Audit Committee. The HEFCE recommends that once every seven years retendering should take place and that an audit partner should not hold that position in respect of an institution for more than seven continuous years contrasts sharply with the SHEFC recommendation of a three-year period between formal reviews and the recommendation in Wales of external competition at least once every five years.

External audit of an HEI's related companies

An HEI will normally wish to have any wholly owned subsidiary companies audited by the same firm that audits the HEI as this will assist the audit of both the HEI's consolidated accounts and those of the subsidiaries. However, subsidiary companies are legal entities in their own right and if not wholly owned, or part of a joint venture arrangement, it is quite possible for the auditors of these companies to differ from those of the HEI. It is also possible for the financial statements of a student union to be consolidated with those of the HEI because of the ultimate control that the HEI is judged to have over the affairs of the student union even though it has no formal shareholding in the latter. In all such cases the auditors of the HEI will need to satisfy themselves through discussions with the auditors of the related company that the financial statements of the latter are prepared on a basis which enables them to be consolidated. The HEI's external auditors will have no right of access to the records of the related company/ies, unless this is part of the agreement between the HEI and the company/ies.

Audit of IT systems

IT systems are an essential part of all corporate and academic processes and no organisation could now operate satisfactorily without them. However, IT systems audit is an area which requires a very high degree of specialisation, knowledge and training.

Audit of these systems is, therefore, of prime importance and requires specialised techniques and processes which may be undertaken through a number of different organisational structures. Generally, ongoing audits of IT systems will be part of the internal audit processes, although such audits will also be used to provide reassurance for the external auditors. It is, however, quite common for one-off studies to be undertaken of the IT organisational structure in an HEI which, while not being an 'audit' as such, can significantly affect the controls in an institution. Given the rapid changes in systems and technology, internal audit also needs to be involved when processes are redesigned, to ensure that essential control elements are in place.

Organisational models for providing IT systems audits include:

- undertaken wholly by in-house internal audit from own staff resources;
- undertaken wholly by externally provided internal audit;
- undertaken as part of an HE audit consortium which has a specialist IT capability;
- separately bought-in by an in-house internal audit service.

It is unusual for an in-house internal audit service to have sufficient expertise to cover all IT audit requirements and hence the last option is a method of providing this additional expertise. An external internal audit provider will usually be well placed to call on other specialists in its organisation to provide this service. The organisational structure for undertaking the audit of IT systems will, therefore, vary greatly depending on the audit structure in place.

The requirements of the auditor in such audits will include:

- technical expertise;
- knowledge of best-practice in the provision of IT services and systems development;

- an understanding of systems integration within the institution;
- the capacity to perform such work in the specified timescale.

These specialist audits can be clearly separated from those more generalist ones which, although requiring a high level of IT understanding, do not require in-depth professional IT training. Such studies would include:

- business recovery planning;
- application controls associated with new systems.

Value for money audit

The 3 E's of economy, efficiency and effectiveness have long been a mantra in management jargon and underpin the more recent phrase of 'value for money' (VFM). For some time, auditors have been seen as having a strong role in relation to VFM in addition to their more conventional audit activities.

HEIs tackle VFM audit in many different ways, depending partly on organisational structure and the extent of devolution of authority, but part of the process is through the involvement of audit committees. The funding councils require audit committees to satisfy themselves that arrangements are in place to promote the 3 E's and a useful starting point is that all managers should try and obtain maximum VFM as part of their ongoing responsibilities. It is usual for internal audit to highlight opportunities for improved VFM in any report they produce and specialist one-off VFM audits of a particular area, for example, on treasury management or catering, can be undertaken either by internal audit or by a specialist firm. Studies can also be undertaken which benchmark performance in closely defined areas of an institution against those of peers. Such studies highlight areas requiring further investigation and conclusions should not be drawn until further investigation has identified possible reasons for any resulting variance.

VFM studies have also been undertaken by a Joint Value for Money Steering Group for the sector, which has produced studies to highlight good practice on treasury management, energy management and building repairs and management.

Therefore internal audit has a specific role to play in obtaining VFM in HEIs which follows directly from the mandatory requirement in the Audit Code of Practice relating to the 3 E's.

Internal and external audit compared

From the above sections some basic differences will be evident.

- Internal audit is an internal service aimed at providing assurance regarding the governance of an institution, for the benefit of the HEI's Board and its management, part of this reassurance being that the HEI is complying with conditions of funding. It also undertakes detailed studies to help improve management effectiveness, to prevent and detect fraud and help improve value for money.

- External audit provides an independent external view, primarily on the veracity of the published financial results of an institution, although as part of this process it needs to satisfy itself that the processing and information systems which generate the figures used in the financial statements are satisfactory. The relevant funding councils and other external partners use the report of the external auditors to provide the required reassurance on the financial position of the institution. Such partners will include those providing loans to the institution, and such loans will often contain covenants on the financial performance of the institution and of its level of debt, known as the 'gearing ratio'.

Corporate governance arrangements in HEIs

Background

The last couple of decades have witnessed a number of widely reported corporate failures or scandals, which have included:

- the Maxwell Corporation;
- the Guinness affair;
- Enron;
- WorldCom.

The failures in the late 1980s generated a number of initiatives to improve the corporate governance of both private and publicly funded organisations. The Cadbury Committee, established in May 1991 by the Financial Reporting Council, the London Stock Exchange and the accounting profession, was the first of these and the one which helpfully incorporated its recommendations into a code of practice. This code highlighted, in particular, the vital role of audit committees in raising standards of corporate governance and also considered the control and reporting functions of executive and non-executive directors.

A number of other influential documents followed, a key one for higher education being the report of the Committee on Standards of Conduct in Private Life, chaired by Lord Nolan. Its first report, issued in May 1995, identified seven principles, as follows:

- '*Selflessness* – Holders of public office should take decisions solely in terms of the public interest. They should not do so in order to gain financial or other material benefits for themselves, their family, or their friends.

- *Integrity* – Holders of public office should not place themselves under any financial or other obligation to outside individuals or organisations that might influence them in performance of their official duties.
- *Objectivity* – In carrying out public business, including making public appointments, awarding contracts, or recommending individuals for rewards and benefits, holders of public office should make choices on merit.
- *Accountability* – Holders of public office are accountable for their decisions and actions to the public and must submit themselves to whatever scrutiny is appropriate to their office.
- *Openness* – Holders of public office should be as open as possible about all the decisions and actions that they take. They should give reasons for their decisions and restrict information only when the wider public interest clearly demands.
- *Honesty* – Holders of public office have a duty to declare any private interests relating to their public duties and to take steps to resolve any conflicts arising in a way that protects the public interest.
- *Leadership* – Holders of public office should promote and support these principles by leadership and example.'

The Nolan Committee's report has been assimilated by the HE sector while simultaneously other high-level reports have influenced the corporate governance climate. The Cadbury report's major reform was to separate the roles of chairman and chief executive which, in principle, is always the case in higher education. The reason for saying 'in principle' is explained more fully later on.

The Greenbury Committee has influenced the governance climate with regard to setting remuneration for directors and top management. The requirement for all HEIs to have a remuneration committee arises from this report.

The implementations of the Cadbury and Greenbury Committee reports and how they were being implemented, was reviewed by the Hampel report, which also re-examined the role of directors, auditors and shareholders. The report led to the Stock Exchange publishing its combined code in June 1998 which covered topics such as responsibilities of directors, their remuneration, relations with shareholders and accountability and audit.

This set of reports was further augmented by probably the most important of all such governance reviews, namely the Turnbull Report, which produced guidelines on internal control, in September 1999. The recommendations of this report have had far-reaching implications for governance of both private and public sector institutions, as they define and expand the responsibilities of company directors. Issues covered include:

- the type of risks which need to be controlled;
- what control systems are necessary to cover such risks;
- how to keep control systems up to date;
- the responsibilities of directors.

The basic approach in the report was, therefore, one of risk assessment and installing mechanisms to cover such risks. HE has taken this approach very much on board, although some would say 'gone overboard', with detailed guidance and requirements on risk management. As has been the case with listed companies, HEIs have had to be compliant to the required level for years ending after 22 December 2000, and be fully compliant by the 2002/03 Financial Statements or risk having their accounts qualified. This is covered further in Chapter 9.

In January 2003, another important report on the governance of companies, entitled 'Review of the role and effectiveness of non-executive directors', prepared by Derek Higgs for the Chancellor of the Exchequer, was published. However, the recommendations of this report appear to have little direct bearing on the HE sector, other than to stress the importance of corporate governance as an issue. The report's main thrust was to considerably strengthen the role of non-executive directors, recommending that at least half the board, excluding the chairman, should be independent non-executive directors, which is always the case in HEIs. Such directors are also to be appropriately remunerated.

A report on audit committees prepared for the FRC (Financial Reporting Council) by Sir Robert Smith entitled 'Audit Committees-Combined Code Guidance' was also published in January 2003 at the same time as the Higgs report. A review of this document would lead one to conclude that the HE sector already complies with the thrust of this guidance through the requirement to establish and operate audit committees in accordance with HEFCE's Audit Code of Practice.

Governance structures in HEIs

The various reports described above have all influenced corporate structure in HEIs and the minimum governance structure which must be in place requires only three formal committees of the Board of Governors/Council: an audit committee, a remuneration committee and a membership nominations committee. Most institutions will also have a finance committee, employment committee or finance and general purposes committee and all institutions will also have an academic board or senate which will advise governors, through the chief executive, on academic matters.

As with all systems, governance structures are only as robust as the individuals operating them and whilst a robust structure goes a long way to establishing a well-run and resilient HEI, instances have been reported where a strong Vice-Chancellor has acted de facto as chief executive and chairman and other cases have been reported where the chairman has interfered excessively in the executive management of an HEI and acted de facto as chief executive. Many of the improprieties in HE which have made headlines in the past couple of decades have had as their root cause the merging or blurring of responsibilities at chairman/chief executive level.

It needs to be stressed that instances of financial difficulty or irregularity in HEIs have been of a completely different and lesser order to the problems encountered in the large corporate institutions mentioned above. However, owing to the use of public (taxpayers') money and the transparent and high-profile accountability through to Parliament and its Select Committee system, minor problems which would go un-noticed in the corporate sector, can become national scandals if they occur in the HE sector.

Annex 1   Model content of an HEI's financial regulations

Financial planning
- Budget objectives;
- resource allocation;
- budget preparation;
- capital programmes;
- overseas activity.

Financial control
- Budgetary control;
- financial information;
- changes to the approved budget;
- virement;
- treatment of year end balances.

Accounting arrangements
- Financial year;
- basis of accounting;
- format of the financial statements;
- capitalisation and depreciation;
- accounting records;
- public access;
- taxation.

Audit requirements
- General;
- external audit;
- internal audit;
- fraud and corruption;
- value for money;
- other auditors.

Treasury management
- Treasury management policy;
- appointment of bankers and other professional advisers;
- banking arrangements.

Income
- General;
- maximisation of income;
- receipt of cash, cheques and other negotiable;
- instruments;
- collection of debts;

- student fees;
- student loans;
- emergency/hardship loans.

Research grants and contracts
- General;
- recovery of overheads;
- costing/transparency;
- grant and contract conditions.

Other income generating activity
- Private consultancies and other paid work;
- short courses and services rendered;
- off-site collaborative provision (franchising);
- european Union and other 'match funding';
- profitability and recovery for overheads;
- deficits;
- additional contributions to departments;
- additional payments to staff.

Intellectual property rights and patents
- General;
- patents;
- intellectual property rights.

Expenditure
- General;
- scheme of delegation/financial authorities;
- procurement;
- purchase orders;
- tenders and quotations;
- post-tender negotiations;
- contracts;
- EU regulations;
- receipt of goods;
- payment of invoices;
- staff reimbursement;
- institution of credit cards;
- petty cash;
- other payments;
- late payments rules;
- project advances;
- giving hospitality.

Pay expenditure
- Remuneration policy;
- appointment of staff;
- salaries and wages;
- superannuation schemes;
- travel, subsistence and other allowances;
- overseas travel;
- allowances for members of the governing body;
- severance and other non recurring payments.

Assets
- Land, buildings, fixed plant and machinery;
- fixed asset register;
- inventories;
- stocks and stores;
- safeguarding assets;
- personal use;
- asset disposal;
- all other assets.

Funds held on trust
- Gifts, benefactions and donations;
- student welfare and access funds;
- trust funds;
- voluntary funds.

Other
- Insurance;
- company and joint ventures;
- security;
- students union;
- use of the institution's seal;
- provision of indemnities.

Source: CIPFA 2003, 'A Model Set of Financial Regulations for Further and Higher Education Institutions'.

Annex 2   The Financial Memorandum

More detailed aspects of the FM

The following points should be noted:

- **HEFCE's powers** – these are clearly defined and it can only make payments to HEIs for activities set out in Section 124 (1) and (2) of the Education Reform Act, consolidated as Section 65 (2) of the Further and Higher Education Act.
- **Chief Executive of HEFCE** – in addition to setting out its responsibilities to institutions, the HEFCE Financial Memorandum also explains that the Chief Executive Officer of the HEFCE has been appointed as its Accounting Officer and is responsible for ensuring to the Secretary of State that funds are properly applied for the intended purposes. He/she is also responsible for:
  - promoting good value for money;
  - ensuring that an institution has appropriate arrangements for financial management and accounting;
  - he/she shall inform the institution's governing body and/or its audit committee if he/she has serious concerns about an institution's financial affairs.
- **Responsibilities of the HEI under the FM** – these include:
  - *stewardship* of funds, clearly set out as a governing body responsibility;
  - designating a *principal officer* who will need to satisfy the governing body that the conditions in the Financial Memoranda are being complied with and who may be required to appear before the Public Accounts Committee.
- **Financial management, value for money and provision of information** – these are included under the HEI's responsibilities and contain, in paragraphs 21 and 22, key conditions relating to the overall financial position and management of a HEI. Summarised, these are that:
  - an HEI remains solvent and taking one accounting period with another;
  - total expenditure is not greater than total income;
  - historical cost deficits must not arise in two consecutive accounting periods, unless discretionary reserves cover the deficit;
  - any negative discretionary reserves must be cleared within three years (i.e., negative discretionary reserves occurring at the end of year 1 must be cleared by the end of year 4).

  The sections on allocation and payments of funds and estate management are generally technical in nature, although specific conditions are outlined which apply when 'exchequer funded' assets are sold.
- **Financial commitments** – The HEFCE considers the protection of public investment to be a major responsibility and clearly sets out commitment limits. The key one is that the annualised cost of all long-term financial

commitments must not exceed 4 per cent of total income without the written consent of the HEFCE.

- **Financial Statements** – 31 December is set as the date for receipt of audited financial statements and HEIs are instructed to comply with any Accounts Directions which are issued. (Financial Statements are prepared to 31 July.)
- **Audit** – this sets out the general rights of various bodies to carry out audits in an institution and also stresses that any requirements which are mandatory under the HEFCE 'Audit Code of Practice' are a condition underlying the receipt of the HEFCE grant funding. The Audit Code of Practice is covered more fully in an earlier section.

Recent amendments incorporated in the FM

HEFCE continuously reviews the FM and amends as appropriate. The October 1 2003 version was updated from the June 2000 version with relatively minor alterations which reflect a combination of changes in government policy, changes within the HE sector and current best practice. The most important changes were:

- *Financial management* – an HEI to notify HEFCE of an event or likely event which may adversely affect the financial position as soon as it is identified.
- *Short-term borrowing* – some relaxation of the rules with written required consent for a negative net cash of 5 per cent of total income for over 35 consecutive calendar days.
- *Long-term borrowing* – the requirement to account for small changes in servicing costs of separate leases to be replaced by looking at the total cost of an HEI's leases.
- *Audit, assurance, risk and control* – a strong paragraph added on risk management reflecting HEFCE's Accounts Direction. Also a paragraph stating that HEFCE's Audit Service will evaluate the risk management, control and governance arrangements in HEIs.
- *Costing and pricing* – HEIs to identify and recover full economic costs of their activities and to integrate costing and pricing methods into decision-making processes. HEFCE funds must not be used for non-public purposes.
- *Widening participation* – HEIs must submit acceptable strategies and action plans to obtain formula funding for this activity.
- *Subscription to quality enhancement agency* – HEIs to subscribe for three years from August 2004 to QAA and HESA as condition of grant.
- *Mergers* – HEI to actively involve HEFCE at early stages of mergers.
- *Compliance with laws including Race Relations Amendment Act and Equal Opportunities, and so on* – under the RRAA, HEFCE has monitoring duties hence a new paragraph and general mention of equal opportunities.
- *Financial sanctions if audit failure* – explicit reserve power that funding can be withdrawn if an HEI fails an audit re-inspection by the QAA.

Annex 3 Typical content of an internal audit plan

- **Academic**
  - systems, for example, quality monitoring systems, transparency review;
  - faculties, covering all their activities.
- **Support systems**
  - IS/IT – particularly control systems;
  - library – purchasing, lending control, and so on.
- **Student systems**
  - particularly related to student records;
  - alumni activities, marketing.
- **Estates**
  - including operation, acquisition and disposal;
  - planning matters, project management and so on;
  - catering, conferences;
  - residences;
  - auxiliary services, for example, catering, cleaning, postal services.
- **Finance and purchasing**
  - income and debtors;
  - expenditure and creditors;
  - cash, banking, treasury management;
  - assets, insurance and so on;
  - management accounting, reporting processes;
  - payroll;
  - grants, including EU and funding councils;
  - purchasing including operation of tendering procedures.
- **Personnel**
  - starters, leavers, premature retirements;
  - health and safety.
- **Business developments** – including operation of subsidiary companies.
- **Student union** – the HEI's involvement will depend on the local arrangements.
- **Investigations and contingency allowance.**

Chapter 9

Financial accounting and accountability

Introduction

All public and private sector organisations will produce a wide range of financial information concerning their activities and use of resources but most of that information will be confidential to the management of the organisation. However, they will have a statutory duty to produce and publish a set of annual financial accounts containing certain defined financial information, relating to the organisation, for the previous 12-month period. This statutory requirement ensures that certain financial information about the organisation comes into the public domain.

In many parts of the public sector (e.g., NHS, local government) the usual period for producing such accounts is for the year ended 31 March but in the private sector, the individual organisation itself will be able to opt for a particular accounting year. In the HE sector, the financial year ends on 31 July and thus broadly aligns with the academic year.

This chapter considers the issue of financial accounting and accountability in the HE sector. However, before considering financial accounting in the HE sector we first address the generic issues of:

- why produce statutory accounts at all – what is their purpose?
- what general principles of financial accounting underpin the preparation of financial accounts?

The chapter then aims to explain what financial information is included in HEI published accounts and how it is prepared.

Purpose of statutory financial accounts

The production of financial accounts is a complex and time-consuming activity with a substantial cost to the organisation both in terms of production of the accounts and their subsequent audit. Hence it is important that there is some purpose behind their production.

User group	Information required regarding
Government departments and agencies	• Accountability for use of public funds • Efficiency of service provision
Employees	• Job security • Future earnings potential
Suppliers	• Scale of potential purchases • Continuity of business • Ability to pay promptly
Students	• Long-term financial viability of the institution • Resources available for investment
Other customers	• Scale of business activity • Continuity
Lenders	• Security of loans made
General public	• Accountability for use of public funds • Efficiency of provision

Figure 9.1   *Potential user groups of HEI accounts*

Fundamentally, accounting theory states that accounts are prepared to put into the public domain financial information about the organisation which will be of relevance to users, and potential users, of those accounts in making decisions about the organisation. In saying this, it must be recognised that different users will need to make different types of decision. However, this requirement must be balanced against the needs of the organisation to protect itself by not releasing information which could be damaging to itself and in not incurring excessive costs to produce the information needed. Thus taking the example of a limited company, the release of information for the benefit of users of accounts needs to be balanced against the release of information which benefits competitors of the company.

From the foregoing it follows that we first need to identify who are the users of accounts and what information they need. Users can be classified into a number of key groups each with its own requirements for financial information and it will therefore vary to some extent from sector to sector. However, for an HEI, we would postulate that the groups shown in Figure 9.1 **might** be potential users.

The primary users of HEI statutory financial accounts are probably Government departments and funding bodies and their primary reasons for needing HEI accounts relate chiefly to their role in accounting for the use of public funds and their need to assess the efficiency of service provision.

Principles of financial accounting

The financial accounts of public and private sector organisations will vary in terms of detailed content and format but, in broad terms, they will comprise a number of different and interlocking statements, the key ones being:

- income and expenditure account (or profit and loss account in the private sector);
- balance sheet;
- cash flow statement.

Before looking at HEI financial accounts in a little more detail it is helpful to consider the fundamental nature of, and relationship between, these three different financial statements. This is best illustrated using the example of a small hypothetical business called 'Abacus'. These same underlying principles can then be applied to the financial accounts of an HEI.

Abacus: basic financial information

Abacus commenced business on 1 April 2002. It purchases wooden toys, paints them and then sells them on at a higher price. The information available about the business is shown in Figure 9.2.

At the date of commencement of business, Abacus had the following financial position

	£000
Owners investment in the business	35
Loan from bank	10
Equates to:	
Cash in the bank	45

During the year, Abacus undertook the following financial transactions

	£000
Purchase of wooden toys	50
Sales of wooden toys	65
Payment of wages	5
Cost of paint	3
Miscellaneous expenses	2
Purchase of equipment	40
New loan taken out	5
Repayment of existing loan	2
Payment of bank interest	1
Owners' drawings from the business	2
Cash received from sales	61
Cash paid for purchases of wooden toys	48
At the end of the year Abacus held stocks of wooden toys worth £3,000	

Figure 9.2 *Information about Abacus*

Abacus: financial statements

As noted above, the organisation will produce three distinct financial statements and these are discussed below.

Income and expenditure (profit and loss) account

The term income and expenditure (I&E) account is more likely to be used in 'not for profit' organisations such as hospitals and HEIs, whereas the term profit and loss (P&L) account will be used in commercial organisations. Whichever title is used the main function of this statement is the same.

The I&E account (P&L account) is a statement of *financial performance*. It shows the financial performance of the organisation, in terms of the surplus (or deficit) of income over expenditure, achieved over a period of a year. The income and expenditure account for Abacus is shown in Figure 9.3.

Income and expenditure (profit and loss) account for 2002/03		
	£000	£000
Sales of wooden toys		65
Purchases of wooden toys	50	
less: stocks at year end	3	
Cost of wooden toys sold		47
Gross surplus (profit)		18
less: Running costs		
Wages	5	
Paint	3	
Miscellaneous	2	
Depreciation of equipment	4	14
Net surplus (profit) before finance charges		4
less: Finance charges		
Bank interest		1
Net surplus (profit)		3

Figure 9.3 *Income and expenditure account for Abacus*

A number of points of clarification need to be made about the structure and content of this statement:

- **Income** – An I&E account differs from a statement of cash flows since it adopts what is termed the accounting **accruals** concept. Under this concept, income is the amount actually earned by the organisation during the year as opposed to the cash actually received. The difference between income and cash received is accounted for by amounts owing (debtors) as the data from the above example illustrates:
  - sales income earned = £65,000 (shown in I&E account) *less*
  - cash received from sales = £61,000 (shown in cash flow statement) *equals*
  - debtors outstanding at the year end = £4,000 shown in the balance sheet.

- **Cost of purchases** – Again under the accruals concept this is the cost of purchases of wooden toys made in the year as opposed to the cash actually disbursed on their purchase. The difference between expenditure and cash spent is accounted for by amounts owed (creditors), as the data from the above example illustrates:
  - purchases made = £50,000 (shown in I&E account) *less*
  - cash disbursed for purchases = £48,000 (shown in cash flow statement) *equals*
  - creditors outstanding at the year end = £2,000 shown in the balance sheet
- **Stocks and cost of goods sold** – The business commences the year with no stocks of wooden toys but at the end of the year stocks of wooden toys amount to £3,000. Hence the amount charged to the income and expenditure account is the cost of the wooden toys actually sold. This is derived by deducting the remaining stocks from the cost of the wooden toys purchased:
  - purchases of wooden toys = £50,000 (shown in the I&E account) *less*
  - stocks held at the year end = £3,000 (shown in the I&E account and balance sheet) *equals*
  - cost of goods sold = £47,000 (shown in the I&E account)
- **Depreciation** – All organisations make use of fixed assets such as buildings and equipment. The wear and tear involved in using these assets means that inevitably they suffer a reduction in value and this reduction in value is as much a cost to the organisation as pay or non-pay expenditure and has therefore to be accounted for in the I&E account under the heading of depreciation. Using the data from the above example, the depreciation charge is computed as follows:
  - cost of equipment = £40,000
  - useful life = 10 years
  - annual depreciation charge = £40,000/10 = £4,000 per annum.
  This depreciation charge does not involve any cash movement into or from the organisation. Instead the surplus (profit) of the organisation is reduced by the amount of the depreciation charge and the value of the equipment is reduced in the organisation's balance sheet by the amount of depreciation charged.
- **Interest charges** – Although the business receives new loans and repays old loans during the year, these just involve adjustments to the capital of the business and are not expenses of the business. However, the interest charges on loans are an expense of the business and are charged to the I&E account. New loans and repayment of loans are shown in the balance sheet and cash flow statements below.

Balance sheet

A balance sheet is often confused with an income and expenditure statement but the two statements are very different. Whereas the income and expenditure statement is a statement of *financial performance over a period of time (one year)*, a balance sheet is a statement of the *financial position* of the organisation *at a single point in time* (usually the year end). It shows the assets owned by the organisation and its outstanding liabilities at that point in time, namely at the end of the financial year. Thus the closing balance sheet for one year becomes the opening balance sheet of the next year. The balance sheet for Abacus is shown as Figure 9.4.

A number of points of clarification need to be made about the structure and content of this statement:

- **Fixed assets** – The fixed assets of an organisation include land, buildings, equipment, vehicles and go on, but in this simple example, only equipment is shown. The normal accounting convention (termed the historic cost convention) is that the gross cost of fixed assets is shown in the balance sheet at their original purchase price (i.e., historic cost). Depreciation (as discussed above) is calculated on this historic cost and deducted from the gross cost of fixed assets to give a net figure for fixed assets. However, even within the historic cost convention some fixed assets such as land and

Balance sheet as at 31 March 2003

	£000	£000
Assets		
Fixed assets		
Equipment	40	
less: depreciation	4	
		36
Current assets		
Stocks of wooden toys	3	
Debtors	4	
Cash	8	
	15	
less current liabilities		
Creditors	2	
Net current assets		13
Total assets		**49**
Financed by:		
Owners' investment	35	
add: profit for year	3	
less: owners' personal drawings	2	
Owners' capital		36
Bank loans		
Original loan	10	
add new loan	5	
less: repayments of existing loan	2	
Outstanding loan balance		13
Total financing sources		**49**

Figure 9.4   *Balance sheet for Abacus*

buildings may be revalued to a current value and included in the balance sheet as a revalued amount.

- **Current assets and liabilities** – Creditors, debtors and cash will be shown at actual values. Under the historic cost convention stocks are shown in the balance sheet at the lower of their original purchase price (i.e., historic cost) or their current value.
- **Owners' investment** – At the commencement of the business this amounted to £35,000. The profits earned by XYZ (£3,000) accrue to the owners and hence increase their investment but drawings from the business of £2,000 reduce their investment by that amount.
- **Bank loans** – The business started the year with an outstanding loan and during the year part of this old loan was repaid while a new loan was taken out. The results of these transactions are reflected as adjustments in the balance sheet and not the I&E account as follows:
  - loans at start of the year   £10,000
  - less repayments   £2,000
  - add new loan   £5,000
  - loans at end of year   £13,000.

In addition, an interest payment of £1,000 was made during the year and has been charged to the I&E account as an expense to the business.

Cash flow statement

A cash flow statement is also a statement of *financial performance* which shows whether the organisation had a net inflow or outflow of cash (as opposed to income and expenditure) over the year. Cash flow is important since organisations generating a financial surplus in income and expenditure terms can still experience financial difficulties if their cash flow position is not also positive. An I&E can show a profit but if cash is not collected, with a resulting high level of debtors, cash flow difficulties may arise. The cash flow statement for Abacus is shown as Figure 9.5.

A number of points of clarification need to be made about the structure and content of this statement:

- **Cash inflows** – In this example, cash receipts from sales of goods and new bank loans constitute positive flows of cash into the bank account of Abacus.
- **Cash outflows** – In this example, negative flows of cash out of the bank account of Abacus are the result of:
  - payments for purchases of stock items;
  - operating expenses (e.g., wages, paint, expenses);
  - bank loans – both interest payments and principal repayments constitute cash outflows but only the interest payments have been charged to the I&E account;
  - purchases of equipment – this is not charged to the I&E account since it is not an operating expense of the business; it is reflected by changes to the fixed asset figures in the balance sheet;

Cash flow statement for 2002/03

	£000	£000	£000
Opening Cash Balance			**45**
Cash inflows			
Sales receipts	61		
New bank loan	5		
Total cash inflows		+66	
Cash outflows			
Purchase payments	48		
Wages	5		
Paint	3		
Miscellaneous expenses	2		
Bank interest	1		
Loan repayment	2		
Purchase of equipment	40		
Owners drawings	2		
Total cash outflows		−103	
Net cash outflow during 1997/98			**−37**
Closing cash balance			**8**

Figure 9.5 *Cash flow statement for Abacus*

- owners' drawings – these are not charged to the I&E account since they are not an operating expense of the business; they are shown as a charge to the owner's capital in the balance sheet;
- depreciation – although this is a cost of production, this is *not* shown in the cash flow statement since it does not involve any flow of cash into or out of the business.

The regulatory framework for financial accounting in the HE sector

No organisations (e.g., companies, local authorities, NHS Trusts, charities) have freedom to decide what financial information should be disclosed in their statutory financial accounts and in what format those accounts should be prepared although they are able to disclose more than the minimum information required. Likewise, HEIs do not have freedom to decide the format and content of their annual accounts but must operate in a regulatory framework which defines the format of their financial accounts and the minimum information they must disclose.

Such an accounting framework applies to all HEIs but many HEIs also, either wholly or partly, own companies and a different regulatory framework of accounts applies to those companies to which HEIs must adhere.

Overall the regulatory accounting framework in which HEIs must operate is complex and comprises three main aspects:

- accounting requirements defined by statute;
- accounting requirements defined by the accounting profession; these are not mandatory in law but are usually complied with;
- accounting requirements defined by funding councils.

Failure to comply with any of these requirements may lead to the HEI's financial statements being 'qualified' by the HEI's external auditor.

These requirements are summarised in the Figure 9.6 and discussed in the ensuing sections.

	HEIs	HEI-owned companies
Accounting requirements defined by statute	• FE and HE Act 1992	• Companies Acts
Accounting requirements defined by the accounting profession	• Statements of Standard Accounting Practice (SSAP) and Financial Reporting Standards (FRS) • International Accounting Standards • Statement of recommended practice (SORP)	• Statements of Standard Accounting Practice (SSAP) and Financial Reporting Standards (FRS) • International Accounting Standards
Accounting requirements defined by funding councils	• Accounts Directions • Other guidance and reporting	

Figure 9.6   *Framework of HEI accounting requirements*

Accounting requirements defined by statute

HE institutions

As previously explained, HEIs have developed, historically, from a number of different backgrounds and these include:

- the old chartered universities;
- the nineteenth-century municipal universities;
- the twentieth-century universities established before the 1960s;
- the 'new' universities (former-polytechnics) and colleges of HE which became independent HEIs in 1989; the former were accorded the use of the university title in 1992 by the Further and Higher Education Act 1992.

All have charitable status, and are 'exempt' charities' which do not need to register separately with the Charities Commission. The key legislation which has led to consistent preparation of the annual financial statements of these bodies was the Further and Higher Education Act 1992 which in S 62(1) established the Higher Education Funding Council for England 'to exercise in relation to England the functions conferred on them'. From this primary legislation the Financial Memorandum and other directions and guidance relating to the accounts of HEIs have developed. In paragraph 5.71, the Further and Higher Education Act also inserts specific 'Accounts' guidance in relation to the HECs (Higher Education Corporations) established under the Education Reform Act of 1988:

It shall be the duty of each corporation to:

- keep proper accounts and proper records in relation to the accounts; and
- prepare in respect of each financial year of the corporation a statement of accounts. The statement shall:
  - give a true and fair account of the state of the corporations affairs at the end of the financial year and of the corporation's income and expenditure in the financial year; and
  - comply with any directions given by the HEFCE as to the information to be contained in the statement, the manner in which information is to be presented or the methods and principles according which the statement is to be prepared.

HEI-owned companies

Although HEIs are 'charities' they undertake significant activities which support their charitable aims but which are not in themselves part of their primary objectives. In order to safeguard the charitable status of HEIs, such activities, some of which are considered as trading activities by the Inland Revenue, need to be undertaken through subsidiary companies. Such an arrangement ensures that the charitable status of the HEI, which can provide taxation benefits, on items such as gift aid, investment income, and reductions in council tax payments is not endangered. The relevant taxation legislation which must be complied with is contained in section 505 of the Income and Corporation Taxes Act of 1988.

The operations and accounting arrangements for such subsidiary companies are governed by the Companies Act 1989, which updated and consolidated the Companies Act of 1985 and other legislation.

In 1985 a rationalisation of company legislation into four main acts took place, namely:

- Companies Act 1985;
- Business Names Act 1985;
- Company Securities (Insider Dealing) Act 1985;
- Companies Consolidation (Consequential Provisions) Act 1985.

However, subsequent changes were necessary to the Companies Act 1985 to incorporate two new EC Directives:

- Seventh Directive – consolidated accounts;
- Eighth Directive – regulation and qualification of auditors.

The opportunity was also taken to make other changes, amendments and additions including legislation relating to insolvency, insurance companies, fair trading, financial services and to the 1985 Companies Act itself.

The fundamental part of the Companies Act 1985 is Part 1, Chapter 1. Part 1 covers the formation and registration of companies and their judicial status and membership and in Chapter 1, section 1 (i) a company can be formed if:

> Any two or more persons associated for a lawful purpose may, by subscribing their names to the memorandum of association and otherwise complying with the requirements of the Act in registration, form an incorporated company, with or without liability.

The Act sets out three different company models:

- a company limited by shares, the liability of members being, if any, the amount paid on their shares;
- a company limited by guarantee, the liability of members being the amount they have guaranteed to contribute in the event of the company being wound up;
- an unlimited company, in which members have no limit on their personal liability.

The 'Memorandum of Association' sets out the objectives for a company and the limits on what is allowed to do. These are often drafted very broadly to avoid a company being accidentally restrained from undertaking a venture in a new but possible related field of activity. The 'Articles of Association' set out the internal workings of a company and the 1985 Companies Act incorporates a model set of articles for companies limited by shares known as 'Table A'.

Company law is extremely complex, and HEIs must comply with legislation, such as that on business names, when setting up subsidiary companies. There is also detailed legislation in the Companies Act on accounting and auditing arrangements for companies. The 1989 Companies Act specifies items such as:

- form and content of accounts;
- directors' emoluments, and higher paid employees;
- consistency of accounting treatment;
- procedures for approving and signing of accounts, directors' report and audit report;

- group accounts – particularly relevant for HEIs with subsidiary companies;
- auditors – qualifications, rights and appointments, resignation and removal.

There is therefore considerable extra administration, management time and cost associated with meeting the legal requirements of subsidiary companies in addition to the complexity of setting up tax-effective systems for transferring profits from subsidiary companies to the HEI. However, there are many similarities in detail in the financial statements/accounts of HEIs and companies, as both have a common foundation in the Companies Acts.

Accounting requirements defined by the accounting profession

Statements of Standard Accounting Practice (SSAP) and Financial Reporting Standards (FRS)

Accounting standards were introduced during the 1970s in response to a series of scandals concerning the way in which the statutory financial accounts of certain companies were being prepared and the inaccuracies and distortions contained in those accounts. The aim was to develop a framework for producing such accounts and to provide for some degree of consistency of accounting practice on various issues. However, even with the advent of accounting standards there is still a fair degree of freedom for organizations to apply differing accounting practices.

Statutory financial accounts are now prepared in accordance with the requirements of SSAPs and FRSs and these standards apply to all companies and other kinds of entities that prepare accounts, with the intention that they show a true and fair view. Currently it is the role of the Accounting Standards Board (ASB) to issue accounting standards and as such it is recognised for that purpose under the Companies Act 1985. The ASB took over the task of setting accounting standards from the former Accounting Standards Committee (ASC).

Accounting standards developed by the ASB are contained in 'Financial Reporting Standards' (FRSs). Soon after it started its activities, the ASB adopted the standards issued by the ASC, so that they also fall within the definition of accounting standards. These are designated 'Statements of Standard Accounting Practice' (SSAPs). Whilst some of the SSAPs have been superseded by FRSs, some remain in force.

A list of SSAPs and FRSs currently in force is shown in Figure 9.7.

As noted, accounting standards apply to all companies and other organisations which prepare accounts, with the intention that they provide a true and fair view of that organisation's financial performance and financial position. Thus they apply, in principle, to HEIs and HEI-owned companies, although the nature of certain standards (e.g., FRS 14 on Earnings per share) means that, although applicable, they are not relevant to HEIs.

SSAP	FRS
• SSAP 25 – Segmental reporting • SSAP 24 – Accounting for pension costs • SSAP 21 – Accounting for leases and hire purchase contracts • SSAP 20 – Foreign currency translation • SSAP 19 – Accounting for investment properties • SSAP 17 – Accounting for post balance sheet events • SSAP 15 – Superceded by FRS 19 • SSAP 13 – Accounting for research and development • SSAP 9 – Stocks and long-term contracts • SSAP 5 – Accounting for value added tax • SSAP 4 – Accounting for government grants	• FRS 19 – Deferred Tax • FRS 18 – Accounting Policies • FRS 17 – Retirement Benefits • FRS 16 – Current Tax • FRS 15 – Tangible Fixed Assets • FRS 14 – Earnings per Share • FRS 13 – Derivatives and other Financial Instruments: Disclosures • FRS 12 – Provisions, Contingent Liabilities and Contingent Assets • FRS 11 – Impairment of Fixed Assets and Goodwill • FRS 10 – Goodwill and Intangible Assets • FRS 9 – Associates and Joint Ventures • FRS 8 – Related Party Disclosures • FRS 7 – Fair Values in Acquisition Accounting • FRS 6 – Acquisitions and Mergers • FRS 5 – Reporting the Substance of Transactions • FRS 4 – Capital Instruments • FRS 3 – Reporting Financial Performance • FRS 2 – Accounting for Subsidiary Undertakings • FRS 1 (Revised 1996) – Cash Flow Statements • FRSSE (Effective June 2002) Financial Reporting Standard for Smaller Entities

Figure 9.7   *Current SSAPs and FRSs*

However, of particular recent concern to the HE sector, as it is to the corporate sector, is the impact of FRS 17 on the reporting of pension funds in financial statements. The sector operates three main national pension schemes, the USS (Universities Superannuation Scheme), the TSS (Teachers Superannuation Scheme), and the LGPS (Local Government Pension Scheme), and many pre-1989 HEIs have in-house pension schemes for administrative staff. Some HEIs are also involved with the NHS superannuation arrangements. This is too complex an issue to consider at depth in this book but readers need to be aware that different schemes are treated differently in accounting terms and this can produce different effects in the financial statements of the different HEIs. Key factors in determining the accounting treatment are whether schemes are 'funded' or 'not funded' (such as the TSS) and whether the pension is related to the final salary of the individual or the contributions made into the scheme.

International accounting standards

International accounting standards are prepared and issued by the International Accounting Standards Board (IASB). One of the roles of the IASB is to promote the convergence of domestic accounting standards around the world to achieve greater harmonisation of global accounting practices particularly in relation to multi-national companies. The pressure for convergence means that from time to time, UK domestic accounting standards may need to be amended.

Statement of recommended practice (SORP)

The need for HEIs to comply with best accounting practice consistently across the sector led to the production initially of a SORP covering just HE. However, in view of the similar accounting principles and needs in both FE and HE, a document covering both sectors was first issued in June 2000 (which applied from 1 August 1999). An updated version, 'Statement of recommended practice: accounting for further and higher education' was published on 1 September 2003 and has applied from 1 August 2003. The revisions reflected changes in Statements of Standard Accounting Practices (SSAPs), Financial Reporting Standards (FRSs) and in best accounting practice since the issue of the first combined SORP.

The need for a separate FE/HE SORP arose from the distinctive nature of the group of organisations in these sectors and the distinctive nature of their activities. Institutions must also comply with Generally Acceptable Accounting Practice (GAAP) and therefore the FE/HE SORP has to be subjected to a review by the Accounting Standards Board (ASB). The ASB set up a steering committee which included representatives of FEIs and HEIs, the funding councils, the profession, UUK (formerly CVCP) together with its own observer to produce the FE/HE SORP. The FE/HE SORP includes guidance on the format of the mandatory financial statements, namely the income and expenditure account, balance sheet, cash flow statement and the statement of total recognised gains and losses, and includes guidance on items required by HEFCE under its Accounts Directions. The FE/HE SORP also includes a model set of FE/HE Financial Statements for the imaginary 'Casterbridge College'.

Any SORP is required **not to conflict** with accepted accounting practice in any fundamental manner. The ASB, on the basis of its review, gave the required 'negative assurance' in respect of the FE/HE SORP issued in 2003. It was 'fronted' by the ASB which concluded that the SORP did not appear to contain standards which were unacceptable or which appeared to conflict with current or possible planned accounting standards.

Accounting requirements defined by funding councils

HE institutions

HEFCE requires compliance with the SORP but also issues, from time to time, Accounts Directives which are mandatory on the sector. It also sets out in its

Financial Memorandum that each HEI must keep proper accounting records and must submit audited financial statements to HEFCE by 31 December each year, in respect of the 31 July year-end.

The Accounts Directions are issued as necessary by HEFCE to cover specific and general accounting issues for the HE sector which will impact on the annual financial statements. HEFCE also provide guidance on how to present the required information/disclosures contained in the Accounts Directions.

The Accounts Directions 23/2002 issued by HEFCE on 21 November 2002 included directions on:

- restatement of the need to follow the SORP for FE and HE, and also the requirements of the Companies Acts for Institutions which are also companies limited by guarantee;
- the requirement to use the accounting treatment for inherited liabilities provided in the guidance from the BUFDG Accounting Standards Group of March 1995 entitled 'Accounting in Higher Education Institutions' (with any subsequent updates);
- corporate governance – progress towards effective risk management, and other elements of corporate governance (this is a major issue for the sector and is covered in more detail below);
- ensuring that external audit contracts enable external auditors to give a view on the proper application of income, including HEFCE grants;
- the sensitive issue of disclosure of information on the salaries of vice-chancellors or their equivalent and disclosure of compensation paid for loss of office for senior staff (defined as earning over £70,000 a year).

The Accounts Directions can therefore cover very broad and very specific issues. That of corporate governance is worthy of more detailed consideration, and the Council of HEFCE in September 2000 agreed a timetable for compliance with implementing full corporate governance principles which required full compliance statements on internal control for the year ending 31 July 2003.

Effective risk management is also a fundamental element of this process and the Accounts Direction for 2002/03 specifies steps HEIs must have taken to introduce an effective risk management strategy, which include:

- all risks to be covered, but a focus on critical areas;
- policy clearly set out;
- monitoring to be regular and linked to action;
- commitment from the top, and an identified manager;
- embedded into routine operations of the HEI, not an add-on.

Although the financial element will always be important, risk management must cover the wider risks across the whole HEI. The concern of many HEIs was that if their external auditors could not confirm that full compliance had been achieved for the year ended 31 July 2003, then their financial statements for the year 2002/03 might be 'qualified' by their external auditors. In mid-2003 HEFCE's audit service and a number of external auditors were concerned that compliance might not be achieved in all HEIs and HEFCE therefore provided both:

- a restatement that the deadline for full compliance remained as the reporting year ending on 31 July 2003;
- further guidance to assist HEIs in this task and what actions should be taken if, exceptionally, an HEI was unable to comply (see HEFCE Circular letter 16/2003 of 3 July 2003).

HEI-owned companies

In the mid-1990s HEFCE became aware that its guidance did not refer to subsidiary companies of HEIs which were increasing rapidly in number. HEFCE therefore commissioned a report entitled 'Related Companies – Recommended Practice Guidelines' on such companies.

The report stressed a number of key issues of particular relevance to finance directors, including:

- the fundamental importance of the business plan including the capitalisation level of the company;
- the need to take proper legal and taxation advice;
- careful consideration of the constitution of the company (see previous consideration of the memorandum and articles);
- the critical importance of the memorandum of understanding between the parties. This should clearly set out the purpose behind the company/joint venture, the responsibilities of the parties and the management/control framework. This memorandum should also incorporate an unambiguous exit route to enable the company to be closed down if the planned objectives are not being met and in the case of joint ventures to enable each party to terminate its membership/participation in such circumstances.

Financial accounting practices in the HE sector

In this section we outline the structure and content of statutory financial accounts in the HE sector. Firstly we consider HEIs themselves and then consider the accounts for companies owned by HEIs for various purposes.

Annual financial statements of HEIs

The annual accounts/financial statements of an HEI fit into the overall general structure set out earlier as modified by specific section legal and accounting requirements The three fundamental documents in the accounts are the:

- income and expenditure account;
- balance sheet;
- cash flow statement.

However, other reports and opinions are required to complete the full set of financial statements which are submitted to HEFCE.

There are minor changes in the format depending on the management arrangements operating in particular HEIs, but the following list of contents incorporates the full range of required documents:

- Governors' Report and Financial Statement;
- Consolidated Income and Expenditure Account;
- Consolidated Statement of Historic Cost Surpluses and Deficits;
- Statement of Total Recognised Gains and Losses;
- Consolidated Balance Sheet, together with the HEI's Balance Sheet;
- Consolidated Cash Flow Statements;
- Notes to the Accounts.

These financial statements need to be approved by the governing body and signed on its behalf by the Chairman and Vice-Chancellor/Principal of the HEI. The signature of the finance director is also included in some HEIs. A much abbreviated 'model' is set out below to demonstrate these features.

Governors' report

This will comprise the following:

- **Treasurers/Members Report** – financial review, investment performance, operational review, forward look/developments, particular issues/ successes.
- **Corporate Governance Structure/Statement** – explanation of committee structure, frequency of meetings, and so on.
- **Statement of Responsibilities of the Governing Body** – statement that Governing Body has kept proper accounting records, used suitable accounting policies/standards, financial statements prepared on an 'on-going-concern' basis, reasonable steps taken to ensure proper and effective use of and safe guarding of funds.
- **Statement on Internal Control** – this sets out the steps taken by the Governing Body to achieve a high level of internal control of all activities.

It relates to requirements arising from the Turnbull Report and from 2002/03 HEIs have needed to confirm that risk management processes are in place and operational.

- **Auditors' Report to the Governing Body** – the required external audit report, setting out the basis for the audit opinion. HEIs will hope to receive a 'clean' audit report with no qualifications. The opinion will be based on whether or not the financial statements give a true and fair view, if funding has been properly applied in terms of the source of funding and in terms of the HEI statutes.
- **Statement of Principal Accounting Policies** – these will set out the type of policies and may also refer to various accounting standards. These policies may also be referred to in the notes to the Accounts.

Consolidated income and expenditure account

It needs to be highlighted that the I&E Account of the HEI is 'consolidated' which means that it includes the financial results of all subsidiary undertakings. A consolidated I&E account for a HEI is shown in Figure 9.8

The following points should be noted in relation to this I&E account:

- In addition to the above, for many of the HEIs formed in 1989 after the passing of the 1988 Education Reform Act, the information shown in Figure 9.9 will also appear.
- The 'Historical cost surplus/(deficit) after tax' is the figure used by HEFCE to assess the financial position of an HEI which is a surplus of £500,000 in 2002/03 in the example.
- A revaluation reserve arises on the revaluation of assets and many HEIs will have modest balances on this account as the periodic revaluation of assets is a standard accounting procedure. However, the 1989 HEIs generally took over their buildings, equipment and other assets, from the LEAs who had previously managed the HEIs, without making a payment. Such assets were then re-valued with the re-valued amount being included as an asset in the balance sheet and the corresponding entry being the setting-up of a revaluation reserve of an identical amount on the other side of the balance sheet. These reserves can therefore have significant balances in many HEI's established in 1989 and such revaluation reserves are used annually to provide the depreciation on these assets which is included as part of the total depreciation charged to the I&E Account. The depreciation charge in such cases is, therefore, not cash-backed as no cash is set aside to provide for replacement of these buildings.

	Year ended 31 July 2003 £000	Year ended 31 July 2002 £000
Income		
Funding Council Grants	60,000	58,000
Tuition fees and education contracts	29,000	27,500
Research grants and contract	3,000	3,000
Other income	21,000	21,000
Endowment and Investment income	1,000	1,300
Total income	114,000	110,800
Expenditure		
Staff costs	67,000	66,000
Exceptional restructuring costs	4,000	–
Other operating expenses	37,000	36,500
Depreciation	6,000	6,000
Interest payable	3,000	4,000
Total expenditure	117,000	112,500
(Deficit)/surplus on continuing operations after depreciation of fixed assets at valuation and before tax	(3,000)	(1,700)
(Loss)/profit on disposal of assets	–	–
(Deficit)/surplus on continuing operations after depreciation of tangible fixed assets at valuation and disposal of assets but before tax	(3,000)	(1,700)
Taxation	–	–
(Deficit)/surplus operations after depreciation of assets at valuation, disposal of assets and tax	(3,000)	(1,700)

Figure 9.8   *Consolidated I&E Account for an HEI for the year ended 31 July 2003*

Consolidated statement of historical surpluses and deficits

This statement (Figure 9.10) shows the impact of differences in the approach to calculating depreciation and the impact of taxation.

Income and expenditure account	Year ended 31 July 2003 £000	Year ended 31 July 2002 £000
(Deficit)/surplus on continuing operations after depreciation of assets at valuation, disposal of assets and tax	(3,000)	(1,700)
Release from revaluation reserve	3,500	1,600
Historical cost surplus/(deficit) after tax	500	(100)
Balance at 31 July 2002	35,000	35,100
Balance at 31 July 2003	35,500	35,000

Figure 9.9   *Additional I&E disclosure for post-1989 universities*

	Year ended 31 July 2003 £000	Year ended 31 July 2002 £000
(Deficit)/surplus on continuing operation before taxation	(3,000)	(1,700)
Difference between historical cost depreciation and the actual charge for the period calculated on the re-valued amount	3,500	1,600
Historical cost (deficit)/surplus for the period before taxation	500	(100)
Historical cost (deficit)/surplus for the period after taxation	500	(100)

Figure 9.10   *Consolidated Statement of Historical Surpluses and Deficits for the year ended 31 July 2003*

Statement of total recognised gains and losses

This statement (Figure 9.11) shows the gains and losses accruing to the HEI during the year from different sources.

	Year ended 31 July 2003 £000	Year ended 31 July 2002 £000
(Deficit)/surplus on continuing operations after depreciation of assets at valuation, disposal of assets and tax	(3,000)	(1,700)
Unrealised surplus on revaluation of fixed assets (if applicable)	–	–
HEFCE reimbursement of principal element of debt charges (if applicable)	–	–
(Depreciation)/Appreciation of endowment asset investments	–	–
Endowment income retained for year	–	–
Net endowments	500	500
Total recognised (losses)/gains relating to the period	(2,500)	(1,200)
Reconciliation		
Opening reserves and endowments	109,400	
Total recognised gains and losses for the year	(2,500)	
Closing reserves and endowments	106,900	

Figure 9.11   *Statement of Total Recognised Gains and Losses for the year ended 31 July 2003*

Balance sheet

A typical HEI balance sheet is shown as Figure 9.12.

Particular points to note in the balance sheet are:

- **Endowments** – there are separate lines for endowments , that is, donations given to the HEI, in both assets and liabilities which show the same amounts.
- **Deferred capital grants** – this heading is shown in the liabilities section of the balance sheet. The basis of this is complex and is discussed below. The funding councils often provide capital funds to enable HEIs to purchase buildings, equipment and other assets. When the fixed asset is purchased, the cost of the asset will appear in both the asset side of the balance sheet and on the opposite side of the balance sheet to show that the asset has been financed by a capital grant. Following the 'depreciation' principle set out earlier, depreciation on the fixed asset is charged to the Income and Expenditure Account each year to reflect wear and tear on the asset. At the same time an equivalent portion of the capital grant will be released to the income part of the I&E Account (in the funding council grant section) to match the depreciation element expenditure in the depreciation heading of the I&E Account. The balance of capital grants

	Group 2003	HEI 2003	Group 2002	HEI 2002
Fixed Assets				
Tangible assets	154,700	152,300	154,000	153,000
Investments	1,000	1,500	900	1,300
	155,700	153,800	154,900	154,300
Endowment Assets	3,000	3,000	2,500	2,500
Current Assets				
Stock and shares in hand	600	400	400	300
Debtors: due within one year	9,000	11,000	6,700	8,700
Debtors: due after one year	–	2,600	–	2,200
	9,000	13,600	6,700	10,900
Investments and short-term deposits	11,000	10,500	15,500	15,000
Cash at bank and in hand	1,300	600	1,400	300
	21,900	25,100	24,000	26,500
Creditors: amounts falling due within one year	(13,200)	(12,100)	(14,000)	(13,000)
Net current assets	8,700	13,000	10,000	13,500
Total assets less current Liabilities	167,900	170,300	167,400	169,800
Creditors: amounts falling due after more than one year	(41,000)	(42,000)	(45,000)	(46,000)
Provisions for liabilities and Charges	(10,000)	(10,000)	(5,000)	(5,000)
Net Assets	116,900	118,300	117,400	118,800
Deferred Capital Grant	10,000	10,000	8,000	8,000
Endowments				
Specific	1,000	1,000	900	900
General	2,000	2,000	1,600	1,600
	3,000	3,000	2,500	2,500
Reserves				
Revaluation reserve	68,400	69,300	71,900	72,800
Income and Expenditure Account	35,500	36,000	35,000	35,500
Total reserves	103,900	105,300	106,900	108,300
Total	116,900	118,300	117,400	118,800

Figure 9.12 *HEI Balance Sheet as at 31 July 2003*

(referred to as deferred capital grants) is then shown in the balance sheet. This is summarised below.

- Cost of fixed asset = £100,000. Estimated useful life of 10 years.

- Annual depreciation = £100,000/10 = £10,000 charged to expenditure side of I&E account.
- Annual release of capital grants = £100,000/10 = £10,000 charged to income side of I&E account.
- Fixed assets shown in balance sheet after year 1 = £100,000 − £10,000 = £90,000.
- Deferred capital grants shown in balance sheet after year 1 = £100,000−£10,000 = £90,000.

Thus the overall impact of a fixed asset purchased through a capital grant is nil on both the I&E account and the balance sheet of the HEI.

- **Revaluation reserve** – this will include all changes in asset values following formal revaluations.
- **Consolidated position** – the balance sheet has columns both for the 'consolidated' position, – the HEI and its subsidiary undertakings – and for the HEI itself.

Consolidated cash flow statement

For an HEI, this is illustrated in Figure 9.13.

	31 July 2003 £000	31 July 2002 £000
Net cash flow from operating activities		
Returns on investments and servicing of finance	Note: the detailed figures are highly technical and are found in the **notes to the accounts.**	
Taxation	The relevant figures are the totals	
Capital expenditure and financial investments		
Management of liquid resources		
Financing		
Increase/(decrease) in cash in the period	300	900
Reconciliation of net cash flow to movement in net funds/(debt)		
Increase in cash in the period		
Cash inflow from new secured loan	Note: another highly technical section with the key figures being net funds/(debt) position. This will also be in notes to the Accounts.	
Cash inflow from liquid resources		
Movement in net funds/(debt) in period, say	(3,000)	(5,000)
Net funds/(debt) at 1 August ,say	(30,000)	(25,000)
Net funds/(debt) at 31 July	(33,000)	(30,000)

Figure 9.13   *Consolidated Cash Flow Statement for the year ended 31 July 2003*

Notes to the financial statements /accounts

The formats of the above statements are mandatory, although slight variations to the wording are to be found, and on each of the statements references are made to notes in the financial statements. These are an integral part of the financial statements and contain mandatory and discretionary elements which explain in greater detail the item to which the notes refer. There will normally be between 35 and 40 notes to the financial statements, which will be reviewed by the external auditors as part of their audit prior to giving their audit opinion on the financial statements for the year. The notes may also refer to relevant SSAPs and FRSs when explaining particular items.

Other financial monitoring by HEFCE

HEFCE requires copies of the Annual Financial Statements by 31 December for the year ended on the previous 31 July which means that this financial information is historical in nature. To assess the financial performance of HEIs against that which has been predicted, HEFCE requests from each HEI a number of other documents which forecast the likely financial position of the HEI. These include:

Usually in July An annual operating statement and financial forecast together with updated strategic plans, if appropriate. These forecasts are for the year which ends on 31 July, the following year, for which HEFCE will already have announced grants and for the three subsequent years. Therefore the document requesting the forecast for 2002/03 was issued in April 2003 and covered the years 2002/03 to 2005/06. It is a very comprehensive document which includes an I&E Account, balance sheet, and cash flow statement together with analyses of various headings and information on capital expenditure and long-term borrowing. A key element is the detailed information requested on projected student number over the period.

Usually in mid-March A 'mid-year financial return' is normally requested in February which seeks details of the latest forecast the year-end position. The HEI is asked to compare this with that provided the previous July, and requests reasons for any significant variance. Other related information is also requested.

HEFCE requires such information for a number of reasons including to monitor the financial strength of the sector. HEFCE also needs to debate with Government future funding for HE and the financial forecasts are vital documents to enable HEFCE to do this, although they contain one major flaw. HEIs are never given a firm instruction on whether the results being forecast are before or after action has been taken to offset any funding shortfalls, such as shortfalls in inflation funding provided to meet pay awards and other price increases caused by inflation. Some HEIs may therefore show the position before taking any action, which can be interpreted as being alarmist while others will show the position having taken remedial action to cover such shortfalls. Such HEIs will tend to understate the financial difficulties. HEFCE, however, will no doubt decide its own approach to these forecasts in its dealings with Government and this approach may not be consistent with the returns from the sector.

The detailed monitoring of HEIs can lead to those with actual or potential financial difficulties having to report their ongoing results to HEFCE on a regular basis. It is believed that a handful of such HEIs have been subjected to such scrutiny in recent years with a larger number being under less severe reporting restrictions, but having to produce action/recovery plans for approval which have been subsequently closely monitored by HEFCE.

Other information required by HEFCE is collected by HESA and is known as the 'finance statistical record'. It comprises an additional analysis of income and expenditure, together with information on research funding, capital expenditure and other miscellaneous expenditure. The expenditure analysis includes a pay and non-pay analysis per academic department, using guidelines provided to attempt to achieve consistency. However, as discussed in Chapter 3, many consider that this HESA analysis is not robust, and hence the wish of a number of HEIs to develop their own more robust forms of benchmarking data.

Finally, mention should be made of the need for all HEIs to submit TRAC returns a discussed in Chapter 6.

Associated companies

Reasons for them and issues arising

The HE sector is continuing to become more diverse in nature and reasons for HEIs to undertake activities through a 'related' company include the need for a mechanism to protect the HEI's charitable status when undertaking commercial activities, the wish to undertake a specific activity or joint venture in a controlled environment, with one or more partners, and the need to establish effective tax compliance arrangements.

Such companies may be wholly-owned subsidiaries of the HEI or the HEI may be a shareholder, possibly a minority shareholder. The objectives of such companies will have to be consistent with the powers of the HEI in order to ensure that the associated company is not acting in an 'ultra vires' manner. Legal opinion exists which advises that if an activity is being undertaken which is not directly related to the objectives of the HEI – for example, a spin-off project arising from a PhD study – then such an activity should be undertaken by a subsidiary company of the HEI's subsidiary company and not by the direct subsidiary itself.

A subsidiary company exists where the HEI:

- has a majority of the voting rights;
- is a member of the company and can appoint or remove directors as it has the majority of votes on the board;
- can legally exert a dominating influence over the undertaking;
- is a member of the company and has an agreement with other share-holders by which it exercises that control;
- owns an interest and exercises dominant control.

Therefore there can be a wide range of associated companies whose financial results may need to be incorporated into an HEI's consolidated financial statements. A number of cases exist where the financial results of an HEI's Union of Students are consolidated into those of the HEI as the HEI has specific rights of ultimate control in prescribed circumstances.

The setting-up of a subsidiary company will normally limit the liability of the parent HEI and its governors, but care has to be taken to ensure that the HEI does not retain too much control, as personal liability may still reside with the governors or senior staff if this is the case. The finance director of the HEI will often be involved in setting up associated companies and may well be a director of the associated company. He or she therefore needs to be mindful of this danger of retaining power in the HEI outside the formal company structure. This is generally referred to as the issue of 'shadow directorships'.

Business planning and management arrangements

An HEI should undertake a full option analysis before establishing an associate company, and the production of a full business plan is an essential part of this process. This will set out clearly:

- the objectives behind the venture together with the background to date;
- the services and/or products which will be delivered;
- the market research and strategic plans (R and D input may be an essential element);
- how the company is to be run and managed and how it relates to the HEI;
- a SWOT analysis will be needed together with detailed risk scenario modelling;
- the HEI's finance director will need to ensure that the financial information necessary to produce a robust business plan is available and that financial projections have been prepared for a number of years ahead. He or she may also need to consider financing arrangements with banks and

venture capitalists and where appropriate this information will need to be presented to the Board of Governors for their approval.

In summary, associated company arrangements should not be established without a very realistic appraisal of the need for such an arrangement, as they can needlessly divert management time from other activities. Even the unavoidable administrative and audit arrangements entailed can add to the overall management load and therefore associated companies need to be established on a sound and robust basis.

HE financial accounting practices: comparisons with other sectors

In this section we undertake some brief comparisons between financial accounting practices in the HE sector compared to that in other sectors. There are three main aspects to this.

Types of financial statement produced

In looking at other sectors and other organisations in those sectors, at a high level, financial accounting practices will be similar, as most organisations will produce the same or similar types of financial statement, namely:

- income and expenditure account (or profit and loss account in the commercial sector);
- balance sheets;
- cash flow statements (or statement of source and application of funds).

Additional statements may also be produced in the various sectors and these will vary from case to case.

Accounting conventions

Basically, in preparing statutory financial accounts one of two accounting conventions might be applied:

Historic cost convention

Under the historic cost convention the following approaches applies:

- The gross amount for the fixed assets (buildings and equipment) of the organisation are shown in its balance sheet usually on the basis of the original purchase price paid to acquire them (i.e., historic cost).

- In some cases, the organisation might decide to revalue certain items of land and buildings to reflect a current value and the balance sheet will contain these revalued amounts. However, the general principle is one of historic cost.
- Annual depreciation charges are calculated on the basis of these mainly historic cost figures.
- Items of stock which are charged to the income and expenditure account of the organisation are charged on the basis of the original purchase price paid to acquire them (i.e., historic cost) unless their current value is lower than the historic cost.

Valuation convention

Under the valuation convention the following approaches apply:

- The gross value of the fixed assets (buildings and equipment) of the organisation is shown in its balance sheet usually on the basis of their current value (i.e., what it would cost to purchase then today or the amount that would be obtained from selling them). This differs from the historic cost approach which show assets at their original purchase price.
- Annual depreciation charges are calculated on the basis of these current values of fixed assets.
- Items of stock are charged to the income and expenditure account of the organisation at their current value irrespective of whether that current value is above or below their historic cost.

The differences between these accounting conventions are illustrated in the simple example (Figure 9.14) based on the same organisation but applying the different accounting conventions.

Thus it can be seen that using a different accounting convention for the same organisation can produce a significantly different financial performance result. In general terms the use of the valuation convention will produce lower financial surpluses than the historic cost convention.

Disclosure requirements

The range and type of detailed financial information required to be disclosed in the statutory financial accounts of organisations will vary substantially from sector to sector. The minimum level of financial information requiring to be disclosed is laid down in aspects of the regulatory framework described earlier and this will differ from sector to sector.

If we compare the mandatory disclosure requirements for HEIs with that of other sectors we obtain the picture shown in Figure 9.15.

In summary, the table suggests that there is variation across all sectors in terms of required disclosure of information. The main areas where the HE

Historic cost convention
● Buildings at historic cost = £50.0 million
● Equipment at historic cost = £3.5 million
● Cost of stock items charged to the income and expenditure account = £21.4 million
● Income = £40.0 million
● Other costs = £10.0 million

Therefore charges made to the I&E account to establish surplus/deficit position are as follows:

● Buildings depreciation (over 50 years) = £1.0 million
● Equipment depreciation (over 5 years) = £0.7 million
● Stock = £21.4 million

The I&E account would be as follows:

	£m
Income	40.0
Costs of stock	21.4
Other costs	10.0
Depreciation	1.7
Surplus	6.9

Valuation convention
● Buildings at current value = £75.0 million
● Equipment at current value = £5.5 million
● Current value of stock items charged to the income and expenditure account = £24.4 million
● Income = £40.0 million
● Other costs = £10.0 million

Therefore charges made to the I&E account to establish surplus/deficit position are as follows:

● Buildings depreciation (over 50 years) = £1.5 million
● Equipment depreciation (over 5 years) = £1.1 million
● Stock = £24.4 million

The I&E account would be as follows:

	£m
Income	40.0
Costs of stock	24.4
Other costs	10.0
Depreciation	2.6
Surplus	3.0

Figure 9.14   *Impact of different accounting conventions*

sector tends to provide less information in its financial statements than other sectors are:

● the amount of information within the treasurers, members' report. In addition to the differences identified in the above table, other information included in the equivalent reports for other sectors, especially, companies and charities but which is not consistently included by HEI's includes:
  – management/activity structure;
  – creditors payment policy;
  – outline of principal activities;
  – significant relationships with other organisations (if not disclosed elsewhere);
  – interests of senior staff/directors in subsidiary companies.
● expenditure analysis which is variable across the HE sector;
● average numbers of staff employed;
● analysis of senior staff costs other than the head of institution.

Disclosure requirement	HEI's	FE Colleges	Companies	Local Authorities	NHS Trusts	Charities
Income analysis						
Detailed income/ expenditure analysis on I&E or equivalent	Yes	Yes	No	Yes	No	Yes
Expenditure analysis						
Pay expenditure analysis by type, salary, NI etc	Yes	Yes	Yes	No	Yes	Yes
Non-pay expenditure analysis by type, consumables, support etc	Varies	No	Yes	No	Yes	Yes
Pay expenditure by activity, e.g., teaching departments etc	Varies	Yes	No	Yes	No	Yes
Non-pay expenditure by activity, e.g., teaching departments etc	Varies	Yes	No	Yes	No	Yes
Staff disclosures						
Average numbers of staff	Varies	Yes	Yes	No	Yes	Yes
Analysis of senior staff costs (other than VC, Principal etc)	No	Yes	Yes	No	Yes	Yes
Details in directors'/ treasurers'/members' reports						
Donations	No	No	Yes	No	No	Yes
Employee involvement in the organisation	Varies	No	Yes	No	No	Yes
Corporate governance/ statement of internal control	Yes	Yes	Plcs only	Yes	Yes	Yes

Figure 9.15 *Comparative accounting disclosure requirements*

Finally, in discussing disclosure requirements two other points should be noted:

- HEIs also voluntarily disclose other financial information beyond the mandatory requirements such as the publication of annual reports. Thus the total level of disclosure by HEIs will extend well beyond the mandatory requirements and this also applies to many other types of organisations, in both the public and private sectors.
- HEIs also provide a range of publicly available information in addition to the financial statements which goes beyond the requirements of private companies and has similarities with some of the information requirements in various public sector organisations.

Chapter 10

The organisation and staffing of the HE finance function

Introduction

The finance function is the term used to cover the HEI's central finance department plus financial activities undertaken by finance staff outposted in academic or support departments. In this chapter we deal with the organisation and staffing of the HEI finance function itself. We consider the following issues:

- the organisation of the HEI finance function;
- roles and responsibilities of the HEI director of finance (DOF);
- staffing of HEI finance departments;
- strategic trends in finance functions;
- organisational change in the HEI finance function.

The organisation of the HEI finance function

There are two key aspects, namely the activities of the finance function and the organisation of those activities.

Finance function activities

Although details will vary between HEIs, finance functions will usually control and be responsible for the following:

- **Payroll** – the payments of salaries, wages and other benefits to employees.
- **Travel expenses** – the payment of travel and subsistence expenses to employees including, in some cases, international payments and payments in advance.
- **Payments** – payments to suppliers and contractors for goods and services received, including payments for utilities. Integral to this function will be

the processes of ordering of goods and services and confirmation of receipt of those goods and services. Also included will be payments made to contractors in relation to capital projects.

- **Income collection** – the collection of income from a range of different sources. Key functions include: issuing invoices for the income due, credit management and recording and banking of payments made. Two important features are prompt and accurate billing and rapid collection. In recent years, a major development in this area has been the collection of fees from students and dealings with the student loans company.
- **Financial control** – this involves creating the basic financial control framework for the institution to ensure that income due is collected, expenditure is controlled, the assets of the organisation are protected and proper financial practices are applied. Integral to this will be the formulation of procedures, the conduct of training and the monitoring of compliance with those procedures.
- **Financial accounting** – this involves maintaining the basic accounting records of the organisation during the year and preparing the annual statutory accounts and statements of the institution.
- **Management accounting** – this includes a variety of activities such as the provision of financial information and advice, development of a financial strategy, budgetary control, costing and pricing and investment appraisal, all of which require liaison with departmental line managers.
- **Treasury management** – this involves liquidity control and managing cash balances and other aspects of working capital, such as creditor and debtor levels. This mirrors the commercial world where company failures can arise due to cashflow problems rather than poor profitability.
- **Internal audit** – as noted in an earlier chapter, internal audit provides a continuous examination of the application of standards of financial control and value for money. In practice the internal audit function may not report to the director of finance but may report to another individual such as the bursar.

Finance function organisation

All (or most) of the above activities will be found, to some extent, in all HEI finance departments, although their precise size and organisation will vary according to the institution. Two particular organisational themes which must be mentioned concern decentralisation and outsourcing. In a later section, also considered will be various strategic trends which will have implications for the future organisation of HEI finance function.

Decentralisation

Traditionally most HEI finance functions have operated a centralised model where all of the above activities have been undertaken in a central finance department. However, in recent years some institutions have taken steps to devolve certain finance activities to academic or support departments. Accompanying this would be the outplacement of certain staff who hitherto had been based in the central finance department. These outposted staff might retain a direct managerial link to the finance department but would work closely with staff in the department where they were based, but it is possible that they might be managerially accountable to the head of the department while retaining professional accountability to the DOF.

The most usual finance activity to be outposted is that of management accounting and the provision of financial advice to departmental managers. However, it is also possible for such activities as payments or income collection (and the associated finance staff) to be outposted and, as will be noted later, modern financial systems would facilitate such a trend. However, certain other tasks such as financial accounting are always likely to be undertaken, largely, centrally.

Outsourcing

Traditionally, most finance function activities have been undertaken in HEI's premises by the HEI own staff. However, in recent years there has been an increasing trend towards outsourcing certain activities to a private company. Examples might include:

- Payroll – the bulk of the payroll function could be outsourced to an external contractor. However, the need for some form of internal payroll liaison function would remain and the DOF would retain responsible for the security of payroll systems including such external services.
- Internal audit – many HEIs have outsourced their internal audit service to private accountancy firms.

We will return later to possible trends in outsourcing of finance activities.

The role and responsibilities of the HEI director of finance

In the HEI, the title Director of Finance (DOF) is often given to the most senior finance manager in the organisation. However, other titles may still be used such as finance officer or head of finance.

As noted in Chapter 1, there are significant variations, between HEIs, in terms of their overall organisational arrangements. Thus in some HEIs, the DOF will be directly accountable to the vice-chancellor or principal of the HEI while in other HEIs the DOF will be accountable to a pro-vice-chancellor, a bursar or a registrar. Also, the DOF role may also be combined (particularly in smaller institutions) with other roles, and thus there may be posts, such as

Director of Finance and Information or Director of Finance and Legal Services and so on.

Whatever the organisational arrangements, there are certain roles and responsibilities which attach to the post of DOF and these are now substantially greater than they were (say) 10–15 years ago and can be summarised as follows:

Financial control

The DOF must ensure that adequate standards of financial control operate in the organisation. This will need to cover the areas outlined above including for example, payments to staff and suppliers, the control of expenditure, the collection of income, and the management of investments. Linked to this, the DOF may be responsible for ensuring access to an adequately skilled and resourced internal audit function. Finally, the DOF is personally responsible for reporting to the Governors on the adequacy, or otherwise, of financial control in the organisation and the remedial action required.

Financial services

The DOF is usually responsible for ensuring that there are effective and efficient financial services. However, it is not obligatory for financial services such as payroll and creditor payments to be directly managed by the DOF. For example, payroll may be managed by the personnel section or contracted out to an agency or contractor while creditor payments may be managed by the supplies department. Irrespective of who actually manages the various financial services, the DOF is always responsible for ensuring that adequate standards of financial control prevail.

Financial systems

The DOF is responsible for providing adequate and robust financial systems which record details of the income, expenditure, assets and liabilities of the organisation. These are needed for two main purposes:

- to prepare the annual statutory accounts of the organisation;
- to provide ongoing financial information throughout the year for HEI managers.

Financial information and advice

This must be provided by DOF and the staff of the finance function. This advice could be at an operational level concerning, for example, budgetary trends or at a strategic level covering, for example, the financial implications of a major capital investment or the implementation of a new pay structure.

The DOF and finance staff are responsible for the provision of this information and advice to managers throughout the organisation and at a more personal level, the DOF will provide financial information and advice to the Governors about all aspects of the HEIs activities.

Strategic development

In addition to managing their ongoing day-to-day activities, all HEIs will have a strategic agenda which can take a variety of forms such as:

- campus rationalisation;
- academic restructuring;
- expansion of teaching and/or research provision;
- expansion of commercial activities.

All these trends have major strategic financial implications and must be considered carefully. The DOF has direct responsibilities for the financial appraisal of any proposed strategies in addition to making a general contribution as a senior manager.

Corporate management

The DOF is usually a member of the HEI senior management team and thus has corporate responsibilities for the management and performance of the organisation. In this role the DOF must be able to contribute towards all matters which affect the organisation, including public and press relations, management of change, performance review and strategic development. These matters must not be regarded as the exclusive province of a single senior manager.

Consequently, the DOF requires a wide range of skills and competencies and traditional financial and accounting skills form only one part of the required skill set for a DOF in today's HEI. These can be summarised as:

- technical financial and accounting skills and knowledge;
- knowledge of the higher education sector;
- strategic vision;
- inter-personal and communication skills;
- team working skills.

Staffing of HEI finance departments

The staff of an HEI finance function can be classified into three main types:

- professional accounting staff;
- technical staff;
- support staff.

Professional staff

Professional accounting staff are professionally qualified accountants, usually a member of one of the six UK chartered accounting bodies:

- Chartered Association of Certified Accountants (ACCA);
- Chartered Institute of Public Finance and Accountancy (CIPFA);
- Chartered Institute of Management Accountants (CIMA);
- Institute of Chartered Accountants in England and Wales (ICAEW);
- Institute of Chartered Accountants in Scotland (ICAS);
- Institute of Chartered Accountants in Ireland (ICAI).

It is unusual today to find an HEI DOF who is not a qualified accountant. Beyond that, the numbers of professional accounting staff in HEI finance departments will vary according to the size and type of the organisation involved. At the risk of over-simplifying, it is probably preferable that professional accounting staff in the HEI are, or should be, largely concerned with issues of strategic financial management and the provision of financial information and advice to managers. They should not be involved in the operation or maintenance of routine financial systems and bookkeeping since this would not be making the best use of their skills developed through long and costly training as professional accountants.

Technical staff

Below the professional accounting staff level there will be technical accounting staff. Some of these staff may hold qualifications such as the Association of Accounting Technicians while others may hold their posts by virtue of many years' experience. These staff are often the bedrock of HEI finance departments. They undertake the various finance function activities such as paying the bills, running the payroll, collecting income and maintaining accounting records.

Support staff

Finally, there is a variety of other staff such as clerical officers, secretaries and receptionists termed support staff who undertake important functions.

Strategic trends in the HEI finance function

There are a number of strategic trends in HEIs which will affect the organisation, staffing and working arrangements of HEI finance functions in the medium term. The precise timing of these changes will vary from place to place.

The main trends which we foresee include:

Managerial decentralisation

In many HEIs there has been a strong trend towards managerial decentralisation with greater devolved authority being given to deans and heads of departments and this seems likely to continue. In this environment the finance function will need to undertake two main roles. Firstly, to provide the necessary financial information and advice to departmental managers in running their units. Secondly, to ensure there is adequate financial and managerial control operating in such a decentralised environment These roles are often assisted by outposting certain finance department staff to the department.

Strategic pressures

HEIs are becoming more strategic in order to deal with the ongoing challenges facing the sector. As finance is a key resource there will be an expectation for the finance function to contribute to this strategic agenda by providing information and advice to managers, which has a strategic dimension. As we have seen in earlier chapters, the development and operation of financial models, dealing with a range of scenarios for strategic planning, will be of great relevance.

Commercialisation

There are several particular trends which require HEIs and their finance functions to operate in a more commercial manner than hitherto. Some of these were further emphasised in the HE White Paper and include for example:

- the pressure for increasing links with the business community;
- the need to generate a wide range of third stream income;
- the increased application of outsourcing to the commercial sector;
- increased use of commercial partnerships.

Furthermore, decisions made by an HEI on the level of variable top-up fees it charges will be critical to its future well-being but in making such decisions an HEI will need to consider possible decisions competitor HEIs may make and much 'inside information' will, no doubt, be flowing in the sector. The key implication for the finance function is that financial modelling must be very flexible, speedy but robust. Answers to 'what if' scenarios must be available quickly, and different scenarios routinely run through the model(s).

Thus overall, the finance function will need to ensure it has the necessary skills to operate in a more commercial environment.

Market testing and outsourcing

HEIs have shown an increasing tendency to market test and, possibly, outsource certain services to the private sector. This has two implications for the finance function:

- the finance function will need to provide financial input into any market testing/outsourcing evaluation;
- the finance function will need to consider to what extent it should outsource some of its own activities. The most likely candidates for such market testing are payroll, creditor payments, debtor control and collection and internal audit.

Standards of financial control and accountability

Recent financial scandals in the public and private sectors have increased the emphasis on high standards of financial control and accountability. This is manifested in a number of ways, such as increased emphasis on corporate governance, application of rules on business conduct and improved standards of internal audit.

Cost pressures

Continual cost pressures in service delivery will affect the work and organisation of the entire HEI. Some examples of such cost pressures include:

- shortfalls in funding to cover nationally agreed pay awards;
- additional costs arising from pension provision;
- costs of maintaining the estate and of updating IT and library functions.

The finance function itself will be under pressure to reduce costs and, as an overhead to the main functions of the HEI, may be required to generate a disproportionate level of cost savings, which will need to be generated while maintaining or even improving the quality of services provided by the department. Many finance departments are now being benchmarked which involves comparing their performance with other finance departments in the public and private sector on matters such as:

- cost per invoice paid;
- percentage of manual cheques issued;
- percentage of journal vouchers raised manually.

Organisational change in the HEI finance function

In response to the above trends, we foresee significant changes in the organisation of HEI finance functions. The processing work of finance departments is likely to be radically restructured to allow time to be released which enables DOFs and their senior staff to become more strategically focused.

Organisational arrangements

A number of changes in the organisational arrangements of the traditional HEI finance function will result from the strategic trends referred to above. Not all occur in all finance departments and not all will occur at the same rate. Nevertheless, all are likely to be seen to some extent. The three main changes are:

- *fewer hierarchies of management* – this is a worldwide phenomenon happening in many different types of organisation but which has applicability to HEI finance departments. Often, many middle-management posts do little more than supervise lower-level members of staff and pass information from a lower tier to a higher tier within the organisation. Investment in improved training and development among lower levels of staff and improved internal audit will reduce the need for close supervision of lower-level staff, while substantial investment in IT will facilitate the direct flow of information. The net effect of this will be to reduce the need for middle management posts in finance departments resulting in flatter and leaner organisational structures and lower costs.
- *decentralisation* – we have already discussed the potential decentralisation of certain finance department staff. As a consequence of increasing managerial decentralisation within an HEI, an increasing decentralisation of finance staff roles seems likely to continue.
- *outsourcing* – as already discussed, this could involve certain finance function activities, traditionally done in house, being undertaken by an external contractor.

Increased investment in IT

No function is immune from the impact of IT. There are a number of aspects of the finance function where IT investment can lead to improved services at lower cost. Some examples are:

- *direct input of pay*: where such systems are implemented, payroll data can be directly input by line managers using a computer terminal rather than paper details being sent to a central payroll section for input to the payroll system. This would reduce the number of staff needed in payroll sections.
- *direct payments*: the traditional ordering and payment process is for an HEI to place a paper order with a supplier, for the supplier to supply the

goods/services and issue an invoice and for that invoice to be paid. This is a cumbersome process both in terms of paperwork and staff time. The whole process can be streamlined by investment in modern systems which operate along the following lines:
- once the quantity of goods held in stock falls below a pre-determined re-order level, the system automatically issues an order to a supplier;
- the order is processed by the supplier whose own systems automatically issue the goods;
- the suppliers system's automatically requisition payment for these goods from the HEI's bank account.

For such an approach to work the HEI must have established links with relatively few suppliers and to make the necessary investment in IT. This simplification of ordering and creditor payments processes would lead to staff reductions in the finance and supplies functions.

Case study 10.1   Reorganisation of a finance department

The finance department of Oakdene University has problems. A benchmarking exercise indicated that the costs of its finance department are significantly in excess of comparable institutions. Also, there are concerns about some aspects of departmental performance. Finally, the department is under pressure to provide greater financial support to budget managers in the university as a consequence of a shift towards greater budget delegation. The finance department plans to do a number of things:

- Invest in a new financial accounting and reporting system. Such a system will enable staff in academic and support departments to enter, directly, transaction data such as payment of invoices and payroll data rather then send the data, in paper form, to the finance department for input into the system. The new system will be expensive to implement and has ongoing support costs of several hundred thousand pounds per annum.
- Substantially reduce staff in its payroll and payments section consequent on the development of direct data input by staff in academic and support departments.
- Reorganise the department to enable professional accounting staff to be released from transactional accounting work thus facilitating the provision of greater financial support to managers.
- Improve standards of internal audit by entering into a shared service agreement with another HEI or a contract with a private firm.
- Improve training for staff in the department.

The success in implementing these changes is the key to improving the status and reputation of the finance department in the university.

- *user-friendly financial systems:* investment in financial models and expert systems which can easily be operated by managers may reduce the need for financial analysis and advice from financial managers, leading to a reduction in the numbers and skills base of those financial managers.

All these developments have major implications for financial control, internal audit and financial management in HEIs, but do not produce any insurmountable problems. However, there may be significant capital investment requirements and cultural change issues in the HEI.

Changing skill mix

The various changes described above are likely to lead to significant changes in the staffing of finance departments, as follows:

- *more professional/technical staff* – meeting the challenges of providing more strategic and commercial information in a decentralised management structure, and the need for better financial control in an IT environment, is likely to require a greater range of specialist financial and business skills from more professional and technical staff; linked to this will be greater investment in training and development to enable those staff in the finance department to maintain their skills;
- *less support staff* – the impact of IT and market testing is likely to lead to a lower number of support and clerical staff in finance departments.

As a consequence of these changes, it is likely that future finance departments will have a considerably different skill mix from that at present.

Chapter 11

Improving performance in the HE sector

The finance function contribution

Introduction

In the public sector and the publicly financed sector which incorporates HEIs, there has been a continuous drive, for many years, to improve the performance of the organisations in the particular sector. Although performance improvement is not the sole province of the finance function in the organisation, the finance function often has a critical role to play in many (but not all) aspects of performance improvement.

This is so in an HEI where the finance function can contribute to performance improvement in the organisation. In this chapter we consider what is meant by performance improvement in the HEI context. We then consider the contribution that can be made by the HEI finance function.

What constitutes improved performance

'Performance improvement' in an organisation is a term capable wide interpretation but we suggest that the following might be regarded as performance improvements in the HEI context.

Improvement in the 3Es

The term 3Es is shorthand for economy, effectiveness and efficiency, and in the context of a HEI, each can be regarded as follows:

- **Economy** – this is often referred to as doing things more cheaply. It is concerned with purchasing real resources such as equipment, consumables and staff at the lowest possible cost. Thus, if one HEI pays 5 per cent less for stationery than the other HEI is paying for identical stationery, the former HEI can be said to be more economic.

- **Effectiveness** – this is often referred to as doing the right things. It is concerned with the extent to which an organisation is achieving its own pre-ordained objectives. In an HEI effectiveness could mean the extent to which the organisation is achieving its student recruitment targets. For example, consider two HEIs. If HEI A is much closer to achieving its target objective than HEI B it can be regarded as the more effective. Note, however, that the amount spent in each HEI in pursuing the objective is not considered as this does not form part of effectiveness measurement.
- **Efficiency** – this is probably the most misunderstood and misused term of the 3Es. Basically it is the ratio of outputs achieved (effectiveness) to resource inputs applied. In the above example, efficiency measures would compare how much has been spent in achieving the relative effectiveness in each case.

Improved customer satisfaction

HEIs have a range of different 'customers', the main ones of which might be thought to be: students, businesses and research councils. Many HEIs have formal systems for assessing the degree of satisfaction among their various customers with the services being received. In this way they can identify improvements or reductions in the level of customer satisfaction.

Improved expert assessment

Improvements in performance might be identified and assessed by some form of expert assessment. In the HE sector there are already two forms of such expert assessment and these are:

- the teaching quality assessments undertaken by the QAA;
- the research assessment exercise undertaken by the HE funding councils.

In both assessments the quality of teaching and research in a HEI is assessed by relevant panels of experts.

Improved public standing

Another measure of performance might be the standing or esteem of the institution in the eyes of the general public. This may be related to the national image of the HEI or the local or regional image. In either or both cases this may be assessed by undertaking some form of public opinion poll.

Performance improvement and the role of the finance function

The above discussion indicates how HEI performance may be improved in any number of ways. Clearly, such improvements will require inputs and resources from many different departments and disciplines within the organisation and the role of the finance function will, therefore, be limited to its areas of expertise. Nevertheless, there are many areas where the finance function can make a significant contribution and in some of these areas it may even be seen as the lead function.

In the remainder of this chapter we discuss some of the ways in which the finance function can contribute towards improved organisational performance. The detailed aspects of each of these approaches are discussed more fully in the preceding chapters of the book and this section just aims to bring them together and emphasise the important role that can be played by the finance function in relation to performance improvement. These roles are categorised as follows:

- strategic management of the HEI;
- operational management of the HEI;
- improved financial services.

Strategic management of the HEI

There are a number of strategic areas where a HEI can achieve significant performance improvements and the modern finance function has a major role to play in key areas which are discussed in the following sections.

Organisational reconfiguration

As discussed in Chapter 12 a future trend might be for HEIs to reconfigure the numbers and types of departments and the activities which they have. Such a reconfiguration might be undertaken to resolve some existing financial problems in certain departments or to provide the HEI with a strategic advantage in terms of attracting students or research funding. In either case, it is important that the various proposals developed are subject to robust financial scrutiny to ensure that a reasonable degree of confidence exists that they will produce the expected financial benefits. Too often, proposals are put forward and implemented without any robust financial appraisal, and not surprisingly the proposals fail financially to achieve what was expected of them.

Going further, an HEI may consider whether to remain as a stand-alone organisation or whether it should consider having collaborative arrangements with one or more other HEIs (or even FE colleges) which might possibly result in a full merger. The financial benefits of such can be:

- cost savings resulting from rationalisation of certain activities;
- increased income streams deriving from synergies generated.

Again, the various proposals must undergo robust financial scrutiny to ensure that there is a reasonable degree of confidence that they will produce the expected financial benefits.

Strategy development and appraisal

A robust strategy is a key foundation of organisational success and good performance. As discussed in Chapter 4, this involves identifying various strategic options and subjecting those options to a rigorous strategic and resource feasibility study. Thus a robust financial analysis is key to a robust corporate strategy. This will involve the financial evaluation of strategic options including an assessment of the degree of financial risk posed by each of the options. In Chapter 4 we outlined how the finance function can contribute to this process through the use of such tools as financial benchmarking and financial modelling.

Outsourcing and shared services

Increasingly, HEIs are considering alternatives to the provision of certain services by in-house staff. These alternatives could involve:

- **Outsourcing** – this would involve contracting the provision of certain services to an external organisation such as a private company. Traditionally, a number of HEIs have contracted services such as catering, cleaning and security to the private sector, but recently HEIs have also contracted services such as IT management and internal audit to private companies.
- **Shared service provision** – this would involve two or more HEIs sharing service provision. For example, two or more HEIs might set up a purchasing department which would serve both organisations and for which they would share the running costs. However, some HEIs have also decided to re-insource (take back inhouse) certain services after a period of outsourcing possibly for reasons such as better service standards, greater reliability and lower costs. The true of cost of outsourcing includes a VAT element of 17.5 per cent on top of the basic charge from the provider and this can make an outsourcing option financially unacceptable.

Outsourcing or shared service provision should never be seen as a panacea, however, and

- in some cases outsourcing might be appropriate;
- in other cases continued in-house provision is more appropriate;
- in other case re-insourcing might be more appropriate.

Outsourcing issues can become very emotionally charged and the finance function has a key role to play in subjecting each option to a rigorous analysis of the costs involved, both capital and revenue and assessing the financial risks associated with each option.

Other non-financial issues will also need to be assessed but these fall outside the financial appraisal.

Operational management

The finance function can contribute to improved financial and resource performance in a number of operational areas in an HEI.

Resource allocation and budget setting

In any organisation, financial, human and physical resources are always finite and improved performance can be achieved by a better utilisation of existing resources. This might involve using resources in a different way or transferring resources from one part of the organisation to another.

The key to achieving better resource utilisation in an HEI lies with the resource allocation and budget systems it operates and the finance function has a key role to play in continually improving these processes. Such improvements could involve more appropriate workload measures, better priority setting, improved RAMs, and so no, and is more fully discussed in Chapter 5.

Financial information systems

To manage budgets and to take financially oriented decisions, managers in academic and support departments will require financial information. For maximum effectiveness, it is extremely desirable that this financial information is integrated with information from other systems (e.g., student data systems, estates systems).

In Chapter 5 we discussed the nature and attributes of the financial information that might be required. It is the primary role of the finance function to identify weaknesses in financial information systems (and its links with other systems) and to put forward suggested improvements and evaluate the likely costs and benefits of those developments.

However, any proposed developments in financial information systems must involve extensive user consultation. Many examples can be quoted of financial information systems which involved considerable investment but which failed to meet the needs of users because of inadequate consultation at an early stage.

Financial advice

In an HEI, most budget managers in academic and administrative departments will not be financially trained and may have limited experience of managing budgets and therefore may require financial advice to run their departments effectively. The main source of such advice will be the staff of the finance function. As discussed in Chapter 10, different HEIs will organise their finance functions differently, some having outposted finance staff who may be located in the departments they serve. In other HEIs, the finance function will be centralised and so advice and support will come from the central department. In either case, the finance staff providing the advice and support can play a major role in improving managerial performance in the HEI.

Improved financial services

There are a number of basic finance areas where the finance function can make a contribution to improved performance.

Improved financial transaction services

These will include the following:

- payroll;
- payments;
- income collection;
- provision of financial information and advice.

There is often considerable scope for improving performance in these areas and examples could include:

- faster services in terms of prompter expense payments, quicker response to queries, and so on;
- lower transaction costs such as cost per invoice paid and cost per payroll transaction;
- improved satisfaction among customers of financial services such as employees and creditors;
- greater flexibility in providing services.

In Chapter 4, we discussed the use of benchmarking as a means of identifying potential performance improvements. Financial services, being a generic activity, is an area where there is scope for HEIs to try and benchmark them against other public and private sector organisations as well as other HEIs.

Improved financial control

Weaknesses in financial control in an organisation can have two negative implications:

- They can lead to waste of and loss of scarce resources (e.g., overpayment of bills, inefficient procurement, poor staff utilisation).
- If made public, such weaknesses can impact on the public image of the organisation. If this is serious it could impact on the attitude towards the HEI of potential research funders and even potential students.

Thus the finance function should continually review systems of financial control to ensure that they are appropriate and effective in today's rapidly changing environment. This is not always done and there are examples of HEIs whose systems of financial control are weak and have not been reviewed or modified for many years. Staff in the organisation (particularly academic staff) should realise that effective systems of financial control are not a bureaucratic burden but are an essential requirement for effective management and the maintenance of public confidence in the organisation.

Improved financial awareness and knowledge

Many finance staff in HEIs would probably be critical of the attitudes of academic managers and staff to issues of financial control and financial management while many academic managers and staff are no doubt critical of finance departments as being bureaucratic.

Whatever the truth of this matter, a key role of the finance function should be to improve financial awareness and financial skills among academic and non-academic managers and staff in the HEI. It is for the individual HEI to decide how this should be done and it could involve any number of approaches such as:

- the development of briefing papers on HE financial issues;
- the delivery of internal training courses on HE finance issues for non-finance staff in the HEI;
- the provision of financial information about the HEI on the organisation's Intranet;
- pro-actively meeting with non-finance staff to promote financial awareness.

It is probably important not to set too high an aspiration level as it would be naïve to expect all staff in the HEI to become enthusiastic about financial matters overnight. The key thing is to aim for ongoing improvements across the organisation.

Efficient tax arrangements

Most forms of taxation impinge upon HEIs and it is in the interests of each HEI to manage its tax affairs to reduce taxation to a minimum and thereby maximise funding available to the HEI. It is a primary role of the finance function to advise on tax issues in the HEI. Separate considerations apply to corporation tax, capital gains tax, VAT and, where appropriate, to stamp duty.

HEIs, as charities, bear no tax on income when it is used for the purposes of the charity and under section 505 of the Income and Corporation Taxes Act 1988 rental income and a number of defined trading profits are not subject to tax. However, trading profits outside those defined are liable to tax and hence the practice of establishing trading subsidiaries and covenanting/gift-aiding the profits to the HEI has become the norm in the HE sector. The distinction between trading and non-trading income is a fundamental concept in respect of corporation tax.

Again, capital gains tax is not charged if the gain is applied for charitable purposes, this dispensation being included in section 256 of the Taxation of Chargeable Gains Act 1992.

VAT is probably the most complicated tax which affects HEIs and the one about which there is the most uncertainty. HEIs will make supplies of goods and services which may be taxable at standard or zero rate, exempt or possibly completely outside the scope of VAT. Generally, HEIs pay, and are unable to recover, VAT on purchases but can recover VAT paid on costs incurred in making taxable supplies – those on which VAT is charged. It is therefore in the interest of a HEI to ensure that it can calculate the VAT it incurs on such taxable supplies. A 'partial exemption' method has been that most commonly used to reach agreement with HM Customs and Excise. This is based on agreeing a percentage of taxable expenditure to total expenditure and this percentage is then used to calculate the amount of VAT which is recoverable. VAT can also impact adversely on estate projects and transactions should be carefully structured to minimise its impact as the amount involved can be very large. VAT will also be payable to providers of outsourced services which should provide the in-house service with a significant cost advantage when evaluating options. Stamp duty can be of relevance in estate transactions and many of the projects relating to the estate, such as those outsourcing student residences, are legitimately structured to minimise the stamp duty payable.

From the above it is clear that effective tax planning is a must for any HEI and given the complexities of taxation law it is essential for an HEI to retain the services of a specialist who can advise proactively on the management of its tax-planning arrangements. Many HEIs will appoint separate advisors for different aspects of taxation, with the choice of the VAT advisor often being the most critical one.

Chapter 12

Future trends in the HE sector

The financial implications

Introduction

The HE sector has become increasingly complex in recent years, and at the same time the influence of Government has become more evident. These two themes were highlighted in the Government's White Paper 'The future of higher education' published in January 2003. The White Paper was open for consultation until 30 April 2003 but only relatively minor changes were made following this process. The White Paper clearly set out Government thinking on HE, and more overtly than ever before stressed **its** view that HE could not exist in an academic vacuum but must relate to the world of business and the community. Following this, in March 2003, HEFCE produced a Strategic Plan for the HE Sector in England which took into account the White Paper. Consultation on this plan closed on 27 May 2003.

The Government's White Paper was aimed at ensuring that HE in the UK remain both competitive internationally in academic and research terms, and play a fundamental part in maintaining the UK as a major economic force. It therefore analysed various weaknesses in HE in the UK and proposed methods of correcting such perceived weaknesses. Many of the proposals were inter-linked and all are likely to have some impact on financial management and control in the HE sector.

This chapter aims to consider future trends in the HE sector and their financial implications. Some of these trends are driven by White Paper proposals but others have other sources. The future trends are discussed under the following main headings:

- Longer-term funding trends;
- Student fees;
- Student finance arrangements;
- Teaching and learning;
- Research;

- HE and business;
- Partnership arrangements;
- Organisational and sector re-configurations;
- HEI resourcing patterns;
- Student finance arrangements;
- Improved HEI management practices.

Longer-term funding trends

In this section we consider some longer-term funding trends regarding the HE sector. This effectively sets the financial context in which the other issues can be considered.

Governmental funding for HEIs

The longer-term governmental funding trends for the HE sector are outlined in the HE White Paper. At face value the White Paper suggests that HE resources will grow at an annual rate of 6 per cent per annum in real terms (10 per cent in cash terms) during the period. This indicates a substantial level of growth but this growth projection conceal a number of trends as follows:

- it combines growth in recurring funds and growth in non-recurring (capital) funds;
- it includes funds for student support which accrue to the student and not HEIs;
- there are considerable variations in growth rates between different funding strands;
- there are different funding trends for different funding bodies;
- the distribution of the growth in funding will not be evenly spread across the sector; different funding streams will have different degrees of dispersion;
- different mechanisms will be used to distribute the different funding sources.

Each of the above issues is discussed further below. The figures shown are calculated after excluding the effects of inflation and thus they represent real growth. Any shortfall in funding as a consequence of, for example, nationally negotiated pay awards being greater than the inflation allowance reduce this growth. Thus, individual HEIs should assess these figures carefully and judge how they might be affected individually as the sector wide results can be misleading.

Recurrent/non-recurrent trends

Excluding student support (since this accrues to students and not to HEIs) the average annual growth in recurrent funding (3.8 per cent) is significantly lower than the average annual growth in non-recurrent (capital) funding (31.2 per cent). Most of the capital funds are research based and will probably accrue to the research intensive institutions.

Trends in recurrent funding

If we consider the different elements of recurrent funding, Table 12.1 shows the following trends.

Table 12.1 White Paper growth projections – recurrent and non-recurrent funding analysis

	Base level 2002/03 (£ million)	Average annual growth in funding (£ million)	Average annual growth rate (%)
HEFCE funded research	990	37	3.7
OST funded research	664	58	8.8
Knowledge transfer	62	13	21.2
Human resources	110	48	44.0
Teaching excellence	0	21	n/a
Expansion	0	9	n/a
Access/Widening Participation	86	10	12.2
Management/ Leadership	15	5	33.8
Other Teaching and Learning	3678	9	0.23

Source: Analysis by Authors

Magnitude

- significant growth in research funding;
- substantially greater growth in OST research funding compared to HEFCE research funding;
- substantial growth in knowledge transfer funding from a low base;
- substantial growth in earmarked funds for Teaching and Learning, from a low base;
- limited growth in general teaching and learning funding.

Dispersion

It is clear that the various stream of funding will not be distributed equally across HEIs. We have tried to suggest the degree of dispersion of the different funding streams across the sector. This is shown in Figure 12.1.

Funding stream	Degree of dispersion	Likely distribution pattern
Research	Narrow	High quality research institutions only
Knowledge transfer	Medium	HEIs with a track record
Access/WP	Medium	Post-92 universities
Human resources	Wide	All HEIs
Teaching excellence	Medium	Those HEIs who can demonstrate excellence
Expansion	Medium	All HEIs but may involve considerable franchising to FE Colleges
Management and leadership	Medium	Innovative projects only
Mainstream T&L	Wide	All HEIs

Figure 12.1 *White Paper growth dispersion*

Resource allocation mechanisms

The various funding streams will be distributed by different mechanisms and this will impact differently on HEIs. For example, we would suggest the following:

- research – the use of competitive bidding (OST) and the use of RAE scores (HEFCE);
- scheme submissions – for example, knowledge transfer;
- funding formula – general T&L;
- performance criteria – for example, teaching excellence.

Student fees

The most fundamental aspect of the White Paper was the extension of the concept of students paying towards the benefits they receive from HE. Tuition fees when introduced in 1998 at £1,000 (2003/04 – £1,125) met approximately 25 per cent of the overall average costs of a degree. (The tuition fee would have met 20 per cent of some course costs and 40 per cent of others.)

The White Paper extended the above concept and linked this with the need to increase funding in HE as a whole to keep UK HE competitive in international terms. The White Paper accepted that underfunding had taken place, that a drop of 36 per cent in funding per student occurred between 1989 and 1997, and that there is a maintenance backlog and an annual underfunding of maintenance. It also argued that those with an HE qualification are substantially better off, to the tune of 50 per cent, than non-graduates. In addition to the two 'givens' of underfunding of HE and that those who are HE qualified are financially advantaged, the White Paper developed a proposal to try and answer all the problems by one mechanism. The proposal, which is revolutionary for a UK HE system, was:

- from 2006 to allow HEIs to set their own UG tuition fees of up to £3,000;
- to eliminate any up-front fee payments; the Graduate Contribution Scheme will recover the fees once students are earning over £15,000 a year;
- to continue to pay the first £1,100 (2002/03) of the fee of those from low-income families;
- from 2004, to provide a grant for such students from lower-income families of £1,000 towards maintenance costs. This is in addition to full student loans which will continue to be available for all, although the repayment level will also be raised to an income of £15,000 a year.

The Graduate Contribution Scheme will require payments through the tax system of 9 per cent of the graduate's income over the threshold, initially set at the £15,000 a year. Given the Treasury's long-held opposition to hypothecated taxes, many HEIs are fearful that the additional funding raised by 'top-up' fees levied – £1,900 on a fee of £3,000 (2002/03 price levels) – would simply be taken by Government. Although the timing and means by which the top-up fees are returned to individual HEIs is unclear from the White Paper, paragraph 7.43 appears to confirm that such additional tuition fees will be received by the individual HEIs. The paragraph anticipates that students will expect better tuition and services for their increased personal contributions and therefore HEIs will need this funding to deliver these expectations. It then explicitly states that the Government will provide HEIs with the fee levels they have set and later recover these fees from students.

The effect of the introduction of these variable top-up fees is difficult to assess and to many older universities a £3,000 fee, implying an increase of only £1,900 per student, is completely unacceptable. Tuition fees of £10,000 plus a year have been quoted as being desirable by some of the more prestigious universities. HEIs will also have to decide whether to differentiate the fees in relation to the costs incurred or possibly to the potential earnings capabilities of different courses. It is also possible that every HEI will set tuition fees at £3,000 and the 'market' factor would therefore be largely eliminated. It is also possible that some HEIs will set fees at £0 in certain unpopular subjects to encourage recruitment.

The complexity of the possible UG tuition fee scenarios has one further element – the Access Regulator. The White Paper proposes that HEIs wishing to charge differentiated fees will have suitable access arrangements in place. These arrangements will be monitored by the Access Regulator who will be able to apply financial penalties if such agreements are not operated as agreed, or withdraw approval for the differential fees. This last possibility is of great concern to the sector as it could impact on the freedom of HEIs to decide their own tuition fee levels.

Student finance arrangements

In HE, prior to 1997 no fees were chargeable to full-time undergraduate students (fees were chargeable to their local authority), although fees were chargeable to post-graduate students. In addition, full-time undergraduate students were eligible for means-tested maintenance grants although the real value of such grants had declined substantially over a period of time. To compensate for the declining value of grants, undergraduate students obtained loans or income from other sources.

In 1998, the Government initiated substantial changes in the arrangements for student finance which involved three main elements:

- Following the recommendations of the Dearing Committee, the introduction of a flat-rate fee, across all HEIs and all subject areas, for each undergraduate student. Students whose parental income falls below a threshold limit would be exempt such fees.
- The complete abolition of maintenance grants.
- The enhancement of the student loans system.

It is often argued that these policy changes have had a detrimental effect on the recruitment of students from poorer families. Unlike students from middle-class families whose fees and living costs would be met, in full or in part, by their parents, students from poorer families would have to rely upon such loans and the possibility of large loans being outstanding on graduation might deter many students from entering higher education.

The Government has now, effectively but not explicitly, recognised the error of these policies and at the time of writing it seems likely that some form of means tested maintenance grant for poorer students will be introduced although undergraduate fees will remain in place with exemptions for poorer students. In addition, the student loans system will remain in place.

However, this policy has to be considered alongside the development, discussed above, of allowing HEIs to levy top-up fees on undergraduate students. Although the re-introduction of student maintenance grants might encourage students from poorer families to enter higher education they might, effectively, be prevented from entering the more prestigious universities unless top-up fees are waived for them or some alternative source of finance (such as bursaries or scholarships) can be found.

Teaching and learning

Expansion of the HE sector

Arguably this is the flagship policy for the HE sector over the next few years. Underpinning the policy is the Government's stated aim that by 2010, 50 per cent of 18–30 year olds are to have participated in higher education. This is seen as relating to the needs of the economy for a skilled and educated workforce but international evidence from OECD suggests little correlation between the per capita GDP of a country and the proportion of GDP it spends on HE.

This increased participation may not mean enrolling for a full-time traditional degree but might involve part-time and shorter-course study, including that of foundation degrees. This is a challenging aim which implies increasing student numbers by some 35 per cent over current levels and recruiting an additional 350,000 students. In considering this policy objective there are two aspects to consider:

Demand-side issues

For these policy objectives to be achieved there must be:

- large increases in the numbers of students recruited into higher education;
- improvements in the rate of student retention and thus the numbers of students completing programmes of HE.

It is often argued that the market for traditional student recruitment, namely the school-leaver with 2 or 3 A levels, is largely saturated. Hence substantial growth in student numbers can only be achieved by recruiting students from 'non-traditional' sources. This approach, often referred to as the widening participation policy, implies recruiting students from sources such as:

- mature students;
- students with vocational qualifications rather than A levels;
- returners to work;
- ethnic minorities.

To access these additional students from non-traditional backgrounds, HEIs are having to adopt new approaches to recruitment such as building stronger relationships or compacts with local schools and FE colleges to encouraging students to progress from schools/colleges into higher education.

In addition to recruiting more students, HEIs also have to take actions to help those students to complete their course of study. Consequently, improvements need to be made in areas such as personal counselling, remedial teaching and student services.

Case study 12.1   Costs of widening participation

Newchester University is a post-1992 university based in a large city where there is another prestigious pre-1992 university. In recent years NU has struggled to attract sufficient numbers of full-time undergraduate students and so has concentrated on the provision of part-time courses and the recruitment of students from non-traditional backgrounds. To achieve this it has had to commit resources to:

- various forms of local marketing (e.g., posters, flyers, shops) but also the development of links with local schools and colleges; the latter has involved existing staff committing unknown amounts of time to these new activities;
- the development of course provision tailored towards local needs including the extension of modularised courses;
- the provision of enhanced learning support and student services to encourage retention of students from non-traditional backgrounds.

The university believes there are significant resource implications associated with these activities but it has not been in a position to assess what these might be.

As it is following the Government's widening participation policy, NU aims to continue to try and recruit more part-time students and students from non-traditional backgrounds. However, the absence of information about the cost implications inhibits the accuracy of financial planning in the university.

Supply-side issues

The other side of the coin is the supply side and the HE sector must expand if it is to meet the increased demand which it hopes will materialise. This could involve any combination of the following options:

- expansion of student numbers at existing HE campuses;
- construction of new campuses for existing HEIs;
- creation of new HEIs;
- expansion of HE delivery within the FE sector through partnerships and franchising;
- expansion of e-learning at existing HEIs;
- expansion of distance learning at existing HEIs.

At the time of writing the supply side strategy for delivering the additional student numbers is unclear but there is a clear expectation that much of the additional HE provision will be delivered by FE colleges, particularly through the Foundation Degree route. Whatever combination of the above approaches is eventually adopted a number of financial implications arise related to the above policy. In summary these include:

- **Capital expenditure** – this would be required for the construction of any new HEIs or new campuses and for the expansion of the sector's distance and e-learning capacity.

- **Student teaching and support costs** – additional expenditure will be needed both to teach and provide support to substantially increased student numbers.
- **Curriculum development costs** – substantial expenditure is likely on curriculum development.
- **Recruitment costs** – additional costs are likely to be necessary to recruit students from non-traditional backgrounds.

Many in the HE sector also claim that substantial additional costs are incurred in teaching and supporting students from non-traditional backgrounds which are well in excess of those for traditional students.

At the time of writing the magnitude of these expansion-costs cannot be estimated with any degree of certainty because of major uncertainties concerning the policy of expansion. For example,

- Will higher educational provision be delivered at FE colleges or HEIs? Evidence suggests that the unit costs of provision (for the same or similar HE courses) is higher in HEIs than FE colleges.
- Any under-utilised capacity in HEIs will enable them to absorb some growth in student numbers with limited increases in costs. What is the extent of this under-utilised capacity?
- What is the scope for efficiency savings in HEIs?
- What are the cost implications of teaching and supporting students from non-traditional backgrounds?
- What new buildings and equipment will be required and how will this be financed?

Widening access to HE

Many, including most of the HE sector, have been puzzled since the introduction of tuition fees at the apparent inconsistency between aiming to increase participation in HE among economically disadvantaged groups and the deterrent effect on a debt-averse part of the population of introducing those fees. The White Paper of January 2003 appeared to recognise this anomaly in its section on fair access by reintroducing maintenance grants for students from low-income families, defined as families with household incomes under £10,000 a year. This maintenance grant is to be accompanied by changes in tuition fee arrangements which tilts the HE system towards a market-based system and this could have fundamental implications for the whole sector including for financial management and control.

Other proposals for improving access generally relate to improving administrative practices, measuring a HEI's performance on the admission of specific socio-economic classes against set benchmarks and on drop-out rates. The HEFCE has proposed various targets for monitoring these in its Strategic Plan for 2003/08.

Increased overseas students

For many years most HEIs have actively sought to recruit students from non-EU overseas countries to increase revenue. For such recruitment, HEIs can charge whatever fee levels they consider students will pay as they are not constrained by the standard undergraduate fee set for home students. However, such recruitment tends to be focused in a limited number of subject areas such as IT and business related areas.

Although clearly an important activity and a potential source of funds, such overseas recruitment has a number of risks which need to be taken into account. These risks include:

- economic downturn in overseas markets can result in a sudden drop in recruitment;
- substantial bad debts from overseas students who cannot or will not pay their fees;
- increased, and often hidden, costs associated with overseas students in such areas as student welfare and English Language tuition;
- a tendency to skew course provision too much towards business and IT related courses at the expense of other areas of activity.

However, the focus on recruiting overseas students will continue and most HEIs probably have plans to increase the numbers of such students. Greater emphasis has been given to this activity following statements by the Prime Minister encouraging HEIs to increase recruitment of such students. The possible introduction of variable top-up fees for home students would reduce, but possibly not remove, the financial attractiveness of recruiting overseas students.

Teaching and learning standards and methods

The Government wishes to ensure that teaching and learning standards are maintained or improved and a number of relatively minor specific financial inducements were proposed in the HE White Paper. However, the most fundamental part of this section of the White Paper was that which stressed that the California State University system delivered excellent teaching without also having a research-based objective. This has been used to support the Government's view that T and R can be separated in many HEIs without damaging teaching and learning excellence.

Most HEIs are investing significant sums in various forms of teaching and learning technologies. To some extent this investment will involve the purchase of various sorts of audio-visual equipment, computers, and so on, but investment is also being made in new learning technologies. Although these various technologies are based around different models of teaching and learning, a key theme involves student-centred learning. This could involve individual students having a personal web page on the institution's Intranet, and material such as timetables, course notes and assessment exercises could be placed on these web pages. Ultimately, once copyright issues have been resolved, digitised versions of key textbooks could also be placed on individual web pages.

There are significant resource implications in such developments of student-centred learning:

- **Personal computers** – under such an approach all students must be able to access the IT networks of the HEI either by PCs based at workspaces or via PCs operating remotely from the institution. This will require significant investment in PCs as it seems unlikely that a HEI will be able to insist that potential students should own their own PCs. This would clearly be discriminatory and would probably work against widening HE participation to non-traditional groups.
- **IT infrastructure** – an HEIs IT infrastructure will require significant investment in capital and running costs. A major reason will be the need to upgrade networks and servers to cope with the increased volume of PC users described above.
- **Teaching staff** – this is an area where a considerable degree of uncertainty and contentious debate exists and it appears to be far too early to make any assessment of the effects of student-centred learning on teaching staff numbers. However, the shift towards student-centred learning, and greater self-learning by students, could have any number of effects in relation to teaching staff. For example, it could mean:
  - fewer teaching staff will be needed for the same number of students;
  - the same number of teaching staff will be able to teach a greater number of students;
  - the same numbers of teaching staff will be able to teach the same number of students but will be able to devote more time to personal coaching and counselling; this would be important in relation to non-traditional students;
  - there would be no change in the numbers of teaching staff for the same volume of students.
- **Teaching accommodation** – a shift towards student-centred learning and self-learning could have significant implications for the volume and type of teaching accommodation. There could be a substantial reduction in the number of large lectures given (in lecture theatres) and an increase in the numbers of tutorials (in small rooms). Thus there may need to be significant investment in the construction or alteration of existing buildings.

Research

Research is a key activity of HE and most HEIs undertake some research. However, the bulk of research activity and funding is already concentrated in a relatively small number of universities. Research (particularly in the science and technology fields) is seen by the Government as an important contributor to the economic health and development of the UK economy. However, there is clearly some concern in government circles that the research output of universities is not sufficiently focused on the needs of the country and the economy. The analysis in the HE White Paper indicates that competitors such as the USA, Japan and Canada are increasing research expenditure and that the UK will need to do so to remain competitive. Such expenditure relates to both infrastructure and staffing. The White Paper analysis also highlights that international comparisons show that a number of countries such as the USA, Germany, the Netherlands, China and India either concentrate, or are planning to concentrate basic research on a limited number of HE sites. In the USA research and research degrees are only undertaken in 200 of the 1,600 institutions which provide four-year HE. Hence, one can anticipate certain changes in various aspects of HEI research including the following:

Profile and concentration

Research funding is already highly concentrated with approximately 75 per cent of HEFCE and research council funding being allocated to just 25 HEIs (16 per cent of total HEIs). The HE White Paper takes this specialisation a step further by stating that it proposes that non-research intensive HEIs will be encouraged to concentrate on the non-research parts of their mission although, as has already been noted, funded research is already concentrated in a fairly small number of HEIs. Thus a further concentration can be anticipated. Nationally the above approach may seem sensible until it is viewed against the policy in operation since 1992. That policy has encouraged all HEIs to undertake research and has encouraged them to enter into the RAE. The sector view has very much been that a 'proper' university needs to undertake research to achieve academic credibility and to inform teaching. This is not, however, a view necessarily shared by HE in the USA. So what are the likely implications for HE finance of an increasing concentration of research in fewer institutions? There will be short- and longer-term consequences. In the short term research staff may be on contracts for which funding is removed, as has already happened following the 2001 RAE. Hence there will be increased financial pressures on such institutions. The reduction in research might discourage individuals from applying for academic posts which might ultimately influence course profiles. In the longer term it is likely to lead to greater segmentation in HE with different tiers of HEIs and possibly the grouping together of certain HEIs with FECs for specific purposes, as outlined in other parts of the White Paper. Therefore, there is likely to be a flow of funding to research-intensive universities and a restructuring of HEIs into different tiers as a result of the current proposals. In financial management terms, those HEIs not undertaking basic research will need to decide whether to undertake more applied/commercial research to support their research infrastructures or whether to withdraw from research activities. The loss of funding would necessitate a review of the financial position of the HEI.

Collaboration

Most types of scientific and technological research are expensive and involve large-scale expenditure on equipment. Moreover, equipment usually gets increasingly expensive as time goes by. Thus it does not seem sustainable in the longer term for identical scientific research equipment to be replicated in many different HEIs, and there is likely to be pressure for improved collaboration and sharing of such equipment between researchers from a number of HEIs. It should be noted that such collaboration is already widespread (both nationally and internationally) in such areas of research as astronomy and particle physics where the equipment costs are prohibitively expensive.

Targeting

For most HEIs, the two main sources of income are the research funding provided by HEFCE and various research grants provided by the research councils. Although the research council income can be targeted towards certain subject areas and even certain specific types of research the HEFCE funding cannot easily be targeted. Even if funding decisions are taken to reward those HEIs with high-performing research departments, the nature of internal resource allocation and budgeting mechanisms in HEIs mean that there is no guarantee that those rewards will accrue to the departments who have earned them. Thus it seems likely (and the HE White Paper makes a start on this) that in distributing future growth in Government research funding, such funding is likely to be allocated via the research councils rather than through HEFCE.

Relationships between HE and business

The Government emphasises the value to the UK of the HE sector and the White Paper states that in 1999/2000 HEIs were responsible for generating nearly £35 billion of income and employing over 560,000 FTE jobs. However, links between HEIs and business are not universally strong and there is seen to be considerable room for improvement in several areas.

Knowledge transfer

The most obvious impact for HE finance is the allocation of additional funding to the HEIF (Higher Education Innovation Fund). Total HEIF funding from all sources will increase in cash terms from £62 million in 2002/03 to £104 million in 2005/06. The theme of working with partners is emphasised by the intention of bringing RDAs into the collaborative discussions and their role will be augmented from 2004/05. The HEIF is aimed at assisting in knowledge transfer and innovation, and the non-research-intensive HEIs are seen as being an integral element of the process of knowledge transfer as, for example, they often provide consultancy services to local companies. Other innovative projects would qualify for funding from this source and a number of HEIs have developed incubator units to assist inventors/innovators to develop their ideas to the company formation stage.

Knowledge Exchange

The Knowledge Exchange concept is a distinctive part of this complex set of business inter-relationships. Funding is being provided to enable two-way communication processes to be established between less research-intensive institutions to enable best practice to be identified and knowledge of it shared. Around 20 Knowledge Exchanges will be established with funding of up to £500,000 each for five years. Again there will be an obvious financial impact for those attracting this funding, but this might well be offset by the complexities of managing such Exchanges and the relationships they generate.

Regional partnerships

The third leg of the business-relationship objective is the integration of RDAs into the outreach work of HEIs for the benefit to the regional economy. RDAs are being encouraged to become involved in the development of New Technology Centres announced in the Government's 2001 White Paper on innovation, enterprise and skills. Two are to be established in each region to provide specialist ICT and high-tech education and HEIs, FECs, RDAs and business are seen as partners in such activities. The Government also considers that HE has social and cultural roles to play in the community and is seeking ways of developing their role in this direction. The overall implications for financial management and control of all these business and community related objectives is to significantly increase the complexity of financial management and control in HEIs. The additional workload will be out of proportion to the additional direct funding received by the HEI, but over a period it is to be hoped that the non-public funding proportion of an HEI's income will increase significantly as a result of such initiatives. The finance director will need to be outwardly-focused and an effective networker to help the HEI maximise the benefits from such relationships.

Developing skills in the workforce

An obvious link to knowledge transfer is the up-skilling of the population and workforce, and the Government is anxious to increase the supply of graduates with industry-related skills. The two-year foundation degree linked closely to employer needs is seen as a way both of providing HE to those not wanting to study for a three-year degree and of providing an immediate benefit to the economy. The theme of 'developing the workforce' is a constant one in the

White Paper. The intention is to fund such foundation courses in FECs, with collaboration taking place with HEIs. This will immediately alter the dynamics and financial pattern of the HE sector.

The Lambert Report

An important report was commissioned in November 2002, by the Chancellor of the Exchequer, from Richard Lambert, a former editor of the *Financial Times*, on ways of improving collaboration between business and HE. The report reviewed:

- the benefit to both sectors of increased links, how to promote these links and the identification of barriers to such links;
- how national, regional and local links can be supported by RDAs and Sector Skills Councils to produce economic benefits;
- how to develop existing best practice;
- how businesses can improve their communications with the sector and be more attractive to graduates, especially in technological areas;
- incentives to encourage R&D by tax credits, and so on;
- business views on governance, management and leadership in HEIs and their effectiveness in delivering the desired benefits for business and the economy.

The report was published in December 2003 with the general theme that links between HE and business had improved greatly in recent years but that there was still considerable scope for improvement Some of the key recommendations are set out below under the chapter headings in which they occur.

- **Demand for research from business** – the main challenge is seen as raising the demand from business for R&D which is low compared with that of many competitors. A number of proposals are made regarding new or enhanced networks which could help achieve this objective and a recommended priority is the need to identify SMEs which do not undertake R&D work. Better publicity of R&D tax credits within industry and better marketing of the TCS scheme is also recommended.
- **Knowledge transfer** – the review recommends that third-stream funding to help promote knowledge transfer should be substantial and permanent and allocated to assist long-term planning of third-stream activities. The report supports the recommendations of Sir Gareth Roberts and the CBI that such funding should increase to £150 million a year in England. Model contracts for IP are also recommended to simplify communications between HE and business.
- **IP and technology transfer** – the review considers that the ownership of IP and its exploitation should be reviewed in order to facilitate an increase in third-stream income. The review also considers that there has been too much emphasis on developing HE spinout companies at the expense of developing licensing agreements with industry.

- **Regional issues** – a greater emphasis for English RDAs to assist in establishing industry/business links with HEIs is recommended, and it is also recommended that RDAs should move away from job creation schemes to more value-added activities such as collaborative R&D projects with HEIs.
- **Funding university research** – the review is conscious of other reviews taking place into research activities in HEIs but has some reservations about the existing dual support system for research which tends to polarise and standardise types of research activity. The review believes that local SMEs will not necessarily be able to obtain benefit from working with geographically remote HEIs. An international table of leading research universities is also recommended.
- **Management, governance and leadership** – the governance processes are seen as too cumbersome in much of HE and this is not helped by overlarge governing bodies (a maximum board size of 25 members is recommended) and too many regulations. Management is seen in many cases as un-coordinated and the earmarking of major income streams reduces management flexibility. The review sets out a possible code of governance for HEIs for further discussion and also recommends how HEIs can assess their effectiveness by periodic reviews which involve their major stakeholders.
- **Skills and people** – The review assesses that the quality of graduates from HE is generally acceptable to industry but recommends possible improvements. As its last recommendation (8.3) it suggests that HEFCE should include the views of employers and public and voluntary sectors when finalising its teaching funding model and should not rely only on historical cost data. HEFCE should also assess whether HE is producing graduates in subjects which match national economic needs.

Partnership arrangements

A key future policy trend for the HE sector is the development of enhanced partnerships between HEIs and a number of other organisations. There are a number of possible aspects to this which might be mentioned:

Partnerships for progression

This is a major policy plank in the objective of increased participation in HE. It would involve local and regional partnerships between; HEIs, FE colleges, schools, learning and skills Councils, local education authorities, and so on, in order to develop comprehensive strategies for increasing HE participation.

Regional development

As already noted, this would involve partnership arrangements between HEIs and their local RDAs as a means of promoting local economic development.

Research

This could involve partnership arrangements between HEIs and other research organisations in the public, private and charitable sectors as a means of maximising the quantity and quality of research output in certain areas and improving efficiency in the use of expensive research resources. Maintenance and development of these partnership arrangements often has significant resource implications for the HEI which may well impact more on the use of staff time than on costs.

Organisational and sector reconfigurations

Over the next few years, changes can be anticipated in the configuration of individual HEIs, and, to some degree, in the HE sector as a whole. We would anticipate that one driver for these changes will be the financial problems being faced by many HEIs in the country. The main aspects of this are as follows:

HEI reconfigurations

Individual HEIs may undertake certain internal organisational reconfigurations as follows:

- **Rationalisation of activities** – certain HEIs will make strategic decisions to specialise in certain areas of activity and two particular aspects of such specialisation might involve the following:
  - a decision to rationalise certain subjects or curricular areas;
  - a decision to specialise further certain aspects of research.

  Changes in student perceptions and employment prospects have meant that some subject areas in HEIs have had difficulty in recruiting sufficient students. Other changes in the research field might also mean that the same departments are struggling to earn sufficient research income. Such departments, therefore, appear financially non-viable in the short and longer term and many HEIs are having to consider whether such discrete and traditional departments can continue to exist. A consequence of such decisions will be the rationalisation of the current range of activities with the consequent impact on the resource base and organisational structure of the HEI.

- **Rationalisation of sites** – many HEIs operate from multi-site campuses often with large distances between sites. Often some of the outlying sites are under-utilised, expensive to operate and not fit for purpose. Thus an HEI may rationalise its estate and concentrate on a smaller number of sites. However, such an approach must be undertaken cautiously. There are often political and community pressures against site closures and the closure of certain sites may affect HEI student recruitment.

Case study 12.2   Organisational reconfiguration of an HEI

Blankshire University is a prestigious and research-intensive university. Within the university there are a small number of science and technology departments which, in line with national trends, are having severe student recruitment problems and thus are projected to generate substantial financial deficits over the next few years. Furthermore, the overall financial outlook of the university is not good and financial deficits of around £3 million per annum are being predicted over the next few years. Thus the financial deficits of these science departments are not sustainable in the longer term.

It is not felt that these departments can resolve their financial problems individually and so a series of departmental mergers is being considered. One such merger would involve science and engineering departments which have combined financial deficits of £1.7 million. It is estimated that merger of the two departments could produce cost savings of some £0.7 million due to reductions in the numbers of support staff and some academic staff. Hence to reduce the magnitude of the combined financial deficit below the current £1.7 million it would be necessary for the combined department to supplement these cost savings by a further £1 million in additional income generation. This additional income could be derived from a combination of teaching income, research income or other income. Thus the key to the merits of merger is to identify whether the synergies create by the merger will enable the merged department to generate this additional £1 million income in a way that the separate departments cannot.

Institutional collaborations and mergers

In many parts of the UK there can be two, three, four or more HEIs within the same city or region. Such a concentration suggests the possibility of duplication of effort and, not surprisingly, HEIs are being encouraged to collaborate more with each other to make better use of public funds and ultimately to merge. However, care is needed. Firstly, experience from other sectors has shown that often the scope for cost savings through collaboration and merger is over-estimated. More often than not the main benefits of merger come from the creation of synergies which can lead, in turn, to new streams of income. Secondly, unlike mergers of FECs, potential mergers of HEIs should not just look at teaching synergies but should also consider potential synergies in research and third-stream activities. Thirdly, collaborations and mergers in the HE sector are strongly inhibited by the culture of status. The academic staff of older HEIs are often resistant to merger with a newer HEI since they see this as a dilution of their academic excellence. Whatever the merits of or errors in such an argument, the reality is that many of the possible mergers that could take place within UK cities would necessitate an old–new merger arrangement. This is likely to act as a severe brake on such mergers taking place unless the financial position of the older institution is so dire that merger is the only realistic option.

HEI resourcing patterns

Over the next few years it can be expected that there will be considerable change in the pattern of resources employed by HEIs. Some of these changes will be merely the continuation of past trends while others will eventually become new trends. Furthermore, it must be strongly emphasised that the magnitude of these trends will vary substantially between HEIs and in some they may not even be discernible. Some of the trends which can be envisaged are as follows:

Diversification of income base

Many HEIs already have a very varied income bases with substantial streams of income from HE funding councils, research councils, commerce and industry, and so on. However, other HEIs will rely predominantly on funds from HE funding councils. Most HEIs probably have an objective to further diversify their funding base and reduce their reliance on public funding but the extent to which they can achieve this remains to be seen. Clearly the introduction of top-up fees will have significant implications as it is likely to significantly change the income base of most HEIs.

Realisation of intellectual assets

Most HEIs are becoming increasingly aware that through their research activities they are generating a substantial amount of intellectual assets. Substantial efforts are being made to identify these intellectual assets and to protect them by devices such as patenting or licensing. Ultimately, of course, HEIs will want to realise the value of these intellectual assets in financial terms either as a capital sum (through, e.g., the sale of an HEI-owned company) or through a revenue stream (through, e.g., licensing). Experience has shown that these can be difficult transactions to achieve.

Use of private finance

For the last ten years or so the use of private finance in public service provision has expanded greatly with many large construction projects (e.g., hospitals, schools) being financed by private sources of funding with the ensuing buildings being leased back to the public authority. Such an approach has also been employed, to some degree, in the HE sector particularly with regard to students residences. The need for substantial capital investment in HEIs coupled with the limitations on future borrowings and internal finance (due to lack of usable cash balances) suggests that there may be a continuing increase in the use of privately financed capital projects in the HE sector

Cost structures

In Chapter 6 of this book we discus the issue of cost behaviour and the distinction between those costs which are fixed and those which are variable. To a large extent it is probably the case that in most HEIs the balance, at least in the short to medium term, is strongly towards the fixed cost end of the spectrum. However, this is not always the case and in many HEIs (particularly the former polytechnics) it is already the case that a large proportion of academic staff will be hourly paid (rather than paid an annual salary) and hence, to a large extent, become basically a variable cost. Nevertheless, to deal with the problems which would result from fluctuations in income levels it can be anticipated that most HEIs might try to alter their overall cost structure such that a larger proportion of costs are variable in nature and thus capable of being easily reduced in line with reductions in income. Some aspects of this might be an increased use of contracted services rather than in-house staff and an increased range of short-term employee contracts. However, changes to employment laws might, in future, place a limit on what can be achieved in this area.

Efficiency improvements

Although, has already been noted, the unit of resource for HEIs has decreased by over 50 per cent in the last ten years, this does not mean there is no further scope for efficiency improvements in the HE sector. In common with other largely publicly funded services there is likely to be ongoing pressure to improve the efficiency of service provision. However, it is probably the case that in many HEIs the easy cost savings have already have been made and further cost savings can only be achieved by more radical measures such as:

- rationalisation of sites in a multi-site HEI; this would require substantial capital investment but should realise substantial cost savings;
- investment in streamlined and technologically driven administrative systems designed to reduce administrative running costs;
- organisational simplification which would involve reducing the number of tiers in the HEI itself and in individual departments;
- outsourcing of certain services where this can achieve a lower cost base than in-house service provision.

Improved HEI management practices

In recent years there has been continued pressure to improve management practices within HEIs and various initiatives have been pursued by the funding councils. Also, the comments of the Lambert Report discussed above should also be noted.

Some examples of these initiatives are as follows:

- **Costing and pricing** – under the auspices of the Joint Costing and Pricing Steering Group (JCPSG) there have been a number of initiatives to improve costing and pricing practices in HEIs.
- **Risk management** – in line with best practice in public and private organisations, HEIs are encouraged to developed risk management strategies which identify their key business risks and the means of dealing with those risks. The preparation of risk management strategies should involve senior executives and governors of institutions.
- **Financial strategy** – all HEIs need a financial strategy to underpin their corporate strategy and a recent report from HEFCE provided guidance as to what such financial strategies should contain and how they should be developed.
- **Human resource management** – in recent years HEFCE has provided funds to give an incentive to HEIs to develop human resource strategies, and a great many have developed such strategies. The next stage is, of course, for HEIs to implement these strategies.
- **Estates management** – HEIs have large and varied land and property portfolios and the effective management of these portfolios is essential for good performance. Hence HEIs have been encouraged to develop and implement estates strategies. Such strategies often involve the large-scale disposal of existing land and buildings and the construction of new buildings.

The extent to which these initiatives have achieved real improvements in managerial practices is debatable and it seems likely that there will be considerable variations within the sector as to the degree of improvement which has taken place.

Looking ahead it seems likely that there will continue to be a policy of promoting improved managerial practices within the HE sector and the various funding council initiatives will continue. However, much of the capability for improving managerial practice rests with the HEIs themselves and it remains to be seen to what extent HEIs will take on board the following:

- the recruitment of vice-chancellors/principals from outside the HE sector by appointing experienced senior managers from large complex commercial and public sector organisations;
- the appointment to senior academic management posts (e.g., heads of schools) on the basis of managerial abilities as well as academic abilities;
- large-scale investment in improved and more efficient administrative and management systems such as: manpower planning and e-procurement.
- effecting a cultural change to eradicate the divide between academic staff and non-academic staff.

Appendix
Recent developments

The manuscript for this book was completed at the end of January 2004. Subsequently there have been a number of significant developments affecting the HE sector which are in need of further discussion.

Progress of the Higher Education Bill

Following the publication of the HE White Paper in March 2003, the Government published an HE Bill which was laid before Parliament. This Bill has been very controversial and, as is well known, only achieved its second reading in the House of Commons by a margin of six votes in an environment of immense political controversy. The most controversial aspect of the Bill is the proposed introduction of variable top-up fees for domestic undergraduate students.

Subsequently, the HE Bill obtained its third reading in the House of Commons on 31 March 2004 by a majority of 61 votes. Following this it is assumed that the main principles of the Bill will ultimately become law. The Bill entered the House of Lords on 1 April 2004 where it is possible that detailed changes might be made to parts of the Bill. The Government does not have an overall majority in the House of Lords and therefore will have to rely on the support of crossbench (i.e., party unaffiliated) members to get the Bill through. The normal timescale would anticipate the House of Commons considering any amendments made by the House of Lords in July 2004. Therefore by the end of July the HE Bill could have received Royal assent.

A particular issue which seems likely to generate considerable debate in the House of Lords is the role of the Office for Fair Access (OFFA). As the Bill passed from the House of Commons to the House of Lords there was a belief that debate would move from that on variable tuition fees to other matters, particularly the powers of this regulator. In the HE Bill universities need to agree an access plan with the regulator before being allowed to levy variable tuition fees from 2006 and part of the regulator's role is to assess the manner in which universities are attracting students from poorer backgrounds. Given that there are over thirty university chancellors or pro-chancellors in the House of Lords the debate on this topic could be very robust and while the chancellors are likely to support the principle of variable tuition fees they are likely to be less enthusiastic about the powers given to OFFA.

Public funding aspects of variable top-up fees

As has already been described in the book the main points of the top-up fee proposals can be summarised as:

- HEIs can charge top-up fees to domestic undergraduate students up to a limit of £3,000;
- students will **not** pay these fees 'up front' but their accumulated fees will be recovered over a period of years once they are earning over the threshold limit.

Clearly there are timing differences here. HEIs will receive the proceeds of top-up fees with effect from 2006/2007 but students will not begin to repay their accumulated fees until probably some time after 2010/11. It has been estimated that it could be 11 or 12 years before the first batch of top-up fee graduates fully repay their debts. Thus for many years there will clearly be a gap between the sums being advanced to HEIs for top-up fees and the sums being repaid by graduates. Thus in some shape or form, the exchequer will have to guarantee or finance that outstanding debt. Presumably the student loans will be repaid to some form of student loans company who will advance funds to HEIs on the basis of an exchequer funding guarantee.

Little has been said about this 'funding gap' but what is critical is not the existence of the gap but the potentially large size of that gap and its impact on public finances. A recent journal article (*Prospect*, February 2004) has suggested that on the basis of reasonable assumptions concerning student numbers, student fees, length of degree courses, graduate salaries, and so on, it could be 2019 before the inflows and outflows of funds are in balance and by that time the cumulative fund deficit to date will be of the order of £11 billion. Subsequent to that, the inflows will exceed the outflows but it could be 2030 before the accumulated fund deficit has been discharged. Clearly such financial projections thirty years ahead are hugely prone to changes in the basic assumptions such as student numbers and length of courses, but on the face of it, it hardly seems to be an effective means of attempting to reduce the burden of HE finance on taxpayers.

Financial implications of European Union students

Undergraduate students from other EU countries pay the same level of fees as English students which is substantially lower than that for other overseas students. The public funding made available to English HEIs for such students is estimated to be around £188 million which equates to an average of £3,750 for each EU undergraduate student.

The introduction of top-up fees into the English HE system will have financial implications relating to current and future UG student numbers of EU students studying in the England. When the top-up fees take effect in 2006, all EU students will be eligible to borrow this amount through the state-run student loan scheme. However, it is not easy to predict how collectible will be some of these loans once students have returned to their own country. The government claims to be working on bilateral agreements with student-loan agencies in other countries where they exist and if necessary it hopes to recover money through tax systems. It regards this as feasible by 2010, when the first repayments become due but it remains to be seen if this is the case.

Another financial issue arises from a case currently before the European Court of Justice, where a French citizen is arguing that all EU students should be entitled to the same grants and loans paid to English citizens on low incomes. These loans will increase after 2006 to make the new tuition fees more palatable. The UK Government argues that such aid to poor students is a social benefit, not an educational one, but the Court traditionally tends to favour arguments based on equal treatment of all EU citizens over those based on national sovereignty. Judgment is expected by early 2005.

Impact of EU accession

After 1 May 2004, the same financing arrangements described above will also apply to the eight countries of Eastern Europe, plus Malta and Cyprus who will then join the EU. A recent report (Higher Education Policy Institute March 2004) suggests that this could result in there being between 12,000 and 19,000 additional undergraduate students from the new member countries by 2010. Depending on the ability of HEIs to expand their capacity, there is some possibility that these additional student numbers might displace potential UK students and therefore prejudice achievement of the Government's 50 per cent participation target. However, there would be two main financial implications of this phenomenon:

- all the UG students from the new EU countries will be eligible for student loans relating to top-up fees;
- if Britain loses the court case referred to above, given how poor many of the new EU countries are, then at least half and possibly more of the new applicants would be eligible for the money intended for disadvantaged English students. The combined grant, maintenance loan and tuition-fee loan for a poor student studying in London will be around £10,000 a year by 2008.

However, although these costs are substantial it is argued that there are some counter-benefits. For example:

- EU students spend on average £7,500 a year when they are studying here and there are VAT tax receipts deriving from this;

- those students that work pay taxes on their income;
- traditionally around a quarter of EU students stay on and get a UK job after graduating.

It is sometimes argued that the direct and indirect taxes they pay will more than make up for the taxpayer-subsidised tuition and loans. However, this is a debatable point and a rigorous analysis would be required to justify this assertion.

Developments in the transparent approach to costing (TRAC)

In Chapter 6 there was discussion about the development of HEI costing systems under TRAC. It is probably true to say that in most HEIs the production of financial information under TRAC was not seen as being of great relevance to the HEI itself but was seen as more an aspect of central reporting of financial information. In February 2004 Volume III of the TRAC Guidance Manual was published and the detailed requirements this manual places on HEIs are likely to have significant implications with regard to the costs they can charge to funding bids to research councils and other public bodies such as Government departments.

The requirements of Volume III mean that with effect from early in 2005 funding bids to research councils and other public bodies must identify and show what is termed the full economic cost (fEC) of the project concerned. The rationale for this is to encourage HEIs to undertake research on an economically sustainable basis. The detailed aspects of the procedures that must be followed to establish the fEC for such bids are described in the relevant TRAC manual but three key areas should be highlighted:

- **Estates costs** – Under the fEC regime considerable improvements must be made in the degree of sophistication by which HEIs attribute estates costs (i.e., premises, equipment, technicians and the infrastructure adjustment) to individual research projects. Rough and ready apportionments of cost must be replaced by more sensitive methods and a series of minimum costing standards have been laid down. If HEIs cannot demonstrate that they can achieve these minimum standards then they will **not** be permitted to includes any estates costs in their bids.
- **Indirect Costs** – Each HEI must establish a minimum of one indirect cost rate for support services (excluding estates costs) which is specific to research activity. This will be used to attribute indirect costs to individual research projects. However, if they wish they can establish several such rates provided they are specific to research activity. If HEIs cannot establish such rates in accordance with the deadlines laid down, they will be required to use default rates for their research council bids. Such default rates may be below the actual rates.

- **Time of principal investigators** – Traditionally in making bids to research councils, HEIs have **not** been permitted to include the costs of the time of the principal investigators (PI) on the project. Clearly the PIs do contribute towards such projects and their time inputs represent a cost. Under the fEC regime HEIs will be permitted to include PI time inputs in the bid but in order to do this, they must be able to show that they have systems robust enough to identify and possibly to verify such time inputs. Clearly such time recording systems will go beyond the time allocation systems used under TRAC.

A number of points need to be made about these fEC requirements:

- Bids for funding to public bodies such as research councils must be based upon the fEC of the proposed project in accordance with the rules. Thus HEIs will not be permitted to cross-subsidise to and from other activities. While there are good reasons for encouraging HEIs to base their bids on the fEC of a proposed project it must also be noted that in the private sector cross-subsidisation is a permissible and is a common business practice albeit in the context of overall business sustainability. For bids to private sector organisations such rules will not apply and HEIs will be free to bid on whatever basis they think fit. However, they will still be encouraged to base their bids upon the fEC of the project. Although the fEC mechanisms will only apply to publicly funded research activity, it is easy to see how they could be extended to publicly funded teaching activity.
- Clearly the use of default rates and the risk of exclusion of certain costs (e.g., estates costs) from funding bids mean that it is beneficial for HEIs to be in a position to meet the full fEC requirements as soon as possible. Implementation of the requirements of fEC will have staffing and resource implications for HEIs. The TRAC manual estimates that development and implementation costs associated with fEC in a research intensive university will be in the range £100,000 to £250,000. Projected to the sector as a whole, this probably means additional costs to the HE sector of the order of £6–7 million.
- Although bids to research councils will incorporate the fEC of the project, the research councils will only fund projects on the basis of approximately 65per cent of the fEC. This is for the simple reason that the research councils could not, at present, fund projects at fEC since only limited additional funds have been made available to them for this purpose. The higher costs associated with fEC may mean that the volume of other (non-research council) publicly funded research may be reduced since again no additional funds are available to meet the fEC. Thus the use of fEC may have significant implications for the distribution of research funds across the HE sector depending upon the focus placed on the projected costs of projects as opposed to other features. It is by some suggested that

the use of fEC to prepare funding bids will assist HEIs to argue for more research funding from Government, but this remains to be seen.

- Finally, although the achievement of economic sustainability in HEIs is clearly desirable, the fEC approach might be seen as an attempt to micromanage HEI activities with significant costs involved. Alternative macroapproaches involving the achievement of overall rates of return might be less intrusive and resource efficient.

References

The National Committee of Inquiry into Higher Education (July 1997) (The Dearing Committee) – Chairman Sir Ron Dearing, HMSO.

HEFCE Practical Guide to PFI for higher education institutions (November 1998) HEFCE 1998/69, Bristol.

HEFCE Practical Guide to PFI for higher education institutions: Revised (February 2004) HEFCE 2004/11, Bristol.

HEFCE Public/Private Partnership (PPP) and Private Finance Initiative (PFI) projects – our approach (19 March 2003). HEFCE Circular 07/2003, Bristol.

HEFCE PFI Case Studies (December 1998). HEFCE 1998/71, Bristol.

HEFCE Student accommodation projects; a guide to PFI contracts (October 2000) HEFCE 2000/47, Bristol.

David Greenaway, Michelle Hayes (2000) Funding Universities to Meet National and International Challenges, University of Nottingham.

David Greenaway, Michelle Hayes (2000) Funding Universities to Meet National and International Challenges, University of Nottingham.

David Greenaway, Michelle Hayes (2000) Funding Universities to Meet National and International Challenges, University of Nottingham.

Nicholas Barr (June 2003) Financing higher education: Comparing the options. London School of Economics and Political Science.

Secretary of State for Education and Skills (January 2003) Cm5735.

The Future of Higher Education. The Stationery Office.

Universities UK (February 2001) New directions for higher education.

Richard Lambert (December 2003) Lambert Review of Business University Collaboration, HMSO.

HEFCE Funding higher education in England: How HEFCE allocates its funds (9 June 2003) HEFCE 2003/29, 2003/29 Guide.

HECFE Funding Method for Teaching from 1998–99 (November 1996), HEFCE Circular C 21/96.

HEFCE Developing the funding model for teaching from 2004–05: Consultation. (August 2003) HEFCE 2003/42, Bristol.

Sir Gareth Roberts (May 2003) Review of research assessment. (Report to the UK funding bodies).

HEFCE Review of research funding methodology (August 2003), HEFCE 2003/31, Bristol.

Secretary of State for Education and Skills (January 2003) Cm5735.

The Future of Higher Education. The Stationery Office.

Richard Lambert (December 2003) Lambert Review of Business University Collaboration, HMSO.

Sir Gareth Roberts (May 2003) Review of research assessment. (Report to the UK funding bodies).

HEFCE Model financial memorandum between HEFCE and institutions. HEFCE (December 2003). HEFCE 2003/54, Bristol.

Chartered Institute of Public Finance and Accountancy (CIPFA) (2003) A Model set of Financial Regulations for Further and Higher Education.

Lord Nolan (1995) Committee on Standards in Public Life, HMSO.

HEFEC HEFCE Audit Code of Practice (May 2002). HEFCE 2002/26, Bristol.

HEFCE Institutional audit and accountability: HEFCE Code of Practice – draft for consultation. HEFCE 2003/60, Bristol.

HEFCE Accountability and Audit: HEFCE Code of Practice. HEFCE 2004/27, Bristol.

Chartered Institute of Public Finance and Accountancy (CIPFA) (1996) – Handbook for audit committee members in further and higher education.

Institute of Chartered Accountants in England and Wales (1997) Audit Committees: a framework for guidance.

HEFEC-HEFCE Audit Code of Practice (May 2002). HEFCE 2002/26, Bristol.

Sir Adrian Cadbury (December 1992) Report of the Committee on the Financial Aspects of Corporate Governance: The Code of Best Practice (Cadbury Code).

Lord Nolan (1995) Committee on Standards in Public Life, HMSO.

Sir Richard Greenbury (1995) Directors' Remuneration: Report of a Study Group (The Greenbury Report).

The Committee on Corporate Governance: Final Report (1998) (Hampel Committee Report).

Nigel Turnbull (1999) Internal Control: Guidance for Directors On the Combined Code (The Turnbull Report). ICAEW.

Derek Higgs (2003) Review of the role and effectiveness of non executive directors.

Sir Robert Smith (2003) Audit Committees Combined Code Guidance.

Statement of Recommended Practice for Further and Higher Education (SORP), 2003.

HEFCE The HEFCE's Accounts Direction to higher education Institutions for 2002/03. (November 2002). HEFCE Circular 23/2002, Bristol.

HEFCE HEFCE's Accounts Direction to higher education Institutions for 2002/03, update, (July 2003). HEFCE Circular 16/2003, Bristol.

Robson Rhodes: RSM International (March 1996) Related Companies: Recommended Practice Guidelines. Manchester.

HEFCE- HEFCE Strategic plan 2003–08, (March 2003).

HEFCE Consultation 2003/12, Bristol.

Secretary of State for Education and Skills (January 2003) Cm5735.

The Future of Higher Education. The Stationery Office.

HEFCE HEFCE Strategic plan 2003–08, (March 2003).

HEFCE Consultation 2003/12, Bristol.

Secretary of State for Education and Skills (January 2003) Cm5735.

The Future of Higher Education. The Stationery Office.

Secretary of State for Education and Skills (January 2003) Cm5735.

The Future of Higher Education. The Stationery Office.

Secretary of State for Education and Skills (January 2003) Cm5735.

The Future of Higher Education. The Stationery Office.

Secretary of State for Education and Skills (January 2003) Cm5735.

The Future of Higher Education. The Stationery Office.

Secretary of State for Education and Skills (January 2003) Cm5735.

The Future of Higher Education. The Stationery Office.

Richard Lambert (December 2003) Lambert Review of Business University Collaboration, HMSO.

Richard Lambert (December 2003) Lambert Review of Business University Collaboration, HMSO.

Transparent Approach to Costing. Volume 3. Full Economic.

Costs of Projects. Produced for JCPSG by J M Consulting Ltd.

Further information and reading

A very large amount of official information and guidance about the HE sector is available on web-sites of Governmental bodies. These include the following:

DfES	www.dfes.gov.uk
HEFCE	www.hefce.ac.uk
TTA	www.tta.gov.uk/php/read.php?sectionid=1
LSC	www.lsc.gov.uk

HE statistical information can be obtained from HESA (www.hesa.ac.uk).

For those interested in detailed aspects of HE in other parts of the UK, the following sites are relevant:

Wales

National Assembly for Wales	www.wales.gov.uk
HEFCW	www.hefcw.ac.uk

Scotland

Scottish Parliament	www.scottishparliament.uk
SHEFC	www.shefc.ac.uk

Northern Ireland

Northern Ireland Assembly	www.ni-assembly.gov.uk
Northern Ireland Office	www.nio.gov.uk
HEFCE (agents)	www.hefce.ac.uk

In terms of publications, the interested reader might consider the following:

- CIPFA Higher Education Finance – published by CIPFA, London (2002)
- Higher Education Yearbook – published by Caritas Data Ltd.

Index